India's Look East Policy and the Northeast

India's Look East Policy and the Northeast

Thongkholal Haokip

$SAGE www.sagepublications.com
Los Angeles • London • New Delhi • Singapore • Washington DC • Boston

First published in 2015 by

SAGE Publications India Pvt Ltd
B1/I-1 Mohan Cooperative Industrial Area
Mathura Road, New Delhi 110 044, India
www.sagepub.in

SAGE Publications Inc
2455 Teller Road
Thousand Oaks, California 91320, USA

SAGE Publications Ltd
1 Oliver's Yard, 55 City Road
London EC1Y 1SP, United Kingdom

SAGE Publications Asia-Pacific Pte Ltd
3 Church Street
#10-04 Samsung Hub
Singapore 049483

Published by Vivek Mehra for SAGE Publications India Pvt Ltd, typeset in 10/13 pts Berkeley by Diligent Typesetter, Delhi and printed at Sai Print-o-Pack, New Delhi.

Library of Congress Cataloging-in-Publication Data

Haokip, Thongkholal.
   India's Look East Policy and the Northeast / Thongkholal Haokip.
     pages cm
   Includes bibliographical references and index.
   1. India, Northeastern—Economic policy. 2. India, Northeastern—Politics and government. 3. India—Economic integration. 4. India, Northeastern—Foreign economic relations—Southeast Asia. 5. Southeast Asia—Foreign economic relations—India, Northeastern. I. Title.
       HC437.N57H36   337.54059—dc23   2015   2014048850

ISBN: 978-93-515-0101-5 (HB)

The SAGE Team: Rudra Narayan, Sanghamitra Patowary and Vaibhav Bansal

This book is dedicated to my beloved mother,
Mrs Lhingkhonei Haokip.

Thank you for choosing a SAGE product! If you have any comment, observation or feedback, I would like to personally hear from you. Please write to me at <u>contactceo@sagepub.in</u>

—Vivek Mehra, Managing Director and CEO,
SAGE Publications India Pvt Ltd, New Delhi

Bulk Sales

SAGE India offers special discounts for purchase of books in bulk. We also make available special imprints and excerpts from our books on demand.

For orders and enquiries, write to us at

Marketing Department
SAGE Publications India Pvt Ltd
B1/I-1, Mohan Cooperative Industrial Area
Mathura Road, Post Bag 7
New Delhi 110044, India
E-mail us at <u>marketing@sagepub.in</u>

Get to know more about SAGE, be invited to SAGE events, get on our mailing list. Write today to <u>marketing@sagepub.in</u>

This book is also available as an e-book.

Contents

List of Abbreviations

AFTA	ASEAN Free Trade Area
AGP	Assam Gana Parishad
APEC	Asia-Pacific Economic Cooperation
ARF	ASEAN Regional Forum
ASEAN	Association of Southeast Asian Nations
BATD	Bodoland Autonomous Territorial Districts
BCIM	Bangladesh–China–India–Myanmar Regional Economic Forum
BIMSTEC	Bay of Bengal Initiative for Multi-Sectoral Technical and Economic Cooperation
BIST-EC	Bangladesh, India, Sri Lanka, Thailand-Economic Cooperation
BJP	Bharatiya Janata Party
BPO	Business Process Operation
CLMV	Cambodia, Laos, Myanmar and Vietnam
ECC	European Economic Community
ECOSOC	United Nations Economic and Social Council
EMS	European Monetary System
EU	European Union
FDI	Foreign Direct Investment
FTA	Free Trade Agreement
GDP	Gross Domestic Product
GoI	Government of India
IAS	Indian Administrative Service
ICT	Information and Communication Technology
IFAS	Indian Frontier Administrative Service
IGEG	Inter-Governmental Expert Group
IMF	International Monetary Fund
INC	Indian National Congress
J&K	Jammu and Kashmir
KNA	Kuki National Army
MDoNER	Ministry of Development of North Eastern Region
MEA	Ministry of External Affairs

MERCOSUR	Mercado Comun del Sur, Common Market of the South
MGC	Mekong–Ganga Cooperation
MNF	Mizo National Front
NAFTA	North American Free Trade Agreement
NDA	National Democratic Alliance
NEFA	North Eastern Frontier Agency
NEC	North Eastern Council
NNC	Naga National Council
NSCN	National Socialist Council of Nagaland
R&D	Research and Development
SAARC	South Asian Association for Regional Cooperation
SAPTA	South Asian Preferential Trading Agreement
STEOM	Senior Trade/Economic Official Meetings
ULFA	United Liberation Front of Asom's
UMFO	United Mizo Freedom Organisation
UN	United Nations
UNCTD-III	United Nations Conference on Trade and Development-III
WTO	World Trade Organisation

Preface

The Look East policy has emerged as a major thrust area of India's foreign policy in the post-Cold War period. It was launched in 1991 by the then Narasimha Rao government to renew political contacts, increase economic integration and forge security cooperation with several countries of Southeast Asia as a means to strengthen political understanding. Outside South Asia, India saw Southeast Asia as the only region where politico-strategic and economic conditions offered an opportunity to play a role for itself. India's Look East policy is aimed at greater economic alignment and an enhanced political role in the dynamic Asia–Pacific region in general and Southeast Asia in particular. The Look East policy is pursued to make India an inalienable part of Asia–Pacific's strategic discourse. Hence, the current phase of the Look East policy marks the beginning of a vibrant relationship on the economic, political and strategic fronts. The economic potential of this policy is also emphasised to link to the economic interests of the Northeastern region as a whole.

The beginning of the early 1990s was marked by a transformation in the international political economy, contributed by the end of the Cold War and the resulting spread of globalisation. Globalisation of world economies intensified international competition and has given rise to a new wave of regionalism. As a viable response in a rapidly globalising world, the trend towards regionalism is being espoused by the developed as well as the developing countries. A large number of states in different parts of the world constitute themselves into regions to give fresh impetus to a wide variety of cooperative ventures based on regionalism. Geographical proximity, economic complementarities, political commitment, policy coordination and infrastructure development provide conditions for formation of such groupings.

During this time India, like many developing countries, faced many challenges—both internally and globally. Internally, the country was unsettled by social unrest, serious political instability and poor economic performance. After the disintegration of the Soviet Union, New Delhi lost a major economic partner and its closet strategic ally. India became aware of the growing trend towards regionalism and due to fears of being marginalised from the global economy, she emphasised on weaving a web of durable cooperative ties with various countries in the region.

The first ever regional economic cooperation that India joined in her own neighbourhood is SAARC. However, it has become a non-starter due to political tensions between India and Pakistan. India also cannot look towards West Asia and Africa for intensive economic cooperation, as the countries of this region look up mainly to the West. During this period, India has got attracted to the high-performing economies of East Asia. Forced by the economic crisis and the dire need of Foreign Direct Investments (FDIs) for rapid economic development, India had enunciated the Look East policy in 1991 and was determined to work with the spirit of regional economic cooperation with her Eastern neighbours. The policy underlines the renewed thrust towards the Asianist perspective of cooperation and development which was undertaken during the Nehruvian era.

The first phase of India's Look East policy was ASEAN-centred, and focused primarily on trade and investment linkages. The second phase, which began in 2003, is more comprehensive in its coverage, extending from Australia to East Asia, with ASEAN as its core. The new phase marks a shift in focus from trade to wider economic and security cooperation, political partnerships, physical connectivity through road and rail links. In India's effort to look East, the Northeastern region has become a significant region due to its geographical proximity to Southeast Asia and China. India's search for new economic relationship with Southeast Asia is now driven by the domestic imperative of developing the Northeast by increasing its connectivity to the outside world. Instead of consciously trying to isolate the Northeast from external influences, as it had done in the past, New Delhi has now recognised the importance of opening it up for commercial linkages with Southeast Asia. In its effort to look East, India has the vision for Northeast as the gateway to the East and a springboard for launching intense economic integration with Southeast Asia.

Northeast India is the northeastern borderland of South Asia, and also the northwestern borderland of Southeast Asia. The region has much more geographical contact with and proximity to other national states than the Indian mainland. The people have distinct ethnic and cultural identities, which are similar to those of the people of Southeast Asia and China than with the people of the rest of India. The region is a storehouse of mineral resources, biodiversity and water resources, and has been known for her natural resources and maintenance of active transborder trade with her neighbours during the pre-independence period. But these natural bounties are yet to be harnessed. The partition of India in 1947 caused the extreme geo-political isolation of the Northeast, making it the most regulated, sensitive border region and the most exposed territory. In addition, the partition also caused the severance of the inland water, road and railway communications through erstwhile East Pakistan, and access to the Chittagong port was lost. The Chinese takeover of Tibet and the virtual closure of the border with Burma added to the isolation of the region. These profound economic and political changes that followed in the wake of independence created a sense of unease among the tribal population of the region. Since the development initiatives of the Indian government in this region have been based on its security concerns, the state-centric security approach has kept the region isolated and underdeveloped.

For several decades, people have talked about economic integration of the Northeastern states with the rest of the country. Over the time, policy-makers, bureaucrats and intellectuals have attributed the numerous armed separatist struggles and political instability in the Northeastern states to the region's underdevelopment and weak economic integration with mainland India. As part of the efforts to integrate the region with the rest of India, developmental funds were poured in and emphasis was laid on infrastructural development. However, the region still has the problem of underdevelopment and faces the problem of a growing and expanding security apparatus. The migration of people from Bangladesh, Nepal and Myanmar has only added to the tensions in the region. Such unrest in the region has resulted in alarming changes, which endanger the security of the region by hindering the development of a strategically significant region of the country. Moreover, there is a relocation of factories and industries towards northern and western India, and hence the cost of transportation of goods to Northeast India has increased. Therefore, the existing policy of development of the Northeastern region needs to be reoriented if its stated objectives have to be fulfilled in due course.

In the recent years, the development of this region is being factored into the overall strategy of national development as well as in the conduct of India's relations with the other countries. India's Look East policy, which identifies Northeast India as the gateway to the East, is one such major initiative undertaken by the Government of India (GoI). One direction that holds out much promise as a new way of development is political integration with the rest of India and economic integration with the rest of Asia, particularly with East and Southeast Asia. In the second phase, the Look East policy has been given a new dimension wherein India is now looking towards a partnership with the ASEAN countries, integrally linked to the economic and security interests of the Northeastern region.

Taking into account its geographical proximity, its historical and cultural linkage with Southeast Asia and China and the primary objective of the Look East policy, it is being widely stated that the Look East policy would result in the rapid development of the region as it promises increased trade contacts between the Northeastern region and Myanmar, China and Bangladesh. The policy also has the potential of solving the problem of insurgency, migration and drug trafficking in the region through regional cooperation.

On the other side, there is pessimism that the policy of integrating Northeast India with its Eastern neighbours would lead to dumping of cheap foreign goods and the region's own industries being adversely affected by it. The region is also being perceived as just a transit region without bringing economic development to the region, as it has no adequate industrial infrastructure to produce goods which can be exported to these countries. There is also a concern that such integration will develop further the feeling of alienation of the people and the region itself would drift away from the mainstream Indian politics. Therefore, there is a need to examine deeply the existing realities and issues. Considerable works have been done on the dynamics of India's Look East policy, but these academic works did not examine the economic potentials of the Look East policy linked to economic interests of the Northeastern region. The works on the economy of the Northeast recommend the economic integration of the region with the dynamic East and Southeast Asia without examining the possible consequences of such a policy in terms of ethnic integration of the communities of the Northeast with the rest of the Indian states.

This book studies the evolution of India's Look East policy, the economic potentials of the Look East policy linked to the economic interests of the Northeastern region, the continuity and change of India's policy towards the Northeast and, in that context, examine whether the Look East policy is likely to attain its goals. It also examines whether it is feasible to adopt a policy for economic development by opening up to the East in the face of possible alienation in ethnic terms.

This book has been divided into eight chapters. Chapter 1 discusses the trend towards regional integration after the end of the Cold War, the growth of regional organisations and its relationship with the United Nations. The chapter then briefly discusses India's attempt at establishing regional cooperation. The main concepts, namely, regional integration and regionalism, as they have emerged, so far have been discussed in this chapter.

Chapter 2 of the book assesses the challenges that India faced, both at the domestic and international levels, during 1990–91 and the compulsions of India to look East. The chapter also discusses the policy objectives of the Look East policy, such as regional integration, reforms and liberalisation, rapid economic growth, development of the Northeastern region and security consideration, and its various approaches, such as geographical focus, sub-regional cooperation and free trade agreements.

Chapter 3 discusses the endeavours of India to reinforce the Look East policy by joining several sub-regional groupings, such as the Bay of Bengal Initiative for Multi-Sectoral Technical and Economic Cooperation (BIMSTEC), the Mekong Ganga Cooperation (MGC) Project and the Bangladesh–China–India–Myanmar Regional Economic Forum (BCIM Forum). It also explores the complementarities that exist between Northeast India and its neighbouring countries, and possible technical and marketing collaborations in various fields.

Chapter 4 provides the historical background of political integration and its fallout in Northeast India since independence.

Chapter 5 attempts to provide the historical background of economic development in Northeast India till the late 1980s. It traces the background of modern economic development in the region, since the discovery of tea in 1823 by East India Company and the subsequent entry of the region into the world economy. It explores whether the plantation economy and modern economic growth raise the standard of living of the people. The consequences of the partition of 1947 and the newly drawn political boundary, the Chinese occupation of Tibet and the virtual closure of border with Burma on the economy of the region and the region's economic condition after independence are also discussed.

Chapter 6 examines the continuity and change of India's policy towards its Northeastern region, and the economic potentials of the Look East policy. It starts with the analysis of *Nehruvian policy framework* for the Northeast to the *politics of political representation* and the *development syndrome*. It then looks into the development of new policy by the GoI, which directs its Look East policy to tap the geo-economic potential of the Northeastern region as a gateway to East and Southeast Asia by converting locational disadvantage into advantage.

As the Look East policy provides a lot of opportunities as well as challenges for the Northeastern region, Chapter 7 examines the possible political impact of the Look East policy vis-à-vis the issues of ethnic integration, insurgency, migration and drug trafficking. These conundrums in the Northeastern region are interrelated and transborder in nature. This chapter also explores whether the transborder nature of these problems can be solved by way of effective regional cooperation through the Look East policy, and examines the nature of sovereignty bargains that the Indian state will be willing to engage in its pursuit of regional integration. The concluding chapter (Chapter 8) recapitulates the major findings of the previous chapters.

Acknowledgements

I am indebted to many people who have helped me in writing this book. First and foremost, I am sincerely grateful to the faculty members of the Department of Political Science, North-Eastern Hill University (NEHU), Shillong, for sharing their views on the subject.

I am thankful to Dr C. Joshua Thomas, Deputy Director, Indian Council of Social Science Research-North Eastern Regional Centre (ICSSR-NERC), for his immense guidance and help which enabled me to avail help from the ICSSR, New Delhi, during my visit to various libraries in New Delhi.

I am grateful for the help received from the staff of NEHU Central Library, ICSSR-NERC and North Eastern Council library in Shillong, Omeo Kumar Das Institute of Social Change and Development in Guwahati, National Library in Kolkata and from other libraries, namely, Jawaharlal Nehru University library, Nehru Memorial Museum and Library, Parliament Library, Research and Information System and the National Social Science Documentation Centre, New Delhi.

I would also like to express my deep gratitude to my parents, Pu Sonthong Haokip and Pi Lhingnei Haokip, for their understanding, encouragement and support during the course of my work.

Last and by no means least, I thank the Almighty God for enabling me to do this piece of work without any difficulties, and for the blessings I have received over all these years.

Thongkholal Haokip
Kolkata: January 2014

1

Regional Integration and India

The beginning of the 1990s was a turning point in international politics. Dramatic events took place at the global level that brought about one of the most significant changes in the twentieth century, and subsequently transformed the nature of international politics. This period witnessed the end of the Cold War between the two military blocs that brought an end to the bipolar world, which was based on confrontation of two politico-economic systems. It also brought an end to the stability of the world based on mutual deterrence. The high-risk–high-stability situation has been replaced by a low-risk–low-stability situation. The end of the Cold War and the collapse of the Soviet Union also brought about the reorientation of former Soviet client states, especially those in the Third World, from centralised to market economies. These global changes have precipitated two consequences in the prevailing international relations. First, there is a growing interdependence between countries and second, economic and trade issues are gaining vital precedence over the political and military ones.[1] With a shift from geo-politics and geo-strategic to geo-economics, the economic dimensions of international politics have become prominent. The world, previously polarised by an ideological struggle, rapidly changed into economic blocs.

With the end of the Cold War and the resultant breakdown of the overarching Cold War structure that underpinned and ordered international relations, nation-states became aware of the need to re-evaluate their place in the international system. As a result individual states began to seek new relations with the emerging group of major powers and with their own immediate neighbours. Many states realised 'how much their own welfare was dependent on the stability and well-being of the region in which they are located.'[2]

The post-Cold War phase in international relations witnessed a distinct trend towards regional integration. As a result, a large number of states from different parts of the world began to make serious attempts to constitute themselves into regions to give a fresh impetus to a wide variety of cooperative ventures amongst themselves. Regional integration, in general, appeared to be an effective device to serve economic and commercial objectives of these states. In the process, old organisations were recasted and new organisations created to suit the changing global political context.[3] All these developments consequently brought about a change in the world policies leading to the development of a new world order, and dramatically altered the basic parameters in which the various relationships had hitherto operated.[4]

Regional Integration: Concept and Growth

The growth of regional integration has been one of the major developments in recent international relations, and has become part and parcel of the present global economic order. This trend is 'now an acknowledged future of the international scene' and 'has achieved a new meaning and new significance.'[5] The nation-state system, which has been the predominant pattern of international relations since the Peace of Westphalia in 1648, is evolving towards a system in which regional groupings of states are becoming more important than sovereign states. Walter Lippmann believes that 'the true constituent members of the international order of the future are communities of states.'[6] E.H. Carr shares Lippmann's view about the rise of regionalism and regional arrangements, and conceives that the concept of sovereignty is likely to become even more blurred in the future than it is at present.[7] The process of regional integration has increasingly affected and even shaped international relations. Trade, economic cooperation and many trans-border issues and problems are increasingly being dealt at a regional supranational level. It is this development of increasing regional cooperation in economic, political and security issues that has gathered momentum in recent years. These integration projects are an increasingly growing phenomenon and occur simultaneously with globalisation.

Regional integration has been defined as 'an association of states based upon location in a given geographical area, for the safeguarding or promotion of the participants', an association whose terms are 'fixed by a treaty or other arrangements.'[8] Philippe De Lombaerde and Luk Van Langenhove define regional integration as 'a worldwide phenomenon of territorial systems that increase the interactions between their components and create new forms of organisation, co-existing with traditional forms of state-led organisation at the national level.'[9] According to Hans van Ginkel, regional integration refers to the process by which states within a particular region increase their level of interaction with regard to economic, security, political, and also social and cultural issues.[10] In the present age of economic globalisation, integration is generally defined as 'the voluntary linking in the economic domain of two or more formerly independent states to the extent that authority over key areas of domestic regulation and policy is shifted to the supranational level.'[11] In short, regional integration is the joining of individual states within a region into a larger whole. The degree of integration depends upon the willingness and commitment of independent sovereign states to share their sovereignty.[12]

Regional integration initiatives, according to Van Langenhove, should promote:

> the strengthening of trade integration in the region; the creation of an appropriate enabling environment for private sector development; the development of infrastructure programmes in support of economic growth and regional integration; the development of strong public sector institutions and good governance; the reduction of social exclusion and the development of an inclusive civil society; contribution to peace and security in the region; the building of environment programmes at the regional level; and the strengthening of the region's interaction with other regions of the world.[13]

Regional integration arrangements are primarily the outcome of necessity felt by nation-states to integrate their economies so as to attain rapid economic development and reduce the conflict between the integrated units by building mutual trust. Integration is not an end in itself, but a process to support economic growth strategies, greater social equality and democratisation. This desire for closer integration denotes the desire for opening to the outside world. Regional integration is being used as a means to boost development by promoting efficiency, rather than disadvantaging others. The members of these arrangements believe that their regional initiative will result in a freer and open global environment for trade and investment.

Regional integration or regionalism is not a recent phenomenon. In the past two centuries, four waves of regionalism have occurred. The first wave started in the mid-nineteenth century and continued until the beginning of the First World War. It was basically a European phenomenon, and the conclusion of a number of bilateral and regional trading agreements contributed to the growth of regionalism in Europe. The First World War disrupted this first wave of regional trade arrangements. The second wave began soon after the end of the War and was highly protectionist and often associated with *beggar-thy-neighbour* policies and substantial trade diversion, as well as heightened political conflict. Some were created to consolidate the empires of major powers; however, most were formed among sovereign states.[14]

The third wave of regionalism occurred soon after the end of the Second World War and took place from the later part of the 1950s till the 1970s. During this episode, a number of regional trading blocs were formed by developed countries in Western Europe, the Soviet Union and its allies, and less developed countries as against the backdrop of the Cold War and decolonisation. Thus, all regional integration projects during the Cold War period were 'built on the Westphalian state system and were to serve economic growth as well as security motives in their assistance to state building goals.'[15] However, the present wave of regionalism relies on high levels of economic interdependence, a willingness by the major economic actors to mediate trade disputes and a multilateral framework that assists them in doing so.[16] In the words of Lawrence:

> The forces driving the current developments differ radically from those driving previous waves of regionalism in this century. Unlike the episode of the 1930s, the current initiatives represent efforts to facilitate their members' participation in the world economy rather than their withdrawal from it. Unlike those in the 1950s and 1960s, the initiatives involving developing countries are part of a strategy to liberalize and open their economies to implement export and foreign investment-led policies rather than to promote import substitution.[17]

As such, regional integration provides an opportunity for the constituent units to increasingly react and settle trans-border disputes within the framework of their regional organisation. Nation-states, especially developing countries, prefer interaction with states outside their region not as a single entity, but as a region or regional organisation so that they can maximise their bargaining power. Therefore, the formation of an organisation based on region for trade, economic, security and political cooperation is on the rise. These countries which venture upon regional integration are usually close neighbours, and, to a certain extent, share a common past and, thus, common history. Common history, in turn, leads them to share common problems and an intensified perception of those problems.

The recent surge of regionalism can, thus, be attributed to the increasing force of globalisation, which in turn is the result of the end of the Cold War. Globalisation has resulted in the growth of world market, increased penetration and domination of the national economies, which makes the nation-states bound to lose some of their *nationness*. This dominance of the world market over structures of local production has resulted in the emergence of a political will to halt or to reverse the process of globalisation,[18] in order to safeguard some degree of territorial control and cultural diversity.[19] One way of achieving such change has been through regional cooperation. Regional cooperation, therefore, is seen as a natural response to the forces of globalisation and a part of the states' effort to cope with pervasive globalisation. In many regions, regional integration has become an important answer to the challenges of the management of globalisation. Regional arrangements do not infringe the barrier of the sovereign state system, but rather provide an impetus and the machinery for much closer cooperation of states on the regional level. In recent years, regional integration projects have become the focal point of discussions, as developing countries are turning to regionalism as a tool for development. Almost all countries are now members of at least one project and may belong to more than one.

Regional integration and regionalism are often used synonymously in international relations. Regionalism may simply be stated as loyalty to the interests of a particular region. It may also be defined as a policy whereby the interests of a nation in world affairs are defined in terms of particular countries or regions. In the economic sphere, regionalism can be defined as 'an agreement among a certain number of states on preferential trade.'[20] Much of the literature on regionalism focuses on the welfare implications of preferential trading agreements, both for members and the world as a whole.[21] On a broader term, regionalism stands for the integration of economies and political systems on a smaller, regional scale, encompassing a few states that are located near each other, with many such regional cooperation or integration processes taking place simultaneously. Regionalism, therefore, promotes the regional integration of closely-knit neighbouring countries.

International Organisations and Regional Integration

The end of the Cold War brought about significant changes in the political, economic and strategic environment of the world. The issues in this new environment are vast and complex that it needs global cooperation and action to tackle them. Nation-states realised that these issues can be best addressed at multilateral agencies, and, therefore, multilateralism is being espoused by the United Nations (UN) and is increasingly regarded as the modus operandi in world politics today. However, the multilateral system is facing increasing challenges. Due to the repeated failure of multilateralism, developing countries have lost confidence in the global multilateral institutions to provide equitable development rules and to give them ownership of development policies. Since multilateralism, the first best option, is not attainable by many countries, both developed or developing and large or small are pursuing the second-best option—regionalism. Regionalism is then considered to be an alternative, at least, for countries geographically close to one another, especially for countries with close economic interests and exchanges. The desire for regional integration evolves as a result of environmental development, compulsions due to common problems and the experiences gained out of the drawbacks and inadequacies of the existing larger international organisations.[22]

The idea of regional arrangements has gained support from many international organisations. Since its inception, the UN has recognised regional arrangements. In its Charter, the UN has one chapter (Chapter VIII, Articles 52–54) entitled 'Regional Arrangements', fully devoted to the subject of regional arrangements. Observing the consistency of regionalism and regional arrangements with the principles of the UN, Article 52(1) of the Charter states that:[23]

> Nothing in the present charter precludes the existence of regional arrangements or agencies for dealing with such matters relating to the maintenance of international peace and security as are appropriate for regional action provided that such arrangements or agencies and their activities are consistent with the Purposes and Principles of the United Nations.

Clauses 2 and 3 of Article 52 also encourage regional arrangements for pacific settlement of local disputes before referring them to the Security

Council. In addition to Chapter VIII, Article 33 calls upon the parties to any disputes, the continuance of which is likely to endanger the maintenance of international peace and security to seek a solution through regional agencies or arrangements. Article 51 of the Charter also provides for an unrestricted regional security arrangements outside its effective control.

The Charter of the UN, however, does not define *regional arrangements* or *regional agencies* and its relationship with such arrangements or agencies. All references relating to regional arrangements are confined to the field of security. It is silent on the possible economic, social, cultural and other potentialities of such groupings. The institutional approach to regionalism and regional cooperation that was incorporated in the UN Charter was founded on the clashing power politics of the two power blocs in the post-war years.

With the end of the Cold War, the main focus of regional organisations has shifted from security to economic cooperation. As it has encouraged regional agencies and arrangements for pacific settlement of disputes during the Cold War period, the UN now encourages regional integration. The UN also believes that a 'relative cultural, economic, political and geographic affinity within a region leads itself to a more effective organisation',[24] and these more effective regional organisations are more supportive to its multilateral objectives. The UN's Economic and Social Council (ECOSOC), which facilitates international cooperation on standards making and problem solving in economic and social issues, promotes regional integration as a perquisite for globalisation. Globalisation not only widened the opportunities for national development, but also brought risks. Danuta Huebner, former Executive Secretary of the Economic Commission for Europe, said that the best response from the European continent to global challenges was its integration, since 'integration and international cooperation were guarantors of peace and stability.'[25] The UN is now increasingly feeling that the regional perspective is necessary for global action.

The UN has five regional commissions which provide inter-governmental frameworks for regional cooperation to assist countries in addressing sustainable development issues. These regional commissions have unique convening power in organising ministerial conferences and high-level meetings to further the implementation of regional and global sustainable development action plans through policy dialogues. The UN Conference on Trade and Development-III (UNCTAD-III) emphasises various aspects of regional cooperation. The Doha Declaration of World Trade Organisation (WTO) in 2001 recognises the fundamental role regional trade agreements can play in fostering the liberalisation and expansion of trade and, thus, in helping development. Apart from the UN, other international organisations also support regional integration for economic development, peace and security of the world. The Non-Alignment Movement Summit held at Algeria in September 1973 also calls for maximisation of trade and economic cooperation among poor countries.

New Wave of Regional Integration and Regional Organisations

There has been a new wave of economic regionalism since the mid-1980s, which reached its peak during the 1990s. The United States, which was the main proponent of multilateralism, has been disappointed with the lack of progress at the world trading negotiations. It decided to switch the course and concluded the Canada–United States Free Trade Agreement, and is now going ahead with the North America Free Trade Area.[26] The United States has also announced its intention to negotiate free trade agreements with other countries. Alongside this, the European Union (EU) continues to widen and deepen its integration. These developments have, in turn, led other countries to reconsider the regional option. East Asia, in particular, is convinced that a regional bloc may be the only way to meet the challenges posed by developments in America and Europe. Even developing countries are beginning to fear that their access to world markets may be curtailed significantly if trading blocs become a reality, and they are left out. Hence, throughout Asia, Africa, Latin America and West Asia, old arrangements are being revived and new ones created with a fresh objective to serve the economic interests of the participating countries. Therefore, this new economic regionalism is manifested by recasting old organisations and forming new economic organisations to suit the changing global context, and the deepening of the existing arrangements. This surge can be attributed to the new environment created by the end of the Cold War and military alliances, and the resulting emphasis given by nation-states on development through mutual economic cooperation with neighbouring states.

The EU is the first regional organisation in the post-war period. The formation of the European Community was critical in triggering integration projects in the 1960s, while the recent deepening and enlargement of the EU has been a key factor in triggering the latest wave of integration.[27] A good example of new regionalism is the development of a model of integration that incorporates political elements in deep economic integration. It has come a long way through decades, where redefining of objectives, priorities, adaptations and institutional changes are the secrets of its survival and prosperity. The EU was originally created by the six founding nation-states—France, Italy, Belgium, West Germany, Luxembourg and the Netherlands in 1957 by the Treaties of Rome, which established the European Economic Community (ECC) following the earlier establishment by the same six nation-states of the European Coal and Steel Community in 1952. The Single European Act in 1986 introduced measures aimed at achieving an internal market and greater political cooperation. The treaty on EU, which was signed in 7 February 1992 in Maastricht, Netherlands, renamed the ECC as EU. The Amsterdam Treaty of 1997 introduced measures to reinforce political union and prepare for enlargement towards the East, and the Nice Treaty (2001) defined the institutional changes necessary for enlargement. Now, in Europe, there is a complex multilevel governance system with deep cooperation between nation-states, with firm devolution of power within states and a strong international legal framework. This has created a political model which challenges assumptions about governance all over the world.

The most comprehensive economic integration project undertaken since the new wave of regionalism emerged in the middle of 1980s is the regional trade and investment agreement between United States, Canada and Mexico called the North American Free Trade Agreement (NAFTA). NAFTA, which is an expanded version of the Canada–United States Free Trade Agreement of 1988, came into being on 17 December 1992. The agreement came into force on 1 January 1994 to implement free trade area. The declared aims of NAFTA primarily deals with the strengthening of economic growth in the territories of the three NAFTA members by phased elimination of tariff and most non-tariff barriers on regional trade, facilitate cross-border movement of goods and services between the territories of the parties and establish a framework for international cooperation, including most-favoured-nation treatment and transparency. It also aims to promote conditions of fair competition in the free trade area and substantially increase investment opportunities in the territories of the parties. Through this regional cooperation, NAFTA countries are expecting positive impact on their nation's economies by way of creating new jobs and enhancing the living standards.

The core of the latest wave of regionalism in Latin America is Mercado Comun del Sur (MERCOSUR; English translation is *common market of the South*). MERCOSUR is a regional trade agreement which was established by the Treaty of Asuncion signed by Brazil, Argentina, Uruguay and Paraguay in March 1991. It has Chile and Bolivia as its associate members. The formation of MERCOSUR was triggered by external events that threatened to inflict severe damage on the economies of the Latin American region.[28] The primary objective of the formation of MERCOSUR is to create a single market for goods, capital and people. Or in other words, MERCOSUR's purpose is to facilitate free movement of goods, services, capital and people among the four member countries. MERCOSUR has become a successful market of about 200 million people, representing about US$1 trillion of Gross Domestic Product (GDP) and $190 billion of trade. It is the fourth largest integrated market after the EU, NAFTA and Association of South East Asian Nations (ASEAN).

The ASEAN, which is one of the successful examples of regionalism, was formed in 1967 with the signing of the Bangkok Declaration by its five original member countries—Malaysia, Indonesia, Thailand, Philippines and Singapore. The remaining Southeast Asian countries—Brunei, Darussalam, Vietnam, Laos, Myanmar and Cambodia joined the regional grouping during the 1980s and 1990s. The aims and purposes of ASEAN are: (a) to accelerate economic growth, social progress and cultural development in the region and (b) to promote regional peace and stability through abiding respect for justice and the rule of law in the relationship among countries in the region and adherence to the principles of the UN.[29] The formation of ASEAN was to promote regional peace, stability and security and the prevention of balkanisation. It was primarily political and security driven, rather than desiring to benefit from economic integration. However, with the end of the Cold War and increasing wave of globalisation, the association has reoriented its objectives.

In 2003, the ASEAN leaders established the ASEAN Community, which comprised of three pillars, namely, ASEAN Security Community, ASEAN Economic Community and ASEAN Socio-Cultural Community. Through the ASEAN Economic Community, ASEAN members try to pursue the end goal of economic integration. Its goal is to create a stable, prosperous and highly competitive ASEAN economic region in which there is a free flow of goods, services, investment and a freer flow of capital, equitable economic development, and reduced poverty and socio-economic disparities by the year 2020. With the aim of creating a Free Trade Area in the region, it formed the ASEAN Free Trade Area (AFTA) in January 1993. ASEAN has come a long way since its formation and survived the passage of time through the reorientation of its goals. The rise of Southeast Asian regionalism can be seen as a response to the larger changes occurring at the global level, such as the politico-economic integration of Western Europe into the EU.

India's Attempts at Regional Integration

India's efforts towards regional integration can be traced back to the pre-independence period. The leaders of Indian independence movement were conscious of the need to develop cooperation among fellow Asians, and closer collaboration with them was one of their main objectives. Indian leaders foresaw the inevitable trend towards regional integration in the post-war period. Jawaharlal Nehru, during his prison days in 1944, said in course of his reference to imminent changes in the structure of world politics, 'It is possible, of course, that large federations or group of nations may emerge in Europe or elsewhere in the Pacific and form huge multi-national States.'[30]

In his inaugural address at the Asian Relations Conference in 1947, Nehru stressed on the need for greater regional cooperation and asserted, 'There was a widespread urge and awareness that the time had come for us, peoples of Asia, to meet together, hold together and advance together. It was not only a vogue desire but the compulsions of events which forced all of us to think along these lines.'[31] There was an expression of great enthusiasm for regional cooperation from countries such as Sri Lanka and Burma. However, the conference which marked the apex of Asian solidarity also marked the beginning of its decline. The underlying causes of failure 'were the intense rivalry between India and China in the conference and the common distrust of the two Asian giants among the smaller countries of the region.'[32] William Henderson observes: 'Neither the Indians nor the Chinese were prepared to concede leadership to the other, the Arabs were uninterested and the South-East Asians frankly afraid that such an arrangement would mean the end of their freedom, almost before it had been won.'[33]

The next attempt towards regional integration by India was the Conference on Indonesia. It was organised to express support to the Sukarno-led armed struggle against the Dutch attempt to re-impose colonial rule in Indonesia in December 1947. The conference was held in New Delhi on 20 January 1949, which was attended by 15 Asian nations. Apart from the Indonesian issue, Nehru made an open appeal for regional integration, where he said: 'We see creative and cooperative impulses seeking a new integration and new unity. New problems arise from day to day which, concern all of us or many of us.'[34] The conference passed three resolutions where the third resolution called for regional integration of the participating nations. It urged the participating governments to 'consult among themselves in order to explore ways and means of establishing suitable machinery ... for promoting consultation and cooperation within the framework of the United Nations.'[35]

The attempts at regional cooperation continued from 1949 to 1955 where many conferences were organised and attended by India to find out the possibilities of such cooperation. A major step towards cooperation of the Afro-Asian countries was taken in the Bandung Conference, in April 1955, to develop a policy and common approach to their problems. In the economic sphere, the conference underscored the need for economic cooperation in the region, of providing mutual technical assistance, of the establishment of regional training institutes, intra-regional trade, etc.[36] The proposal for regional economic cooperation and intra-regional cooperation in Asia and Africa in the Bandung Conference was not materialised. These earlier attempts by India, since independence, towards regional integration in Asia however failed. A number of reasons were responsible for the failure of these attempts. The interstate disputes, tensions, distrusts and apprehensions among the individual countries were the main factors.[37]

The South Asian subcontinent experienced a changing political environment during the later part of the 1970s. The Janata Party came into power in India, Zia took over Pakistan, Zia-ur-Rehman consolidated his power in Bangladesh and Jayawardene took over Sri Lanka. The Janata government did not abandon the main tenets of the Indian foreign policy followed since 1947, but took a more conciliatory approach towards its immediate neighbours. The new leaders, in contrast to their predecessors, wanted closer relationship and cooperation within the region. The deepening of economic crisis, unemployment, poverty and declining growth rates compelled these countries to think for regional cooperation. The smaller countries in South Asia, such as Nepal, Sri Lanka and Bangladesh, were very enthusiastic about regional cooperation. The idea of regional cooperation in South Asia was first mooted by late President of Bangladesh Zia-ur-Rehman. During his visit to India, Pakistan, Nepal and Sri Lanka, Rehman tried to convince the head of the states regarding the prospective future of his proposed regional cooperation. In May 1980, Zia-ur-Rehman sent a formal letter to all the South Asian countries proposing the establishment of regional organisation in South Asia followed by *Bangladesh Working Paper* sent to all countries on 25 November 1980.

The proposal for regional cooperation came from smaller countries as they felt that it could serve two objectives: It could provide a cover against India's domination and it could accelerate the pace of economic development.[38] With initial reservations, India accepted the proposal in principle, but decided to scrutinise it carefully. It is often argued that any attempt towards regional cooperation in the South Asian region is inconceivable without India's active participation, as South Asia is predominantly an Indo-centric region.

After several rounds of meetings and discussions among South Asian countries, the idea of establishing a regional cooperation took a final shape in December 1985. The South Asian Association for Regional Cooperation (SAARC) was formally established when its Charter was adopted on 8 December 1985 by the governments of India, Pakistan, Bangladesh, Sri Lanka, Bhutan, Maldives and Nepal. It provides a platform for the people of South Asia to work together in the spirit of friendship, trust and understanding. The main emphases of SAARC are to:

1. promote welfare of the people in the region;
2. accelerate economic growth, social progress and cultural development;
3. promote and strengthen collective self-reliance among members;

4. contribute to mutual trust understanding and appreciation of one another's problem;
5. development of mutual dependence among member states;
6. strengthen cooperation with other developing countries;
7. strengthen cooperation among themselves in international forums on matters of common interests; and
8. cooperate with international and regional organisations with similar aims and purposes.[39]

In due course of time, it is becoming clear that there is tremendous potential for regional economic cooperation, and a number of such areas can be explored for economic development. In addition, the association attached high priority to the promotion of people-to-people contact in the region to strengthen mutual understanding and goodwill among the people of South Asia.

The coming of a new wave of regionalism in the early 1990s, creation of new trade blocs and deepening of the existing ones raised the fears of protectionism among SAARC countries. The smaller members put forward the proposal for a preferential trading regime, namely, South Asian Preferential Trading Agreement (SAPTA). SAPTA was created in 1993 at the Dacca Summit, and it became operational in December 1995. However, the commodities under SAPTA constitute a fraction of the commodities traded. Therefore, a SAPTA fast-track is being proposed to extend higher tariff concessions. SAARC also decided to create a free trade area (SAFTA) during the 16th session of the Council of Ministers in New Delhi on 18–19 December 1995. To this end, an Inter-Governmental Expert Group (IGEG) was set up in 1996 to identify the necessary steps for progressing to a free trade area. The 10th SAARC Summit at Colombo in July 1998 decided to set up a Committee of Experts to draft a comprehensive treaty framework for creating a free trade area within the region. The SAFTA Agreement was finally signed on 6 January 2004 during the 12th SAARC Summit held in Islamabad, and the Agreement came into force on 1 January 2006 and the Trade Liberalisation Programme commenced from 1 July 2006. The keen interest shown by the member countries since its inception in 1985 shows that there is a vast scope of success for the association. South Asia has good reasons to promote cooperation in the region. The entire region is unified by a common cultural and ethnic outlook, geographical proximity coupled with the overlapping historical experiences, traditions and common problems underlining the need to pool the resources of the South Asian countries.

Although the formation of SAARC was for non-political purposes, the member countries have not refrained themselves from their mutual political conflicts.[40] According to P.V. Rao, the objective factors required for the promotion of regional cooperation are very poorly prevalent in South Asia. Lack of economic complementarity, unequal levels of development, economic nationalism, over regulated trade practices, mutual suspicions and external suspicions and external intrusion are the major constraints on cooperation.[41] The problems posed by ethno-nationalities as well as inter-state borders within the region are stumbling blocks in promoting any cooperative venture. Since the launch of SAFTA Trade Liberalisation Programme in July 2006 till 10 August 2011, the total exports by SAARC countries under SAFTA reached US$1.3 billion, which is far below the potential.[42]

India attempts for a greater regional integration in Asia and the world at large, but she faces a lot of local regional forces which, at many times, are responsible for instability in the country. Since independence, India has witnessed a surge of internal regional forces which manifest itself in the form of ethnic, cultural, political and economic regionalism.

Therefore, India's effort towards regional economic cooperation in its own neighbourhood is encountered with inherent difficulties, which are often political in nature, and the preoccupation of India's dominance. Economic fears and political hostility have constrained the growth of trade, and these obstacles have not been confined to ties between India and Pakistan. As India is not able to forge a successful regional economic cooperation in its own neighbourhood, it became imperative for her to look for a region where she can forge intensive economic cooperation.

The East Asian Miracle

The East Asian countries witnessed a remarkable record of high and sustained economic growth from 1965 to 1990, and their economies grew faster than all other regions of the world during this period.[43] This rapid economic growth of the eight East Asian economies—Japan, the four Asian tigers (Hong Kong, Singapore, South Korea and Taiwan) and three newly industrialising economies (Indonesia, Malaysia and Thailand)—has been termed as the *East Asian miracle*. In these eight countries, the real per capita GDP rose twice as fast as in any other regional grouping between 1965 and 1990. With sustained high growth rates, these countries also simultaneously reduced poverty and income inequality.

The success of the East and Southeast Asian countries is attributed to economic policies made favourable to the business communities and citizens by the leaders of these countries. Economic dynamism displayed by these economies was attributed to their outward-looking development strategies. Their growth performance has been far higher than that of the most developed regions, including North America, EU, other European countries and Japan. Yi Shen labelled the East Asian economies as *relation-based capitalism* which is characterised by personal and implicit agreements that are governed by second-party enforcement and widely based on mutual trust between transaction parties.[44]

The East and Southeast Asian countries have been one of India's priority areas of cooperation under the framework of economic diplomacy. In fact, India's economic ties with these regions were underdeveloped even though it was one of the fastest growing areas of the world because of its friendship with the Soviet Union. India neglected the Southeast Asian region and regarded ASEAN as a *trojan horse* of the United States, and cultivated close ties with socialist Vietnam.[45] Southeast Asian countries too have negative perceptions about India. They regarded Indian decision-making process as very slow, cumbersome and too bureaucratic, which hampers development in the country and consider Indians too much ideologically oriented and less pragmatic in their foreign and economic policies resulting in divergence of approach between India and the countries of ASEAN. Southeast Asian countries also avoided getting entangled with India as they felt that inclusion of India in any of the institutional arrangements would bring the South Asian conflicts into their own region, which in turn will only complicate their own security rather than solving it.[46]

During 1990–91, India was internally faced with social tensions and unrests, political instability and poor economic performance. The external environment was also not conducive to its interests with the fall of India's major economic partner and its closest strategic ally—the Soviet Union. The subsequent breakdown of ideological barriers due to the end of the Cold War has led India to follow a more pragmatic approach. The admiration for economic achievements of East and Southeast Asian countries coupled with the changing global environment caused New Delhi to pay more attention to the rapidly growing economies of East and Southeast Asia.[47] To the Indian liberalisers, East and Southeast Asian countries appeared to be a model of success, and Asianism could be revived under a different garb to serve new purposes.[48] As a matter of fact, East and Southeast Asia became a model for the Indian reform process.

India's Predicament and the Economic Reforms

The collapse of the Soviet system deprived India not only of a valuable economic and strategic partner, but also of an important model of centralised economic planning. The Indian predicament was further accentuated as globalisation made its headway during the early 1990s, and the world economic system rapidly turned towards the capitalistic mode of development. Globalisation of world economies greatly intensified international competition and has, at the same time, given rise to a new wave of regionalism.[49] This *new world* order of globalisation and regionalism has to be accepted and embraced by the developing countries in order to survive.

The success story of ASEAN, the resumption of integration process of the EU and the negotiations for NAFTA and Asia-Pacific Economic Cooperation (APEC) gave India the impression that it was in danger of isolation from the dynamics pushing the global economy.[50] Being aware of the growing trend towards regionalism and its possible marginalisation in the global economy and being faced with a serious balance of payment crisis, the Narasimha Rao government in the middle of 1991 liberalised its economy under the supervision of International Monetary Fund (IMF). The liberalisation process and the opening up to world economy have led to a reshaping of the role of Indian state, not only in economic management but also in foreign policy.

According to C. Raja Mohan, there are five structural changes in India, where these *changes stand out and are unlikely to be reversed*. They are: the transition from the national consensus on building a *socialist society* to building a *modern capitalist* one; the transition from the past emphasis on politics to a new stress on economics in the making of foreign policy;

the shift from being a leader of the *Third World* to the recognition of the potential that India could emerge as a great power in its own right; rejection of the *anti-Western* mode of thinking; and the transition from idealism to realism.[51]

In India's drive towards globalisation, the primary task of diplomacy is to contribute directly to economic development. For that matter, New Delhi has sought to improve the functioning and efficiency of its economic diplomacy. The new emphasis on economic diplomacy has induced some reorientation in the role and functioning of the Ministry of External Affairs (MEA). By the end of 1991, Prime Minister Narasimha Rao issued a note asking the Foreign Office and its diplomats posted abroad to focus more on the economic aspects of India's external relations.[52] As the Indian establishment and the members of the intelligentsia had wanted to escape westernisation, they then became favourably inclined toward Asianism as an alternative to the American capitalist mode.[53] Under the framework of economic diplomacy, the East Asian region has been seen as a priority area of cooperation. With high economic achievements, the Indian leadership became eager to cooperate with the East and Southeast Asian regions.

Notes

1. Shashi Upadhya, *Post Cold War Developments in South Asia*, p. 47.
2. Richard Stubbs, *Political Economy and the Changing Global Order*, p. 231.
3. Rajen Harshe, 'South Asian Regional Co-operation: Problems and Prospects', p. 1100.
4. Poonam Mann, *India's Foreign Policy in the Post Cold War Era*, p. 3.
5. Norman D. Palmer and Howard C. Perkins, *International Relations: The World Community in Transition*, p. 597.
6. Unpublished address on 'the Atlantic Community' at a conference on Regionalism and Political Pacts, Philadelphia, 6 May 1949. Quoted in Norman D. Palmer and Howard C. Perkins. Also see ibid., p. 558.
7. E.H. Carl, *The Twenty Years' Crisis: 1919–1939*, p. 203.
8. Norman J. Padelford, 'Regional Organisation and the United Nations', *International Organisation*, pp. 2003–16.
9. Philippe De Lombaerde and Luk Van Langenhove, 'Indicators of Regional Integration: Conceptual and Methodological Issues.'
10. Hans van Ginkel, 'Regionalism and the United Nations'.

11. Walter Mattli, *The Logic of Regional Integration: Europe and Beyond*, p. 41.
12. Hans Van Ginkel and Luk Van Langenhove, *Integrating Africa: Perspectives on Regional Integration and Development*, pp. 1–9.
13. L. Van Langenhove, 'Regional Integration and Global Governance', p. 4.
14. E.D. Mansfield and H.V. Milner, 'The New Wave of Regionalism', p. 597.
15. H. Hrem, 'Explaining the Regional Phenomenon in an Era of Globalization', p. 70.
16. E.D. Mansfield and H.V. Milner, 'The New Wave of Regionalism', p. 601.
17. R.Z. Lawrence. *Regionalism, Multilateralism, and Deeper Integration*, p. 6.
18. Nicola Phillips, 'The Future of the Political Economy of Latin America', p. 286.
19. Bjorn Hettne, 'Globalization, the New Regionalism and East Asia'.
20. Jagdish Bhagwati, 'Regionalism versus Multilateralism', pp. 535–56.
21. Edward D. Mansfield and Helen V. Milner, 'The New Wave of Regionalism', p. 592.
22. Ghulam Umar, *SAARC: Analytical Survey*, p. 5.
23. All references relating to the Charter of the United Nations is taken from its official website: http://www.un.org/aboutun/charter (downloaded on 07.11.2014).
24. Theodore A. Couloumbis and James H. Wolfe, *Introduction to International Relations: Power and Justice*, p. 294.
25. 'ECOSOC Promotes Regional Integration as a Prerequisite for Globalization', *Regional Commissions Development Update*.
26. Jaime de Melo and Arvind Panagariya, *New Dimensions in Regional Integration*, p. 5.
27. Walter Mattli, *The Logic of Regional Integration: Europe and Beyond*, p. 139.
28. Ibid., p. 152.
29. Overview of Association of Southeast Asian Nations, http://www.aseansec.org/64.htm (downloaded on 28.12.2014).
30. Jawaharlal Nehru, *Discovery of India*, p. 569.
31. Jawaharlal Nehru, *Jawaharlal Nehru Speeches, 1946–49*, p. 300.
32. Warner Levi, *Free India in Asia*, p. 39.
33. William Henderson. 'The Development of Regionalism in Southeast Asia', pp. 463–76.
34. Jawaharlal Nehru, *Jawaharlal Nehru Speeches, 1946–49*, p. 329.
35. Nicholas Manserch, ed., *Documents and Speeches on British Commonwealth Affairs, 1931–1952*, p. 1179.
36. *Foreign Policy of India: Texts of Documents*, pp. 149–54.
37. B.C. Upreti, *SAARC: Dynamics of Regional Cooperation in South Asia* (Vol. 1), p. 9.
38. B.C. Upreti, *SAARC: Dynamics of Regional Cooperation in South Asia*, p. 10.
39. For areas of SAARC cooperation, see SAARC website: http://www.saarc-sec.org/?t=2 (downloaded on 29.12.2014).
40. Devinder Kumar Maadan, 'SAARC: Origin and Development', p. 165.

41. P.V. Rao, 'Globalisation and Regional Cooperation: The South Asian Experience', p. 34.
42. For details of SAFTA, see SAARC official website: http://www.saarc-sec.org/areaofcooperation/detail.php?activity_id=5 (downloaded on 12.11.2011).
43. 'The Making of the East Asian Miracle', *World Policy Research Bulletin.*
44. Yi Shen, 'The Miracle and Crisis of East Asia: Relation-Based Governance vs. Rule-Based Governance'.
45. Isabelle Saint-Mezard, 'The Look East Policy; An Economic Perspective', p. 25.
46. Baladas Ghosal, 'East Asian Miracle and India', p. 12.
47. Sandy Gordon. *India's Rise to Power in the Twentieth Century and Beyond*, p. 299.
48. Christophe Jaffrelot, 'India's Look East policy: An Asianist Strategy in Perspective', p. 44.
49. Rajen Harshe, 'South Asian Regional Co-operation: Problems and Prospects', p. 1999.
50. Isabelle Saint-Mezard, 'The Look East policy; An Economic Perspective', pp. 21–22.
51. C. Raja Mohan, 'India's New Foreign Policy Strategy', 26 May 2006.
52. J.N. Dixit. *My South Block Years: Memoirs of a Foreign Secretary*, p. 58.
53. Christophe Jaffrelot, 'India's Look East policy: An Asianist Strategy in Perspective'.

2

Evolution of India's Look East Policy

The evolution of India's Look East policy can be traced to the changed context of the international system in the early 1990s. The policy launched in 1991 has its genesis in the end of the Cold War, following the collapse of the Soviet Union. Nevertheless, the real genesis of the Look East policy can be traced to the early years of India's independence. India's efforts towards regional cooperation started in the pre-independence period, whereas in the mid-1940s and 1950s there were concerted efforts to develop cooperation with Asian and other developing nations of the world. The importance of Southeast Asia was recognised by one of India's first strategic analysts, the visionary K.M. Panikkar, way back in the 1940s. The prime minister of India, Jawaharlal Nehru, also recognised the importance of Southeast Asia which offered an opportunity for India to forge close political links. Indeed, India's first foray into foreign policy affairs was in Southeast Asia in support of anti-colonial movements in that region.[1]

Even before formal independence, Indian leaders convened the Asian Relations Conference from 23 March 1947 to 2 April 1947 in New Delhi, which was attended by 25 Asian countries, including Egypt.[2] There was an expression of great enthusiasm for regional cooperation from Ceylon (Sri Lanka) and Burma. India called the Conference on Indonesia in New Delhi on 20 January 1949 to express support to the Sukarno-led armed struggle against the Dutch attempt to re-impose colonial rule in Indonesia by launching two major military offensives—*Operatie Product* (Operation Product) on 20 July 1947 and *Operatie Kraai* (Operation Crow) on 19 December 1948. Apart from the Indonesian issue, the conference passed resolutions calling for regional integration of the participating nations. Apart from the major attempts at regional cooperation, there were several other efforts; a number of conferences were organised and attended by India to find possibilities of such cooperation.[3]

Despite the insistence on Asian solidarity by various leaders during the anti-colonial struggles in the post-Second World War period, there was negligible cooperation between the Asian countries. All attempts by India to forge cooperation among the Asian countries did not work well to the satisfaction of the Indian leaders. The interstate disputes, tensions, distrusts, apprehensions among the individual countries and the tussle for leadership between India and China were responsible for the failure of India's attempt towards regional cooperation in Asia and Africa in general, and Southeast Asia in particular.[4] Although India's debut in the international arena had its origin in Southeast Asia, the initiative for pan-Asian solidarity by Jawaharlal Nehru did not materialise, following the Chinese aggression on the North Eastern Frontier Agency (NEFA) in the northeastern region of India in 1962 and the subsequent change of India's policy to strengthen its military capability. As I.K. Gujral said in a speech in Singapore in 1996, every aspect of India's ethos reflects the 'footprints of South-East Asia'; nevertheless, 'the forces of history and circumstances intermittently disturbed this closeness. Colonialism and the Cold War, despite our efforts to come together, drew artificial boundaries between us.'[5] Further, the focus of regional cooperation during the early post-colonial years was more political than economic. Issues such as decolonisation, neutrality and security were the focal point for the leaders of Asia and Africa to rally around a common platform, although some contents of economic cooperation were usually there.

The end of the Cold War has brought about a fundamental change in the international system, which focuses on the economic content of relations and has led to the burgeoning of the formation of regional economic organisations. This change in the international system, the success stories of the East Asian Tiger economies and the radical shift in India's economic and strategic circumstances caused New Delhi to pay more attention to the rapidly growing economies of East and Southeast Asia.[6] From a strategic standpoint, a number of realist political commentators pointed out that the end of the Cold War and the beginning of the Gulf War (1990–91) had created *unprecedented opportunities* for India,[7] although Ross H. Munro argued in the early 1990s that India was the greatest loser from the end of the Cold War: 'India's reach for great power status is in shambles. The keystone of Indian power and pretence in the 1980s, the Indo-Soviet link, is history.... India has no "useful friends".'[8] However, by the latter half of the 1990s, India emerged as a South Asian winner, rather than a loser. Far from being isolated and ineffective as a result of the end of the Cold War, India has gained significant advantages by opening up its economy—advantages that will eventually allow the synergisms inherent in India's circumstances to realise its potential.[9]

India's Domestic and Regional Environment in 1990–91

As nations do not exist in isolation, the domestic as well as external environment have an impact on their foreign policy. The linkage between external elements and foreign policy cannot be wished away, as foreign policy constitutes a set of responses to external challenges and opportunities.[10] Consequently, any change in the environment requires change in the behaviour of nations. Hence, political developments from 1989 to 1991 affected all nations. India was no exception to all these external developments. They had significant impact on India's domestic as well as foreign policy.

The beginning of the 1990s was a turbulent period for India. The country witnessed unstable domestic environment characterised by increasing terrorism and insurgency, political instability, economic doldrums and financial crisis. The unstable domestic environment was compounded by an unfavourable regional environment. Although the *Khalistan* insurgency in Punjab had declined by the end of 1992, there was an increase in the number of violent incidents perpetrated by insurgents in Jammu & Kashmir (J&K) and Northeast India. The militant outfits in J&K became violent and acquired a radical religious ideology in order to legitimise their actions. Most of these militants managed to get logistic support from Pakistan in terms of training, sophisticated arms and ammunition and even finance, which 'in a way gave them some clout to demonstrate their power.'[11] Since the early 1990s, Pakistan adopted a more vociferous anti-India stance which was reflected in encouraging and aiding militants in J&K, and in its attempt to internationalise developments in J&K.[12] The resurgence of Sindhi and Baluchi movements in Pakistan, Nepalis in Bhutan, Terai versus hill people in Nepal, Chakmas in Bangladesh, Tamils in Sri Lanka and various tribal communities in Northeast India, all representing sub-nationalist or ethno-centric tendencies threatening the existing state structure throughout South Asia.[13] The problem was compounded by the emergence of Sagiang Division of Myanmar as a safe haven for the insurgent groups of Northeast India, the underground smugglers market of Cambodia as an important source of arms and ammunition, and the drug smugglers market in the Golden Triangle, a border area comprising Laos, Myanmar, Thailand and Cambodia. This highlighted the threats to India's national security, which could rise from the east and the consequent need to seek cooperation from the governments of these countries in dealing with such threats.

In spite of reforms during the Rajiv Gandhi-led Congress government in the mid-1980s and throughout the latter part of the decade, the percentage of trade in relation to Gross National Product had actually fallen from 12.4 per cent in 1984–85 to 11 per cent in 1988–89.[14] Since there was low level of trade and as a small percentage of the economy was involved in it, there was little scope for adjusting any rise in the prices of oil within the overall trade balance. The small rise in the price of oil, due to the 1990–91 Gulf Crisis, was translated into a 21.9 per cent increase in the import bill in rupee term.[15] The extent of the emerging problem is discernable from the fact that in 1965 India's energy import constituted only about 8 per cent of the value of its merchandise exports whereas by 1990, energy imports constituted nearly 25 per cent of the value of exports.[16]

The 1990 Gulf Crisis had a deep impact on India's economy as it depended much on the West Asian countries for oil and trade. This was followed by economic recession and political turmoil in India. In the Gulf Crisis, India lost remittances of US$205 million from Indians employed in Iraq and Kuwait; it lost an amount of US$500 million owing to it from Iraq at the start of the crisis; and it lost about US$112 million in trade with Iraq and Kuwait.[17] At the same time, trade with the Eastern European countries had suffered severely with the end of communist rule and the collapse of that system. Consequently, by the mid-1991, foreign exchange reserves had fallen barely enough to cover two weeks imports, and India was forced to seek the help of the IMF. An agreement was reached by the Indian government with the IMF in January 1991 on a loan for US$1.8 billion, partly out of the Compensatory Financing Facility (to offset increased oil imports) and partly as a first credit tranche standby.[18]

The political scenario of India during this period was marked by instability, in which three successive governments were formed within two years. The developing economic crisis at the end of the 1980s coincided with the electoral cycle in 1989, in which the Indian electorate chose to express its dissatisfaction by opting for political weakness and instability at the centre by electing a parliament with no party in majority.[19] When the Congress party, which had the largest elected Members of Parliament, refused to form government, Janta Dal took over power backed by two ideologically contradictory parties: the Bharatiya Janata Party (BJP) and the Communist Party of India (Marxist). Instead of taking steps to redress the deepening economic crisis, the parties in power soon launched populist policies, both economically and socially, which worsened the economic situation. Thus, India faced both economic crisis and political instability.

The withdrawal of support to the National Front government by the BJP at the end of 1990 resulted in the collapse of that government. This collapse was followed by a split in the Janata Dal, which was the main constituent of the National Front government. Chandrasekhar abandoned the Janata Dal and formed a new party, the Samajwadi Janata Party. After the fall of the National Front government led by V.P. Singh, a minority government with Chandrashekhar as the prime minister was installed with the support of the Congress party, although Chandrashekhar's party had only 58 members out of 473 in the Lok Sabha. It was so small that it could only survive because nobody in the Parliament wanted another election.[20] The greatest problem of the Chandrashekhar government was the fast disappearance of financial reserves and the inability to formulate any concrete economic policies, even a budget. The withdrawal of the Congress party support within a few months led to the fall of the Chandrashekhar government, and resulted in fresh elections in June 1991. The Congress emerged as the single largest party with 232 seats. Subsequently, a Congress led minority government with P.V. Narasimha Rao as the prime minister, supported by some regional parties was formed in June 1991.

The new government under Prime Minister Narasimha Rao was confronted with the uphill task of putting the derailed economy back on tracks, restoring a semblance of political stability and availing of new opportunities, and facing challenges thrown open by globalisation and the New World Order.[21] There was an enormous increase in non-productive expenditure. Defence expenditure rose from 15.9 per cent of central government's spending in 1980–81 to 16.9 per cent in 1987–88 to nearly 19 per cent in 1990–91. Subsidies grew from 8.5 per cent in 1980–81 to 11.4 per cent in 1989–90.[22] The main thrust of the new government's economic and financial policy was to restructure the framework of economic activity, and move the country towards international market and trade.

Compelled by a severe balance of payment crisis, faced with the gradual erosion of competitiveness of Indian goods in the global market, and recognising the importance of foreign capital in a country's economic development, an economic liberalisation programme was undertaken in June 1991 with a view to firstly attract foreign investments, both portfolio and direct, and secondly to boost exports.[23] The main aim of such a liberal economic reforms programme was to integrate India's economy with the global economy. Sandy Gordon sums up some of the measures taken by the government to reform the economy which were introduced in the budgets since 1991–92 as follows:

1. Devaluation of the rupee by about 30 per cent against the US dollars, with the aim of achieving full convertibility;
2. Raising of the ceiling of foreign ownership to 51 per cent and higher in some instances, with partial repatriation of capital at market rates on a 60:40 basis (with 40 per cent being at the government rate);
3. Removal of restrictive controls on the import of most items and lowering of the tariff. The import duty on capital goods was further reduced to 35 per cent from 55 per cent, with a special 25 per cent rate on capital goods destined for priority sectors. The import weighted tariff was to be reduced to 25 per cent in two to three years;
4. Abolition of the internal licensing system in all but 18 industries;
5. Preparation for sale in principle of up to 49 per cent of the government's share in state enterprises;
6. The floating of the rupee on trade account in 1993;
7. Reduction of the excise duty;
8. Reform of the financial sector; and
9. A substantial reduction in the rate of company taxation in 1994.[24]

The buzzword of the 1991 economic policy was the inclusion of liberalisation, privatisation and globalisation. The main objective of these economic reforms was to bring the derailed economy back on the track by providing a boost to foreign trade and attracting FDI. As a result, market economy replaced the socialistic pattern of society, which the Congress had long cherished as the goal, as well as the means for India's development by building up the public sector domestically while insulating India from international market forces. The economic reforms launched in 1991, thus, constitute a watershed in India's economic history.

Compulsions of India to Look East

The political and economic developments in different parts of the world during the early 1990s brought radical changes in the relations among nations, resulting in the emergence of an era of globalisation. Globalisation brought about an increasing integration of economies and societies, and threw open opportunities as well as challenges to both the developed as well as developing countries. Globalisation of the world's economies greatly intensified international competition and has, at the same time, given rise to a new wave of regionalism.[25] Regionalism, in general, has proved to be an effective device to serve economic and commercial objectives. In the process, old organisations are recast and new organisations are formed to suit the changing global political and economic contexts. Geographical proximity, economic complementarity, political commitment, policy coordination and infrastructure development provide conditions for the formation of such groupings. Consequently, a number of proximate states in different parts of the world constitute themselves into regions to give fresh impetus to a wide variety of cooperative ventures based on regionalism. In this changing political and economic context, India needed to closely examine the evolving international situation and take timely initiatives to adjust its policies in order to reap benefits for herself. At the macro level, India directed its foreign policy at achieving three important objectives: 'Maintaining the territorial integrity of India, ensuring its geopolitical security by creating a durable environment of peace and stability in the region and to build a framework for the well-being of the people by encouraging a healthy external economic environment.'[26]

Within the South Asian region, India and its neighbouring countries have made several attempts for regional cooperation. The SAARC was established on 8 December 1985 to accelerate the process of economic and social development among the seven member states. There have been several attempts to improve trade in the region through SAPTA and SAFTA. Despite such efforts, trade within SAARC countries continues to be abysmally low.[27] Pakistan is yet to ratify the free trade agreement. Economic exchanges and cooperative ties within SAARC were constrained, if not blocked by the India–Pakistan dispute and India's sheer weight.[28] The disappointing pace of SAPTA and SAFTA negotiations forced India to look beyond the confines of South Asia for regional economic cooperation.

The collapse of the Soviet Union had severe repercussions on India. The former Soviet Union had been a time-tested partner for supplies of arms, petroleum and, to some extent, economic assistance. It had also been a leading partner and a big market of Indian consumer goods. The collapse of the Soviet system deprived India of a valuable trading partner; the Rupee Trade Area had accounted for about one-fourth of India's exports. The Soviet Union had always supported India diplomatically through UN's votes, and was an important model of centralised planning.[29] One of the major concerns for New Delhi was that it could no longer rely on Soviet diplomatic support at the Security Council of the UN. Thus, India was exposed to international pressures to vital interests like disarmament, non-proliferation and the Kashmir issue.[30] It was a big loss for India in political, strategic and economic terms.

The temporary disruption of the oil economy in the Gulf region, following the crisis over Kuwait, brought home to India the importance of diversifying its sources of energy supplies in order to reduce its dependence on its traditional suppliers in the Gulf and the erstwhile Soviet Union. In this endeavour, the availability of energy sources in countries, such as Myanmar, Brunei, Indonesia and Australia, provided possible alternatives. Thus, it was natural for Indian decision makers to look for a new international role and to turn to the most economically dynamic region of the world—Southeast Asia.[31]

There are three main issues facing India in the Southeast Asian region. Firstly, stabilising the Northeast, its clandestine flows and foreign connections; secondly, taking advantage of the proximity with Southeast Asian nations, especially Myanmar, to step onto the Asian diplomatic and economic scene; and finally, measuring the impact of China's influence on the Myanmar regime and its consequences for the country's interests.[32] Beijing's growing military and economic penetration in Myanmar and its assertiveness in the Asia-Pacific region renewed India's concerns about the consequences of an antecedent and powerful China and its impact on India's security. India needed various diplomatic, economic and military tools to deal with these sensitive and strategic geopolitical issues. During the Cold War years, the foreign policy of India was driven by ideological or political factors, although it chose to distance itself from the two ideologically opposite blocs by opting non-alignment. Economic dimensions of foreign relations were not given much importance in the MEA.[33] With the end of the Cold War, the main tenets of India's foreign policy, non-alignment, became increasingly obsolete. As India was a co-founder and one of its most influential members, it could assume the status of a leader among the developing countries and enjoy some sort of international reputation in the Cold War period. But with the end of the Cold War, the very concept of non-alignment was undermined. The victory of the United States, its political world view and its free-market economic system posed a new challenge to India's foreign policy. Although military capability still remains one of the primary determining factors of the global power equation, economic power has, of late, begun to exert predominant influence upon it, and the balance of power has tended to shift from military to economic sphere. One of the offshoots of the above-mentioned development has been de-emphasising military orientation and placing more stress on economic orientation of the foreign policy on the part of many countries, both developed and developing including India. Thus, the Nehruvian model of foreign policy autonomy vis-à-vis imperialism and capitalism has come under severe strain, and there are strong pressures from several influential quarters in India and abroad to link it with the Western economy.[34]

With the end of the Cold War and the worldwide trend towards free-market reforms, economics became a major factor in international relations. The international status of a country depends much on its wealth. Therefore, by the end of 1991, Prime Minister Narasimha Rao issued a note asking foreign office and its diplomatic posts abroad to focus more on the economic aspects of India's external relations.[35] Hence, economic diplomacy becomes the new trend in Indian's foreign policy.

Belatedly, the Indian policy-makers became aware of the implications of the 12 years head start which China had in opening up, reforming and developing its economy ahead of India and strengthening the consequent political and economic linkages of China with Southeast Asian countries. There was also a realisation that unless India took steps to reduce China's head start and develop similar linkages with the political leaderships, economies and the elite of this region, it might ultimately find itself with a greatly reduced and barely meaningful political and economic role in the region. Gautam S. Kaji, one of the managing directors of World Bank, expressed the same view in April 1995: 'Certainly, the East Asian nations are still grappling with some of the same problems as India, albeit on a lesser scale. But they have demonstrated with the right commitment, it is possible to move very far. With the same kind of commitment, I am convinced that there can be an "Indian miracle".'[36] In September 1995, Indian Finance Minister Manmohan Singh also noted that '[t]he economic policies of India take into account the dynamism of this region, which shall soon be the tiger economy of the world. We want to participate in this process.'[37]

The policy of India tying India's fortune to the West, with India giving considerable attention to its trading relationships with the oil-rich West Asia, Europe and North America, came under some pressure, with some advocating closer ties with Asia on the ground that it is the centre of growth in the world today.[38] They argued that India has been separated from the East bloc for the purpose of trade and caught in a world in which trading blocs are assuming greater importance. They also maintained that SAARC does not have the critical mass to provide for India's trading needs, even if the political climate were more favourable for regional trade.[39] These views have been reflected in the policies pursued by the MEA, which has been attempting to have India more closely associated with ASEAN and the Asia-Pacific Economic Cooperation (APEC) forum, the loose formation that brings the nations bordering the Pacific together for trade-related discussions.

The emergence of Asian Tigers and the growth of ASEAN as leading economies of Asia provided further impetus for the Indian policy-makers to look at the East as a possible avenue for conducting economic transaction. The onslaught of the liberalisation, privatisation and globalisation processes was on the rise, and there was no escape for the Indian economy. There was also a realisation that India's aspiration of becoming a permanent member of the UN Security Council might not materialise without the overwhelming support of the countries of the East and Southeast Asian region, and that it would be necessary to focus greater efforts on the countries of the East and Southeast Asian regions by strengthening India's linkages with them.[40]

The GoI, while retaining the core concerns in its foreign policy, also recognised the necessity of integrating the Indian economy with the global economy. Policy reforms were immediately undertaken, and the ASEAN region was singled out as an important area with which India sought a formal tie. The GoI, for the first time since independence, turned its attention towards the ASEAN region with economics in mind.[41] The absence of conflict on vital issues and the presence of common challenges made it possible to expand constructive ties between the two peoples.

The change in the international and regional politico-strategic situations in the late 1980s and early 1990s created an environment for positive developments in India–ASEAN relations. The end of the Cold War and the breakdown of ideological barriers led to a more pragmatic approach by India. Since the end of the Cold War, India's strategic world view clearly shifts from an emphasis on moral speak to realpolitik based on acquiring and exercising economic and military power.[42] New Delhi's economic reform programme has changed its equations with many countries. India is letting no chance go by to prove that it wishes to be fully integrated into the global market and to do business.[43] India realised that it is in its interest to go for cooperative venture and utilise the window of opportunity, rather than awaiting initiatives from the side of Southeast Asian countries. According to Prem Shankar Jha, 'the dark side of the East Asian success story is that there will inevitably be a loser and that India could be one of them.'[44] When Finance Minister Manmohan Singh brought about a fresh burst of economic liberlisation to the Indian economy with the 1993 budget, one of his stated goals was to catch up with China.[45]

The Look East Policy

The economic reforms, coupled with the integrative forces of globalisation, frustration with the process of integration within South Asia and the renewed concern about the antecedent and powerful China and its impact on India's security, as well as India's unease at Beijing's growing assertiveness in the Asia-Pacific region, made India to rethink the basic parameters of its foreign policy. While India was opening up to the world market, it became aware of the growing trends towards regionalism and feared that it would be marginalised from the dynamics pushing the global economy. As a result of these compulsions, the Look East policy was officially launched in the year 1991[46] during the tenure of Prime Minister Narasimha Rao, although the term *Look East policy* was mentioned for the first time in the *annual report* of the MEA in 1996.[47] I.K. Gujral had stated: 'What look east really means is that an outward looking India, is gathering all forces of dynamism domestic and regional and is directly focusing on establishing synergies with a fast consolidating and progressive neighbourhood to its East in Mother Continent of Asia.'[48] The Look East policy is, thus, a product of various compulsions, changed perceptions and expectations of India in the changed international environment. It is part of the new *realpolitik* that can be seen in India's foreign economic policy. This renewed interest for regional cooperation with ASEAN was based on the recognition of the strategic and economic importance of Southeast Asia to India's national interests.

As a part of its endeavour to forge closer ties with ASEAN countries, Indian Prime Minister P.V. Narasimha Rao visited some countries of Southeast Asia in 1993 and expounded the new *Look East* policy of India in his much publicised and well-received *Singapore lecture* at the Institute of Southeast Asian Studies. In his lecture, Rao said:

> While in those days, the Cold War was at its peak, and therefore, the super powers were looked upon with some caution mixed with suspicion, it is gratifying to note that the ASEAN can today speak from a position of strength at the same table with the US, Russia, China, Japan ... India has already taken steps to liberalise its currency regime, open the economy to more imports and investment, and educate its people on the benefits of exposure to the outside world. The Asia Pacific would be the springboard for our leap into the global market place.[49]

Since the initiation of the Look East policy in 1991, bilateral relations between India and ASEAN have progressed rapidly. India's ties with ASEAN were upgraded to a Sectoral Dialogue Partnership in March 1993 in three areas, namely, trade, investment and tourism. Indian and ASEAN officials met in New Delhi on 16–17 March 1993 to identify specific areas of collaboration within the designed sectors. Due to its sustained efforts, India–ASEAN relations were upgraded to a Full Dialogue Partnership at the 5th ASEAN Summit in Bangkok, in December 1995. This elevated the interactions between ASEAN and India from the senior official to the ministerial level and enabled India's participation in the ASEAN Post-Ministerial Conference. At the ASEAN Post-Ministerial Conference in Jakarta, in July 1996, ASEAN and Indian ministers outlined a vision of shared destiny and intensified cooperation in all fields, identifying specific areas for cooperation, such as infrastructure, human resource development, science and technology and tourism, among others. I.K. Gujral remarked that he saw India's Full Dialogue Partnership status as a window to India's progressive participation in other ASEAN-like groupings, such as APEC and the Asia–Europe meetings.[50]

The increasingly closer cooperation between India and ASEAN led to the strengthening of not only economic ties, but also security linkages resulting in India's admission to the ASEAN Regional Forum (ARF) in 1996. The ARF is the main forum for security cooperation in the Asia-Pacific region, in which global and regional security issues as well as disarmament and non-proliferation issues are discussed. India's admission to the ARF signifies the acceptance of its role and position in the Asia-Pacific region. The increasing engagement of India in the strategic discourses of the Asia-Pacific region underlines its commitment to the objective of sustaining regional peace and stability. India has been an active participant in the various ARF processes and has hosted several activities. India hosted its first-ever ARF event on 18–20 October 2000, when an Anti-Piracy Workshop was organised in Mumbai by the Indian Coast Guard in conjunction with the MEA and Ministry of Defence. Subsequently, India organised several workshops related to security.

India–ASEAN relations were upgraded to a Summit Level Partnership in 2002. Thus, India became one of the four ASEAN Summit Level Partners along with China, Japan and Korea. At the 2nd India–ASEAN Summit in October 2003, India and ASEAN signed the Framework Agreement on Comprehensive Economic Cooperation, leading to the creation of a free trade area by the year 2011 and India's accession to the Treaty of Amity and Cooperation in Southeast Asia. The third document delineates cooperation to combat international terrorism. India's accession to ASEAN's Treaty of Amity and Cooperation spoke of a growing closeness with Southeast Asia. But of greater significance was the framework agreement aimed at creating a Free Trade Area in 10 years, as provided in the

Agreement on Comprehensive Economic Cooperation. India finally signed the ASEAN–India Free Trade Agreement (FTA) with the 10 members of ASEAN in August 2009.

In 2003, the scope of India's Look East policy was expanded to include the East Asian nations—China, Japan and Korea. Trade and investment ties remain the most important elements, and bilateral trade between India and these countries has increased significantly over the past few years.

Since the shift of international trading activity from Atlantic to the Pacific, India wanted to establish a close relationship with the region. Apart from linkages at the official and governmental level, mutual exchanges of understanding between India and Southeast Asia were initiated by academic institutions, and chambers and industry. Indian Prime Minister Atal Bihari Vajpayee, in his speech on *India and ASEAN: Shared Perspectives*, said the following at Kuala Lumpur in 2001:

> Over the last few years, we in India have consciously focused on rejuvenation of our ties with the countries of ASEAN. This came to be known as our 'Look East' policy. But, even as we looked east, ASEAN moved west. The admission of new countries brought ASEAN literally to India's doors. From a maritime neighbour, ASEAN became our close neighbour with a land border of nearly 1,600 kilometers. This has added a new dimension to India–ASEAN relations.[51]

Delivering a speech on *Resurgent India in Asia* at Harvard University on 29 September 2003, India's Foreign Minister Yashwant Sinha summarised India's Look East policy as follows:

> In the past, India's engagement with much of Asia, including South East and East Asia, was built on an idealistic conception of Asian brotherhood, based on shared experiences of colonialism and of cultural ties. The rhythm of the region today is determined, however, as much by trade, investment and production as by history and culture. That is what motivates our decade-old 'Look East' policy.[52]

Policy Objectives of the Look East Policy

As India move towards maturity in its Look East foreign policy, the policy is moving beyond its initial goal of tapping the opportunity offered by East and Southeast Asia's growth, which is still important. With the continual growth of India's economy, the policy now serves a much broader agenda. Under the Look East policy, four broad objectives have been pursued in the several years since its initiation: regional economic integration, reform and liberalisation, sustained economic growth and development of the northeastern region. The emphasis placed on each of these objectives has been different at different points of time during the past years. More recently, the emphasis has been on developing the northeastern region through economic integration with East and Southeast Asia. The major priority areas of the Look East policy are discussed as follows.

Regional Integration

One of the main objectives of the Look East policy is economic integration with East and Southeast Asia. Of late, India realised that its neighbours in the east achieved rapid economic growth and that it was lagging behind. Enthralled by the East Asian economic miracle, the Indian elite came to realise that the East and Southeast Asian open economic system could be a model for its own development strategy. Thus, New Delhi wanted to expand ties with these high-performing economies with the aim of getting integrated into the process of economic regionalisation in East and Southeast Asia.

The Look East policy, to some extent, is a reaction to the formation of regional economic groupings, such as the NAFTA, EU and MERCOSUR. In this increasingly regionalised world, it is believed that India's grouping with East and Southeast Asian countries would enhance its position in relation to other regional partners. In the words of Indian Prime Minister Manmohan Singh, '[T]his century is going to be Asia's century' and, furthermore, India along with China, 'is going to be a major economy of this century. This is part of our "Look-East" policy.'[53] According to G.V.C. Naidu, India adopted a three-pronged approach in its attempt to forge regional cooperation through the Look East policy. They are:

1. To renew political contacts with the ASEAN member nations;
2. To increase economic interaction with Southeast Asia (trade, investments, science and technology, tourism, etc.); and
3. To forge defence links with several countries of this region as a means to strengthen political understanding.[54]

Reform and Liberalisation

Though the Look East policy is a by-product of India's economic reform and liberalisation in 1991, the policy seeks further reforms to liberalise trade and investment in order to forge deeper economic integration with East and Southeast Asian countries. Thus, India seeks to lower trade barriers and liberalise the investment regime. India has signed a framework agreement during the Bali Summit in 2003 to create a Free Trade and Investments Area with ASEAN by 2016. Since 2003, India, ASEAN and individual ASEAN member countries have agreed to, and begun negotiations on, FTAs after signing the Framework Agreement on Comprehensive Economic Cooperation. India and ASEAN agreed to implement an FTA for the ASEAN–5 by 2011 and for all ASEAN member countries by 2016. The Framework Agreement announced an early harvest programme of immediate deliverables and unilateral trade preferences by India in favour of the least developed members of the grouping. Till date, India has concluded a Comprehensive Economic Cooperation Agreement with Singapore in 2005. India has also entered into a number of pacts with Thailand and Singapore. The ASEAN–India FTA was signed in August 2009 with the 10 members of ASEAN.

Rapid Economic Growth

In the aftermath of India's liberalisation, the Look East policy became more than just a foreign policy alternative as it provided a development alternative as well, in synchronisation with globalisation and the resurgence of Asia as an economic powerhouse. To quote Prime Minister Manmohan Singh: '[I]t was also a strategic shift in India's vision of the world and India's place in the evolving global economy.'[55] It is only with the formulation of the Look East policy in 1991 that India started giving the East and Southeast Asian region due importance in foreign policy planning. Thus, tapping East and Southeast Asia's growth was an important objective of India's engagement with these economies. When the Indian economy started growing at a remarkable rate from the late 1990s, India had increasingly turned its focus to sustained rapid growth. Strong economic ties with East and Southeast Asia would position India well for accessing growth opportunities in Asia.[56] India is also encouraging East and Southeast Asian investment in the transport, communications and power sectors to keep pace with its expanding economy. India believes that East Asia holds a key to India's sustained economic growth, particularly, when international economic activities are becoming more critical to India's own growth and other regions are growing at a much slower pace and becoming more protectionists.[57]

Development of the Northeastern Region

The Look East policy is also a means to reduce India's internal development disparity. The Northeastern states lag behind in economic development and this gap has widened since independence. The sense of neglect has resulted in various forms of unrest in the region. With the launch of the Look East policy, India sees the region not as cul-de-sac but as a gateway to the East, thereby attempting to link the Northeastern region with Southeast Asia through a network of pipelines, road, rail and air connectivity. This is expected to initiate economic development and help the eight Northeastern states to develop infrastructure, communication, trade, investment, logistics, agro-business and other commercial activities. Knowing the potential properly, the Northeastern states strongly support the Look East policy. Indeed, the Look East policy is believed to be the new *mantra* for development of the Northeastern region.

Security Consideration

As the security and prosperity of India is, to a great extent, intricately linked to the well-being of the geographically contiguous ASEAN region, it seeks to 'establish strategic links with many individual countries, evolve closer political links with ASEAN.'[58] With the institutionalisation of regional cooperation with its eastern neighbours through regional and sub-regional agreements, India intends to strategically address its security concerns in its Northeastern region by forging defence links with countries neighbouring the Northeastern region.

Approaches of the Look East Policy

India adopted several approaches in pursuing the objectives of the Look East policy. Geographical focus, negotiation tactics and sub-regional linkages—all played important roles.

Geographical Focus

Since the early 1990s, India started focusing on economic cooperation with the East and Southeast Asian countries. This geographical shift in focus area was primarily due to the success of the East Asian economies, especially the Asian Tigers. India initially chose to focus on ASEAN countries because the ASEAN members were the first to respond favourably to India's Look East policy. In 2003, the scope of India's Look East policy was widened to include the East Asian countries. This was reflected in Foreign Minister Yashwant Sinha's lecture at Harvard University in 2003: 'The first phase of India's "Look East" policy was ASEAN-centred and focused primarily on trade and investment linkages. The new phase of this policy is characterised by an expanded definition of "East," extending from Australia to East Asia, with ASEAN at its core.'[59] Comprehensive Economic Partnership Agreement between India and Korea has been finalised and negotiations are underway with Japan. India and China also have a joint study group, evaluating the potential for a bilateral FTA.

Sub-Regional Cooperation

India's focus on sub-regional economic cooperation, such as Bay of Bengal Multi-Sectoral Technical and Economic Cooperation (BIMSTEC), Mekong–Ganga Cooperation (MGC) and Bangladesh–China–India– Myanmar Regional Economic Forum (BCIM Forum) is with a view to reinforce the Look East policy and boost the development of the Northeastern region. The main aim of these groupings is to create an enabling environment for rapid economic development through identification and implementation of specific cooperation projects in trade and investment, industry, technology, human resource development, tourism, agriculture, energy, infrastructure, technology, transport and communications, energy and fisheries.

Free Trade Agreements

Frustration with the slow pace of WTO negotiations among prominent trading nations and the fear of being marginalised in a world in which economic regionalism is growing, India is now looking towards East Asia for economic cooperation. In its quest for economic regionalism, India chose FTA negotiations as a means to get involved in and shape the course of its economic integration with East Asia. India embarked on bilateral FTA negotiations with individual ASEAN members because bilateral negotiations present an easier path to advancing the FTA negotiations. India has entered into a number of pacts and FTAs with Thailand and Singapore. There were plans to create a free trade area with Brunei, Indonesia, Thailand, Singapore and Malaysia by 2011, and with the remaining ASEAN countries—the Philippines, Cambodia, Laos, Myanmar and Vietnam—by 2016. The ASEAN—India FTA was signed in August 2009 with the 10 members of ASEAN. India is also negotiating with Japan and South Korea that would lead to an eventual East Asia–India FTA.

Since the enunciation of the Look East policy, India started giving priority to Southeast Asia in its foreign and economic policies. The ASEAN member states were supportive of the measures adopted by the Narasimha Rao government. After the Bandung Conference in 1955, it took nearly four decades for India and Southeast Asia to rediscover each other.

Notes

1. G.V.C. Naidu, 'India and Southeast Asia', p. 82.
2. *Keesing's Contemporary Archives*, 1947, p. 8862.

3. For details of India's attempt at regional cooperation during the first two decade of independence, see Sisir Gupta. 1964. *India and Regional Integration in Asia.* Bombay: Asia Publishing House.

4. For details, see (i) Eric Gonsalves (ed.). 1991. *Asian Relations.* New Delhi: Lancer International. (ii) Werner Levi. 1954. *Free India in Asia.* Minneapolis: University of Minnesota Press. (iii) Sisir Gupta. 1964. *India and Regional Integration in Asia.* Bombay: Asia Publishing House.

5. Statement by I.K. Gujral, Minister of External Affairs and Water Resources, Government of India, http://www.asean.org/4338htm (downloaded on 26.12.2014).

6. Sandy Gordon, *India's Rise to Power in the Twentieth Century and Beyond,* p. 299.

7. J. Mohan Malik, 'India's Response to the Gulf Crisis: Implications for Indian Foreign Policy', p. 855.

8. Ross H. Munro, 'The Loser: India in the Nineties', pp. 62–63.

9. Sandy Gordon, 'South Asia after the Cold War: Winners and Losers', p. 879.

10. Poonam Mann. *India's Foreign Policy in the Post Cold War Era,* p. 1.

11. Sreedhar, 'Security Situation in Southern Asia', p. 1437.

12. Government of India, *Annual Report, 1989–90, Ministry of Defence.*

13. Prakash Nanda. *Rediscovering Asia: Evolution of India's Look-East Policy,* pp. 265–266.

14. *Economic Survey, 1989–90.*

15. *Economic Survey, 1990–91,* p. 3.

16. Chart, *Far Eastern Economic Review* (23 July 1992), p. 53.

17. Indian Express, 'Fallout of Gulf Crisis: Indian Exports Suffer.'

18. V. Joshi and I.M.D. Little, *India: Macroeconomics and Political Economy, 1964–1991,* p. 66.

19. Baldev Raj Nayar, 'Political Structure and India's Economic Reforms of the 1990s', p. 343.

20. K. Shankar Bajpai, 'India in 1991: New Beginnings', p. 208.

21. Prakash Nanda, *Rediscovering Asia: Evolution of India's Look-East Policy,* p. 267.

22. B.B. Bhattacharya, *India's Economic Crises: Debt Burden and Specialisation,* p. 1992.

23. G.V.C. Naidu, 'India and Southeast Asia', p. 83.

24. Sandy Gordon 'South Asia after the Cold War: Winners and Losers', p. 121.

25. Rajen Harshe, 'South Asian Regional Co-operation: Problems and Prospects', pp. 1100–05.

26. Government of India, *Annual Report 1991–92, Ministry of External Affairs,* p. 2.

27. Nisha Tajena, 'Informal Trade in SAARC Region', p. 959.

28. India accounts for nearly three-fourths of the population of the association and three-fourths of its GDP. The imbalance is fragrant and often inhibits the proper functioning of the organisation, which is weighted overtly in favour of India.

3

Economic Potentials of the Look East Policy

In order to achieve the policy objectives of the Look East policy, India fervently pursues a structured programme of cooperation with Southeast Asian countries. The pursuance of membership in regional trade blocs, despite its commitment to multilateralism, stems from the fact that most of the major trading economies are members of trade blocs, such as EU, NAFTA and ASEAN. This trend has made India realize that the stimulus for future growth in Asia will increasingly come from within the region. Given the extent of regional integration worldwide, South Asia, India's neighbourhood, remains relatively unintegrated. The slow progress of regional cooperation within South Asia, particularly the inability of SAARC to widen economic linkage within the subcontinent, largely on account of Pakistani intransigence and unwillingness to play by the global rules of the game in trade, has also forced India to *Look East* for more trade opportunities.[1]

Thus, the Look East policy signifies a reorientation of India's foreign economic policy after the Cold War. It signaled the end of India's previous pursuit of self-reliant economic development, and the start of an era in which India strives to take advantage of new opportunities from international trade and investment. The Look East policy also sent a strong signal that East and Southeast Asia would be integral to India's economic opening and the region would no longer be overlooked, as it had been by India's previous foreign economic policy, but would now be regarded as a source of new business opportunity and inspiration for economic development.[2]

India has made a number of attempts at regional and sub-regional cooperation in pursuant with its Look East policy. Through ASEAN and sub-regional cooperation, such as the BIMSTEC, MGC and the BCIM Forum, India intends to forge closer economic relations with East and Southeast Asian countries. These regional initiatives are relevant to the prospect of the emergence of a cross-border region bringing together the Northeast and the adjacent transnational areas on its east.[3] Greater intra-regional trade is expected to benefit the Northeastern states.[4] Thus, economics is the mainstay of the Look East policy.

One of the interesting features of the Look East policy is the continuous pursuance of the policy without any sharp detraction by successive Indian governments. The first phase of India's Look East policy was ASEAN-centred and focused primarily on trade and investment linkages. The second phase, which began in 2003, is more comprehensive in its coverage, extending from Australia to East Asia with ASEAN as its core.[5] The new phase marks a shift in focus from trade to wider economic and security cooperation, political partnerships, physical connectivity through road and rail links. While forging ties with East and Southeast Asian countries, India develops significant policy initiatives in these regions to support linkages with some of the countries through various partnerships. India has had traditional friendship with the countries of Indochina, known as the CLMV (Cambodia, Laos, Myanmar and Vietnam) countries, and engages with them through the MGC, while another pillar of the Look East policy has been the inclusion of some South Asian and ASEAN countries in BIMSTEC and BCIM Forum.

India–ASEAN Economic Cooperation

India and ASEAN are natural partners. Geographically, India is close to Southeast Asia and shares a land border of 1,600 kilometres with Myanmar and maritime borders with Thailand, Indonesia, Malaysia and Singapore. India and some ASEAN member countries have had trading relationships for more than thousand years and have deeply influenced one another in language, religion and culture. The region has been a destination of Indian migrants for centuries. Apart from geographical proximity and the presence of a large Indian-origin population, the fast growing ASEAN market, their greater openness and a larger role in the global market provide a rationale for the new policy thrust.[6] As a part of the Look East policy, India has consciously integrated its economy with East and Southeast Asian countries since the early 1990s.

In order to strengthen its economic links with ASEAN countries, India signed the Framework Agreement on Comprehensive Economic Cooperation with ASEAN at the Bali Summit on 8 October 2003, where FTAs were to be implemented in 10 years. The objectives of this agreement are to strengthen and enhance economic, trade and investment cooperation between the parties; progressively liberalise and promote trade in goods and services, as well as create a transparent, liberal and facilitative investment regime; explore new areas and develop appropriate measures for closer economic cooperation between the parties; and facilitate the more effective economic integration of the new ASEAN member states and bridge the development gap among the parties. With the signing of the framework agreement on FTA between India and ASEAN, India has formally set up a clear institutional framework for operationalising economic cooperation between India and these countries. India finally signed the ASEAN–India FTA with 10 members of ASEAN in August 2009. This agreement is complemented by bilateral agreements signed with Thailand and Singapore. The share of East and Southeast Asia in India's trade is approaching nearly a third, thus, making it a more important trade partner compared to EU or the United States.[7]

The FTA provides an Early Harvest Programme that specifies the areas for collaboration and a common list of items of preferential tariff concessions. In order to establish India–ASEAN free trade, the framework agreement provides the timeframes to negotiate for free trade area. India reduced its tariff for Brunei, Darussalam, Indonesia, Malaysia, Singapore and Thailand by December 2011. For the new ASEAN member states, that is, the CLMV countries, it is fixed as December 2016. Correspondingly Brunei, Indonesia, Malaysia, Singapore and Thailand reduced their tariff for India in 2011, and the CLMV countries will do so in 2016. Philippines, which has expressed its reservations to the FTA has agreed to eliminate its tariff on reciprocal basis for India by 2016. India has agreed to extend unilateral tariff concessions to the CLMV countries on 111 items to extend special and differential treatment to them based on their levels of development.[8]

The existing economic relations between India and ASEAN are wide ranging, involving merchandise trade, trade in commercial cervices, investments, tourism and manpower flows.

Merchandise Trade

India's sustained efforts to engage with ASEAN in the last two decades have shown results. The merchandise exports of India have more than tripled from about US$1.0 billion in 1991–92 (5.7 per cent of its world exports) to US$3.4 billion in 2001–02 (7.7 per cent of its world exports). The overall trend has been upwards, except during the East Asian Crisis where it has declined sharply to only US$1.6 billion in 1998–99. India's merchandise imports from ASEAN have also tripled, from US$1.3 billion in 1992 to about US$4.0 billion in 2001–02. ASEAN accounted for 8 per cent of India's imports from the world in 2001–02.[9] Pharmaceuticals, metal scraps, leather goods, textiles, machinery and electronic components, and gems and jewellery have potential for future merchandise trade expansion between India and ASEAN.

Although ASEAN nation-states imported only 33–40 product groups out of a large number of products that India exported, these products accounted for more than half to one-third of India's global exports and a little less than half to around one-fourth of total imports of the ASEAN nation-states. This means that despite being fewer in number, the complementary products were important in the global trade of the respective countries.[10] Substantial complementarities are yet to be exploited for mutual common benefits. With increasing competition and the need to remain ahead in this era of knowledge-based globalised economy, ASEAN and India have felt the need to expand and deepen their economic linkages. They need to work closely under the Framework Agreement on Comprehensive Economic Cooperation to realise their economic potentials of trade in goods and services, and investment. By doing so, ASEAN and India could enhance their respective attractiveness as FDI destinations, and increase their competitiveness as a producer, exporter and service provider in the global marketplace.[11] As India continues with its economic reforms and has a good macroeconomic performance, ASEAN countries will find further economic opportunities with India. This could, in part, counterbalance adverse impact of China's entry into the WTO on ASEAN's exports and investment flows.[12]

Trade in Commercial Services

Information and communication technology (ICT) services trade is a potential area of cooperation between India and ASEAN. ICT and related services have constituted the major driving force behind services trade in India, and the development of this sector has been primarily market driven and government regulation has been minimal. The growth of this sector has been mainly attributed to the increasing skilled ICT manpower, combined with an increasing international demand for such skilled manpower. Cooperation with ASEAN economies that have developed such capabilities, particularly Singapore and Malaysia, could create synergies for mutual benefits in this area.[13] India has become the leading destination for outsourcing of ICT services, call centre support and other back-end Business Process Operations (BPOs), such as data entry and handling, payroll management, accounting and book-keeping, processing of tax returns and insurance claims, ticketing, coding and organising of documents for major litigation cases and transcription.

Investment Flows

Since the launch of the Look East policy, ASEAN member states, such as Singapore, Thailand and Malaysia, have emerged as important sources of FDI in India. The last two decades also witnessed Indian companies investing in some of the ASEAN member states, such as Thailand, Indonesia and Vietnam. Since the mid-1990s, information technology and computer software sector have emerged as an important source of outward investment for India with Indian companies establishing bases in ASEAN countries, especially in Singapore.

The more advanced ASEAN-6 countries, particularly Malaysia, Singapore and Thailand, are increasingly investing in India in sectors such as telecommunications, fuels, hotels and tourism services, heavy industries, chemicals, fertilizers, textiles, paper and pulps, and food processing. Malaysia has made substantial investments in expanding capacities in selected infrastructural areas, such as logistics, highways and ICTs in India. It has also been cooperating to assist India in providing infrastructure expertise and investments in the energy sector, particularly for oil and gas exploration, and in downstream processing activities.[14] Singapore's private sector companies have invested in health care, real estate and tourism. Indian investment in the region has been wide-ranging, including investments in steel, textiles, chemicals and petrochemicals, cement, sugar, pharmaceuticals and increasingly important, software services and programming.[15] India's strength in software and services fruitfully complement the hardware and manufacturing prowess of East Asia, and East Asian companies have begun to exploit India's strengths in research and development (R&D), software and design by locating their global R&D centres in India.[16] Along with India's economic reforms and liberalisation of regulations on foreign investment permit, the presence of Indian companies in ASEAN is likely to grow. Unlike in the earlier period, their presence will be motivated by economic efficiency and profitability criteria, and not by the desire to escape restrictive business environment at home.[17] The financial crisis of 1997–98 in Southeast Asia thwarted investment process both ways, but slowly there was recovery and rejuvenation of inter-regional investment flows.

Tourism

Tourism is another area which holds potential for expansion of trade in tourism between India and ASEAN countries. Indonesia, Malaysia, Philippines and Singapore have already developed considerable expertise and competitive advantage in tourism. India also realised the potential in this area belatedly, and is taking steps to implement an integrated tourism industry by launching a tourism campaign in ASEAN countries.[18]

During the Bali Summit in October 2003, India offered unilateral liberalisation of air travel for ASEAN carriers. ASEAN air carriers have been permitted to fly to 21 tourist destinations in India directly. In addition, ASEAN air carriers can now fly to four metros in India without any limit during the busy tourist months. These factors are expected to boost tourism flows. The granting of visa on arrival facilities for Indian visitors to Thailand, and recently by Malaysia, are further measures that could enhance such interactions. For the less developed ASEAN countries, Indian visitors could constitute a new source of tourists.

Manpower Flows

Rapid growth of economies of the ASEAN member states, particularly Singapore, Malaysia and Thailand, has led to shortages in skilled manpower. Although the 1997–98 economic crisis did affect the demand for foreign talent in ASEAN countries for a limited period, their resurgence from the crisis revived the need of foreign talent again. In India, on the other hand, supply of manpower has exceeded demand.[19] Hence, there are complementarities between the two in this area. The worldwide shortage of talent, particularly in the ICT sector, has also increased the demand for talent from India as its manpower is internationally competitive, English speaking and accustomed to operating in a multicultural environment.[20] Increasing presence of the same Western multinational companies in both ASEAN and India has also been a contributory factor in manpower flows from India.

Towards Sub-Regional Cooperation

With an endeavour to reinforce the Look East policy and link the Northeastern region to the dynamic economies of East and Southeast Asia, India joined several sub-regional groupings. They are BIMSTEC, MGC and BCIM Economic Forum. Sub-regional cooperation emphasises the complementarities of the resource bases of the different partners and facilitates the spillover of growth across national borders. Furthermore, in sub-regional economic zones, the focus is not only on trade, but also on the promotion of tourism, natural and human resource development and infrastructure.[21] According to this formulation, the countries from the *extended neighbourhood* would rightly become a part of the *immediate neighbourhood*.[22]

Bay of Bengal Initiative for Multi-Sectoral Technical and Economic Cooperation

BIMSTEC is a sub-regional group, involving a group of countries in South and Southeast Asia. The member countries of this group are Bangladesh, India, Myanmar, Sri Lanka, Thailand, Bhutan and Nepal. The initiative to establish an economic group to explore economic cooperation on a sub-regional basis, involving contiguous countries of South and Southeast Asia, was taken by Thailand in 1994. After a number of consultations, the Foreign Ministers' Meeting in Bangkok on 6 June 1997 decided to form BIMSTEC with the initial name BIST-EC (Bangladesh, India, Sri Lanka,

Thailand-Economic Cooperation). The deliberations to form BIMSTEC enjoyed an active support from Asian Development Bank and United Nations Economic and Social Commission for Asia and the Pacific. The inaugural meeting was attended by Myanmar as an observer.

The aims and purposes of the grouping listed in the declaration of the establishment of BIST-EC are:

1. To create an enabling environment for rapid economic development through identification and implementation of specific cooperation projects in the sectors of trade, investment and industry, technology, human resource development, tourism, agriculture, energy, and infrastructure and transportation.
2. To accelerate the economic growth and social progress in the sub-region through joint endeavours in a spirit of equality and partnership.
3. To promote active collaboration and mutual assistance on matters of common interest in the economic, social, technical and scientific fields.
4. To provide assistance to each other in the form of training and research facilities in the educational, professional and technical spheres.
5. To cooperate more effectively in joint efforts that are supportive of and complementary to national development plans of member states which result in tangible benefits to the people in raising their living standards, including generating employment and improving transportation and communication infrastructure.
6. To maintain close and beneficial cooperation with the existing international and regional organisations with similar aims and purposes.
7. To cooperate in projects that can be dealt with most productively on a sub-regional basis among the BIST-EC countries and that make best use of available synergies.[23]

To carry out the aims and purposes of the BIST-EC Declaration, the following institutional mechanisms are provided:

1. Annual Ministerial Meetings, which shall be hosted by the member states on the basis of alphabetical rotation.

2. Senior Officials Committee, which shall meet on a regular basis as and when required.

3. A Working Group, under the chairmanship of Thailand and having as its members the accredited ambassadors to Thailand, or their representatives, of the other member states, to carry on the work in between Annual Ministerial Meetings.

4. Specialised task forces and other mechanisms as may be deemed necessary by the senior officials to be coordinated by member states as appropriate.

Myanmar joined the group as a full member on 22 December 1997, and consequently the name of the grouping was changed to BIMST-EC. Nepal was granted observer status by the Second Ministerial Meeting in Dhaka on 19 December 1998. Subsequently, full membership was granted to Nepal and Bhutan in the Sixth Ministerial Meeting at Phuket, in February 2004. During the first summit in Bangkok on 31 July 2004, the group's name was eventually rechristened as BIMSTEC.

At the Second Ministerial Meeting in Dhaka on 19 November 1998, six areas of cooperation were identified. They are:

1. Trade and investment (led by Bangladesh);
2. Technology (led by Sri Lanka);
3. Transportation and communication (led by India);
4. Energy (led by Myanmar);
5. Tourism (led by India); and
6. Fisheries (led by Thailand).

A number of new areas of cooperation emerged from the First BIMSTEC Summit in Bangkok on 31 July 2004, such as poverty alleviation, counter-terrorism and transnational crime, protection of biodiversity and traditional knowledge, cultural cooperation and people-to-people contact. Besides the identified areas of cooperation, BIMSTEC activities also cover technical cooperation and human resource development, BIMSTEC business travel facilitation, establishment of BIMSTEC centre and cooperation with private sectors.

To institutionalise BIMSTEC and formulate concrete economic agenda, a meeting of BIMSTEC Economic/Trade Ministers was held in

August 1998. It imparted a new dimension to economic cooperation between the member states. It was agreed that BIMSTEC should aim and strive to develop into a Free Trade Agreement, and should focus on activities that facilitate trade, increase investment and promote technical cooperation among member countries. The First Meeting of Senior Trade/Economic Officials of BIMSTEC was held on 26 April 2000 at New Delhi. Senior Trade/Economic Official Meeting (STEOM) is held regularly, at least once a year. The objectives of the Senior Trade/Economic Officials Committee of BIMSTEC are as follows: to oversee, coordinate and expedite the work programmes relating to the field of trade and economic cooperation and to make recommendations to the Trade/Economic Ministers and ensure implementation of the decisions taken by Trade/Economic Ministers. These meetings have identified different steps which need to be taken on priority basis in order to move effectively towards mutual cooperation with particular emphasis on select sectors, namely, trade and investment, technology, transport and communication, energy and tourism.[24]

The need for an FTA to increase intra-regional trade between BIMSTEC countries was also reflected in the first meeting of Inter-Governmental Group of BIMSTEC. It was felt that the ultimate objective of FTA should be to create trade in the region, but should not lead to diversion.[25] As a result, a Framework Agreement on BIMSTEC Free Trade Area was signed on 8 February, 2004 in Phuket, Thailand. The objectives of this agreement are:

1. to strengthen and enhance economic, trade and investment cooperation among the parties;
2. to progressively liberalise and promote trade in goods and services, create a transparent, liberal and facilitative investment regime;
3. to explore new areas and develop appropriate measures for closer cooperation among the parties; and
4. facilitate effective economic integration further among the least developed countries in the region, and bridge the development gap among the parties.[26]

The framework agreement covers FTA in goods, services and investments. Areas of economic cooperation have also been identified for enhancing trade and investment flows. Member countries have agreed upon a plan for a free trade by 2017 and in addition to that, India, Sri Lanka and Thailand have committed themselves to trade liberalisation since 2012. India has also given preferential treatment to a large number of agricultural commodities and rough wood imported from Myanmar.

BIMSTEC is considered to be an important step towards the process of economic cooperation between ASEAN and SAARC countries and an important element in India's Look East policy. Trade and investment in goods and services could accelerate the development of India's Northeastern region by greater cooperation with neighbouring countries, such as Myanmar, China and Bangladesh. As such, India promotes BIMSTEC to establish economic links with the peninsula member countries of ASEAN to boost the development of its Northeastern states.[27]

Mekong–Ganga Cooperation

India has traditional friendship, and share historical and cultural traditions with the countries of Indochina. But it was only after India's economic reforms in 1991 and the consequent enunciation of the Look East policy which led India to reformulate its worldview on the economic and political issues, and also about its strategic space in the Greater Mekong sub-region.[28] The success of India's Look East policy with the original six of ASEAN and their appreciation, and the need felt by them for special economic and social development of Indochina countries greatly facilitate India's engagement with Greater Mekong sub-region.[29]

The MGC is a cooperation initiative established on 10 November 2000 in the Laotian capital Vientiane by India and five riparian countries of the Mekong River, namely, Cambodia, Laos, Myanmar, Vietnam and Thailand. The areas of cooperation include tourism, culture, education, transportation and communications. These four areas of cooperation are emphasised between India and the Greater Mekong countries in order to lay a solid foundation for future trade and investment cooperation in the region. In January 2007, India's Minister of State for External Affairs E. Ahmad, described the MGC as one of the pillars of India's Look East policy.[30]

The working mechanism for MGC consists of the Annual Ministerial Meeting, the Senior Official's Meeting and the five Working Groups, namely:

1. Working Group on Tourism (Thailand is the lead country);
2. Working Group on Education (HRD) (India is the lead country);
3. Working Group on Culture (Cambodia is the lead country);
4. Working Group on Communication and Transportation (Laos is the lead country); and
5. Working Group on Plan of Actions (Vietnam is the lead country).

The first ministerial meeting of MGC was held in Vientiane on 10 November 2000 and concluded with the *Vientiane Declaration*. The declaration underscores the group's determination to develop closer relations and better understanding among the six countries so as to enhance friendship, solidarity and cooperation. The *Vientiane Declaration* outlines the objectives of MGC in four specific sectors: tourism, culture, education, and transport and communications.[31] To be specific, it endeavours to launch the Mekong–Ganga Tourism Investment Guide, establish networks among tourism training institutions and conduct seminars on tourism promotion, common efforts to expand the export market for the handicrafts and traditional textiles of the MGC countries, promote joint research in dance, music and theatrical forms and traditions, conserve, preserve and protect old manuscripts, heritage sites and artifacts, provide scholarships and translate classics. The Vientiane Declaration has committed the member countries to develop transport in the region in order to strengthen inter- and intra-regional linkages between people. The member states are also committed to strengthen cooperation in the development of IT infrastructures and networks.

At the Second MGC Ministerial Meeting held at Hanoi on 28 July 2001, the member countries adopted the *Hanoi Programme of Action*, which provides specific actions to be taken in the four sectors that had been earmarked by the Vientiane Declaration as priority areas of cooperation. The *Hanoi Programme of Action* has six-year time frame covering the period from July 2001 to July 2007, and the progress of its implementation was reviewed every two years in coincidence with the MGC Annual Ministerial Meeting.[32] Amongst others, it highlighted the need for coordination and transparency, and underlined the need for using information technologies and know-how for education and training, and also for making websites to share information and for efficient and effective planning. It also emphasised the need for developing projects involving more than one MGC member countries, but not necessarily all of them.

At the Third MGC Ministerial Meeting held in Phnom Penh on 20 June 2003, the member countries adopted the *Phnom Penh Road Map* as a plan to accelerate the implementation of all MGC projects and activities. The member-states reviewed the progress of the Hanoi Programme of Action and 'noted that the progress was slow and much remains to be done to translate idea to be reality.'[33] They reaffirm the commitment to the implementation of the Hanoi Programme of Action for cultural cooperation and supported the trilateral road linkages among India, Myanmar and Thailand. Apart from the priority areas, member states commit themselves to develop affordable medicine for tropical diseases and help MGC member countries, encourage cooperation and joint venture in pharmaceutical and harmonisation of drug standards, and explore possible new areas for cooperation.

The MGC emphasises the connectivity of India with the Mekong–Ganga countries on cultural and civilisational similarities. In operational terms, the project is an attempt to enhance cooperation in the fields of transport and infrastructure sector with special focus on overland connectivity.[34] The inclusion of Myanmar as member of ASEAN in July 1997 brought the region to India's border and gave an impetus to extending road and rail connectivity. In fact, the India–ASEAN car rally in November–December 2004 is a demonstration of the proximity of India and Southeast Asia, and an endeavour to promote regional connectivity. Under this cooperation, there is a proposal to set up a railway line from Delhi to Hanoi. India has proposed to extend India–Myanmar–Thailand trilateral highway to Laos and Cambodia. When this is done, it will enhance the possibility of setting up special economic zones at borders—India–Myanmar and Myanmar–Thailand.[35] Being land-linked, India's Northeastern region can serve as a *hub* for trade between Mekong and India.[36]

Bangladesh–China–India–Myanmar Regional Economic Forum

The BCIM Forum is a Track II initiative which was a product of the conference on regional cooperation held at Kunming, the capital of Yunnan province in China. The sub-region under this grouping consists of a number of geographically contiguous units, comprising the northeastern states of India, southern provinces of China, Bangladesh and Myanmar. This forum advocates regional cooperation on infrastructure development, and thus it emphasises the importance of improved transport connectivity for efficient movement of goods and people in the interests of both regional and global competitiveness, and in order to promote tourism. Although BCIM forum is organised at the Track II level, they provided practical suggestions and directions as to how the BCIM initiative can be productive at the official level and can evolve into sub-regional programmes at the government levels.

Rather than being involved with China multilaterally, India officially appears to prefer regional organisations, such as the MGC and BIMSTEC, that do not include China.[37] However, in recent times, trade and economic relations have emerged as the trendsetter in the overall India–China relations which is not a mere coincidence, but rather the result of a conscious effort on both sides to bring bilateral relationship in tune with the present realities by building upon mutual complementarities.[38] Therefore, there is an enormous potential for following up the Kunming Initiative, especially the proposal to rebuild the Stilwell Road which was constructed during the Second World War. The Stillwell Road connects Ledo in Assam and Kunming in Yunnan province of China passing through northern Myanmar.

The BCIM initiative has the potential to bring three of India's most important neighbours closer in a joint pursuit of common prosperity through the increasing use of the mechanisms of regional integration. The rationale for BCIM cooperation lies in the potential to generate enormous economic benefits by the integration of these strategically located areas, constituting a natural economic zone, in areas of trade, investment, energy, transport and tourism. The economic dynamism of India and China could offer wide range of opportunities for growth and development in the region.[39] Taking note of the importance of BCIM initiative, Rajiv Sikri observed that:

> [i]t is not just that we are neighbours sharing common borders; all of us also face similar opportunities and challenges in our respective quests for rapid economic growth, national development and prosperity of our people. In our mutual relationships, there is increasingly greater focus on economic issues, which will enable us to realise the untapped potential of our economic cooperation and make it commensurate with the level of our political relationships.[40]

In the *Dhaka Statement 2007* of the Seventh BCIM Forum on Regional Economic Cooperation held in Dhaka from 31 March 2007–1 April 2007, the participating countries reiterated the identification of enormous potential by successive BCIM forums for cooperation in the sub-region which is rich in natural resources, as well as people across an area which represents the interface between East Asia, Southeast Asia and South Asia. It also recognises the necessity to further build on mutual complementarity that exists among the countries of BCIM.[41] The Seventh BCIM Forum also agreed that initiatives should be taken to develop concrete proposals for consideration and follow-up action by the national groups, business communities and the civil society. In this context, the following areas were identified for priority attention: improving trade facilitation, strengthening transport connectivity, enhancing tourism cooperation, promoting educational, scientific, cultural and social exchanges.

Having about 40 per cent of the world population, a huge reserve of natural and other resources and two of the world's fastest growing giant economies—India and China—in the forum, the BCIM sub-regional economic cooperation is perceived to have enormous potentials to generate benefits for the region in general and the weaker parts of the region in particular.[42] Bangladesh, Myanmar, the Northeastern states of India and the Southwestern Chinese provinces could benefit extensively from such regional cooperation. Proper implementation of this sub-regional cooperation could combine the resources of the constituent members in order to gain competitive edge in attracting both domestic and foreign investments, and promoting export for the mutual benefit of the members involved. A regional project on developing energy resources could very well be initiated for efficient and more value added use of these resources. Along with the move in Track-II, Yunnan has been trying to upgrade the cooperation framework to the official level (Track-I), and effort is underway to upgrade the level of cooperation to Track-I.

Northeast India and the Look East Policy

Northeast India has vast potential resources. The region is endowed with rich hydro-power potential, oil and gas, coal, limestone, forest wealth, fruits and vegetables, flowers, herbs and aromatic plants. It has the potential to generate over 50,000 megawatt of hydroelectric power and if fully harnessed, the region could become a major power house not only for India, but also for entire Southeast Asia. The river waters, if fully developed, could not only provide cheap means of transportation, but it can also become a major tourist attraction. Thai companies which have years of experience in managing inland waterway networks could take advantage of the opportunity, thus, offered. The Northeast produces a large variety of organic agro-horticultural products, and is known for handloom and exquisite handicrafts. The competitive edge of Thailand's processed food industry in the world and the awareness and expertise of Southeast Asia's handloom and handicrafts industry to international market offer many opportunities to Northeast India for technical and marketing collaborations. India and Thailand are two of the largest producers of natural rubber, and there exists ample scope for cooperation between Thailand and the Northeast to enhance mutual competitiveness in this industry. Tourism, an industry that can thrive in the Northeast, has much to gain from the Southeast Asian experience. The region's high literacy and a well-educated and hardworking young population is potentially an advantage for foreign and, also, domestic corporates.[43] Cooperation with Southeast Asian countries would help the Northeast explore these potentials. And if all these potentials are harvested it will not only give direct and indirect job opportunities, but will also result in economic development of the region.

The sub-region comprising Northeast India, Bangladesh, Myanmar and Southwest China is a geographically contiguous area, and shares historical and cultural ties. These countries have interacted with each other through the *Southern Silk Road*. The trade on the Silk Road was a significant factor in the development of the great civilisations and in several respects helped lay the foundations for the modern world.[44] There were several minor trade routes linking the region with foreign countries through which substantial trade was carried. Considerable trade was also carried between the villagers of both sides of the international borders.[45] After the hardening of international borders in 1947, which restricted mobility across borders, informal border trade has been continuing across the borders. As per reports, the volume of informal border trade between Northeast India and the neighbouring countries now exceeds several times the official volume of trade.[46] If the informal trade activities are legalised through governmental policy, the complementarities existing between Northeast India and its neighbours can further be exploited.

The border areas of these countries are rich in natural resources. They are at different levels of economic and industrial development, and have different levels of natural endowments. Hence, the complementarities between them are substantial. The geographical contiguity could facilitate the exploitation of the potential of efficiency seeking restructuring of industry, provided conditions for such restructuring are created.[47] Travel agencies in Southwest China's Yunnan province have recently opened a new tourism route—the *Southern Ancient Silk Road*—which attracted an increasing number of tourists.[48] Given the fact that the people of Northeast India have close historical and cultural affinity with its neighbours across the borders, reviving the ancient trade routes through the Look East policy will not only promote trade, but also tourism in the region.

Northeast India, which shares 98 per cent of its border with China, Myanmar, Bhutan, Bangladesh and Nepal, has better scope for development in the era of globalisation. Being located at the centre of the sub-region, it is the natural ground for staging economic cooperation under sub-regional cooperations, such as BIMSTEC, MGC and BCIM forum. Cooperation with the neighbours across the borders can exploit the region's huge, untapped potentials and transform itself into a commercial hub. The region's geographical location and its historical and cultural affinities with its neighbours across the border can be taken into advantage as a *soft power resource* to promote tourism and commercial exchange as a means to galvanise growth and development of the region.

There is vast scope for cooperation between India and East, and Southeast Asia and India's Northeast can benefit enormously from such formalised regional and sub-regional institutional arrangements if infrastructure of the region is improved and its resources geared up to meet the demands of the globalised world.

However, there is a need to examine the historical background of political and economic development of this intricate region before delving into the possible political impact of the Look East policy.

Notes

1. Sanjay Baru, 'India and ASEAN: The Emerging Economic Relationship: Towards a Bay of Bengal Community', p. 21.
2. Dong Zhang, 'India Looks East: Strategies and Impact', p. 15.

3. Shibashis Chatterjee, 'Conceptions of Space in India's Look East Policy: Order, Cooperation or Community?' p. 77.
4. Faizal Yahya, 'BIMSTEC and Emerging Patterns of Asian Regional and Inter Regional Cooperation', p. 392.
5. Yashwant Sinha, 'Resurgent India in Asia', Speech at Harvard University.
6. Atul Sarma and Paadeep Kumar Mehta, 'Indo-ASEAN Trade Prospects: A Study of Trade Complementarity', p. 81.
7. Nagesh Kumar, 'Regional Economic Cooperation in Asia: Relevance and a Possible Roadmap for a Broader Asian Economic Community', p. 12.
8. Framework Agreement on Comprehensive Economic Cooperation Between the Republic of India and the Association of South East Asian Nations.
9. Rahul Sen, Mukul G. Asher and Ramkishen S. Rajan, 'ASEAN-India Economic Relations: Current Status and Future Prospects', p. 3299.
10. Atul Sarma and Paradeep Kumar Mehta, 'Indo-ASEAN Trade Prospects: A Study of Trade Complementarity', p. 84.
11. Ong Keng Yong, 'Advancing the ASEAN-India Partnership in the New Millennium', p. 8.
12. J. Thornhill, 'Enter the Dragon'.
13. Rahul Sen, Mukul G. Asher and Ramkishen S. Rajan, 'ASEAN-India Economic Relations: Current Status and Future Prospects', pp. 3300–01.
14. Mukul G. Asher, Rahul Sen and Sadhana Srivastava, 'ASEAN–India: Emerging Economic Opportunities', pp. 59–60.
15. Sanjay Baru, 'India and ASEAN: The Emerging Economic Relationship. Towards a Bay of Bengal Community.'
16. Nagesh Kumar, 'Regional Economic Cooperation in Asia: Relevance and a Possible Roadmap for a Broader Asian Economic Community', p. 13.
17. Rahul Sen, Mukul G. Asher, Ramkishen S. Rajan, ASEAN-India Economic Relations: Current Status and Future Prospects, p. 3298.
18. Prime Minister's Address delivered at the 5th India-ASEAN Summit Cebu, Philippines.
19. Mukul G. Asher, Rahul Sen and Sadhana Srivastava, 'ASEAN-India Economic Relations: Current Status and Future Prospects', p. 61.
20. T. Tschang, 'The Basic Characteristics of Skills and Organisational Capabilities in the Indian Software Industry.'
21. Isabelle Saint-Mezard, 'The Look East Policy: An Economic Perspective', p. 40.
22. V. Suryanarayan, 'Prospects for a Bay of Bengal community.'
23. Declaration on the Establishment of BIST-EC, Bangkok, June 6, 1997.
24. Rajesh Mehta, 'Establishment of Free Trade Arrangement among BIMST-EC Countries: Some Issues', p. 2.
25. 'Report of the First Meeting of Inter-Governmental Group (IGG) under the aegis of BIMST-EC', 5–6 February 2001.
26. Framework Agreement on the BIMST-EC Free Trade Area.
27. Dong Zhang, India Looks East: Strategies and Impact, p. 19.

28. Swaran Singh, 'Mekong-Ganga Cooperation Initiative: Analysis and Assessment of India's Engagement with Greater Mekong Sub-region', p. 19.
29. H.E. Rodolfo C. Severino, 'The Greater Mekong Sub-Regional and Regional Peace and Security', http://www.aseansec.org/3317.htm (downloaded on 29.12.2014).
30. E. Ahmed, 'Reinforcing 'Look East' Policy', http://www.meaindia.nic.in/ interview/2006/01/17in01.htm (downloaded on 29.12.2014).
31. 'Vientiane Declaration' on Mekong–Ganga Cooperation, 10 November 2000.
32. 'Ha Noi Programme of Action for Mekong-Ganga Cooperation', 28 July 2001.
33. Report of the Third Ministerial Meeting on Mekong-Ganga Cooperation, 20 June 2003.
34. 'Ganga–Mekong Swarnabhoomi Project', http://meaindia.nic.in/onmouse/ ganga1.htm (downloaded on 28.12.2014).
35. *Mekong Ganga Policy Brief No. 1*, Research and Information System for Developing Countries publication on India-Mekong Economic Cooperation, p. 4.
36. Prabir De, 'Connecting Mekong Region with India through Infrastructure linkages.'
37. Sanjib Baruah, *Between South and Southeast Asia: Northeast India and the Look East Policy*, pp. 15–16.
38. Address by Mr. Rajiv Sikri, Secretary (East), Ministry of External Affairs, at the Sixth Bangladesh-China–India–Myanmar Forum, New Delhi, http://www. meaindia.nic.in/speech/2006/03/30ss01.htm (downloaded on 27.12.2014).
39. Mustafizur Rahman et al., 'BCIM Economic Cooperation: Prospects and Challenges', p. 1.
40. Address by Mr. Rajiv Sikri, Secretary (East), Ministry of External Affairs, at the Sixth Bangladesh–China–India–Myanmar Forum, New Delhi.
41. *Dhaka Statement 2007*, Seventh BCIM Forum on Regional Economic Cooperation, Dhaka, 31 March–1 April 2007.
42. Mustafizur Rahman et al., 'BCIM Economic Cooperation: Prospects and Challenges', p. 13.
43. Amita Batra, 'India's Northeast and Southeast Asia: Strengthening and Integrated Space', p. 3.
44. Francis Wood. *The Silk Road: Two Thousand Years in the Heart of Asia*, pp. 9 and 13–23.
45. B.B. Kumar, 'The Border Trade in North-East India: The Historical Perspective', p. 6.
46. B.K. Sharma and S.N. Goswami, 'Border trade in Northeast India: An Overview', p. 96.
47. 'Future Directions of BIMSTEC: Towards a Bay of Bengal Economic Community', RIS publication, p. 2.
48. 'China Opens "Southern Silk Road" Tourism Route.'

4

Political Integration in Northeast India

The history of the Indian nation-state is a history of integration of diverse ethnic groups. At the time of independence, one of the main objectives of the leaders of Indian National Congress (INC), who spearheaded the freedom struggle, was to politically integrate all the princely states and other loosely administered areas into India. This objective was pursued in the next few years so as to secure a territory as much as what the British had handled over to them. In Northeast India, different methods were used to integrate the princely states of Manipur and Tripura, and the adjoining hills areas of Assam. Before dealing with the process of political integration of the present so-called *Northeastern region*, it is first essential to briefly look into the development of the term India's *Northeast*.

The Concept of India's *Northeast*

The term *Northeast* was first used by the British rulers stationed at Fort William, Calcutta, to identify a geographical area located to the northeast of Bengal. Alexander Mackenzie was perhaps the first to use the term *Northeast Frontier* to identify Assam, including the adjoining hill areas, and the princely states of Manipur and Tripura in his book, *History of the Government with the Hill Tribes of the North-East Frontier of Bengal* in 1884.[1] When there was a plan to merge Assam with eastern Bengal in the late 1890s and the beginning of 1900, there were proposals to name the new province as the *North-Eastern Province*.[2] Initially, the term remained a geographical concept, and throughout the colonial period British rulers referred to Assam as the *Northeastern Frontier of Bengal*. Thus, during the colonial period, the area what now constitutes the Northeast was considered to be a frontier of Bengal, a buffer region between India and the neighbouring countries that needed to be protected and defended militarily.

Northeast India became a region merely by a geo-political accident. The separation of Burma from the Indian subcontinent in 1937 and the partition of 1947 virtually created what we now call the *Northeast*. Before partition, there was no idea of a separate Northeastern region. The region does not fulfil the three traditional approaches to the definition of a region, which are homogeneity, nodality or polarisation around some central place. In the words of Barrister Pakem, Northeast India is still a region, and the lack of sophisticated definition of a region for Northeast India does not make it a non-region. It is a region despite its varied physical features and its different economic, political and social systems.[3] J. B. Fuller also observes that '[t]he province of Assam at the far northeastern corner of India is a museum of nationalities.'[4] As such, India's Northeast is a region of diverse geographical features with a population characterised by diverse ethnicity, language, culture, religion, social organisation and levels of economic development.

For more than a decade since independence, *Northeast* basically meant Assam and the princely states of Manipur and Tripura. In order to quell the various ethnic aspirations, new states were carved out of Assam: Nagaland (1963), Meghalaya (1972), Arunachal Pradesh and Mizoram (1987). The concept of India's *Northeast* was formalised politically, and the term became popular with the formation of the North Eastern Council (NEC) in 1971. Since its inception, the NEC has been functioning as a regional planning body for the Northeastern region. Sikkim was included in the NEC in 2002, although the state did not meet the contiguity criteria.[5]

The tendency among scholars and policy-makers to club the whole Northeastern states together as *Northeast*, and use the term as an analytical category for the whole region is always questioned in terms of practical relevance. Udayon Misra pointed out that the use of the term *Northeast* is itself problematic as the region represents a varied cultural mosaic and has never considered itself to be one compact unit.[6] To him, New Delhi suffers from a strong misconception and has failed to appreciate the complex nature of the problem. Wasbir Hussain delineates:

> By bracketing the eight northeastern Indian states, with its diverse tribes, customs and cultures, into what is called the 'Northeast', we tend to ignore the distinct identity and sub-national aspirations of these ethnic groups. More so, such clubbing together of the region, in an attempt to look at it as a single entity, has led to stereotyping of the problems that plague the area.

The fact that each state has a different set of location-specific concerns and grievances often gets blurred in the scheme of things of policy framers and government leaders who are supposed to address these issues.[7]

Historian Manorama Sharma also observes: 'The north-eastern states of India may be looked upon as a political unit for purposes of administrative convenience by the Government of India today, but historically at no point of time has it ever been a political unit, either culturally, economically or politically.'[8] Harping on the region as a political unit of the British and post-independence Indian government, she rhetorically insinuates that 'even a term like pre-colonial creates problems because there is no uniformity even in that phase of development.' Each state and each tribe has different historical experiences.

It is true that the Northeastern region shares certain common problems, such as ethnic unrests, insurgency, immigration, drug trafficking and communication gap. However, there are severe intra-regional differences in social issues and ethno-political aspirations. Not only the hills and valleys are at different levels of socio-economic development; the urban and rural areas of the valleys exhibit social and economic disparities. The region is, in fact, one of the most ethnically and linguistically diverse regions in Asia, and each state has its distinct cultures and traditions. B.G. Verghese commented: 'The Northeast is another India, the most diverse part of a most diverse country, very different, relatively little known and certainly not too well understood, once a coy but now turbulent and in transition within the Indian transition.'[9] Most of the inhabitants consist of peoples who migrated from Southwest China or Southeast Asia via Burma at various points of history. A substantial portion of the population is also composed of migrants during the British rule—one group consists of people recruited to serve the colonial administration in the region and the others are tea planters. Apart from these, there is huge inflow of late immigrants, mainly from Bangladesh, which resulted in constant friction with the local population.

Political Integration

The study of political integration has been one of the major concerns of political scientists. The term is widely used among various fields of political science, such as international relations and international organisation, local and urban government, and operates in the international, national and sub-national level. There has been a new wave in the study of political integration during the post-war years as the newly independent countries of Asia and Africa have to rigorously go through this process in their drive for nation-building.

The rationale of political integration is that there is a need to create a 'territorial nationality which overshadows—or eliminates—subordinate parochial loyalties.'[10] These local allegiances, or the similar primordial attachments, impede development since the national leaders aspiring to expand the functions of the political system need the undivided loyalty of all the population. It is, therefore, one of the challenges to the political system to bring about 'the process whereby people transfer their commitment and loyalty from smaller tribes, villages, or petty principalities to the larger central political system.'[11]

According to Myron Weiner, political integration is the 'integration of political units into a common territorial framework with a government which can exercise authority.'[12] Ernst B. Haas defines it as the 'process whereby political actors in several distinct national settings are persuaded to shift their loyalties, expectations, and political activities toward a new centre, whose institutions possess or demand jurisdiction over the pre-existing national states.'[13] Karl W. Deutsch uses the term integration both as a process and a condition and terms political integration as 'the attainment of a sense of community, accompanied by formal or informal institutions or practices, sufficiently strong and widespread to assure peaceful change among members of a group.'[14] Such an integrated community, according to Deutsch, may or may not be a sovereign state. In simple words, political integration is the integration into the government, the political parties and the pressure group life of a country.[15] In the theoretical treatment of political development and political stability, the concept of political integration is usually employed in a sense that approximates Deutsch's definition,[16] where the focus of interest is on integration within states, or, in other words, on the question whether an amalgamated community is integrated or not.[17]

With the gaining of independence by Asian and African nations during the middle of the twentieth century, the task of nation-building has been left with these nation-states. The first and foremost problem encountered by them was the issue of integrating the vast chunk of people who had been loosely administered in varying degrees by the colonial powers. In large and multinational nation-states, the problem of integrating people inhabiting different regions with varied language, religion, culture and ethnic identities, the task will be an arduous one. As Leonard Binder, while analysing the crisis of political development in new nation-states, pointed out: '[T]he greatest task facing the new nation will be to build a nation out of a collection of tribes or of isolated communities.'[18]

Claude Ake broadly defines the problem of political integration as follows: 'how to build a single coherent political society from a multiplicity of 'traditional societies'; how to increase cultural homogeneity and value consensus; and how to elicit, from the individual, deference and devotion to the claims of the state.'[19] The problem of integration faced by each nation-state differs from others in nature as well as in degree. It varies from country to country 'because of the ambiguity as to what constitutes a nation which is to be integrated' and also because of the 'differences between the countries in their history and ethnic composition.'[20] Therefore, the solution to the problem of integration cannot be uniform even among the developing countries. Some of the most common problem in integration involves the 'problems of national identity, territorial control, the establishment of norms for the handling of public conflict, the relationship between the governors and the governed, and the problems of organising individuals for the achievement of common purposes.'[21] Nonetheless, scholars of comparative politics develop some theoretical frameworks to understand the process of political integration. Much of these theories developed out of concern for nation-building in pluralistic societies.

Theoretical Considerations

There are diverse sources of political integration theories which need to be pulled together for defining the boundaries and characteristics of political integration, and present some tentative hypotheses for future analysis. However, in order to analyse the process of political integration in India's Northeastern states, the conceptual apparatus of Sidney Verba, Claude Ake, Karl Deutsch, Ernst Haas, William Riker and Marxists will be taken as an advantage.

The primary prerequisite of political integration is the existence of political culture. According to Sidney Verba, political culture 'consists of the system of empirical beliefs, expressive symbols, and values which defines the situation in which political action takes place.'[22] Verba pointed out that not all beliefs about political culture are relevant to the concept of political culture, but the concept refers to only those beliefs which affect politics in a fundamental way.[23] In almost all the theories of political integration, cultural homogeneity, especially a homogeneous political culture, is often regarded as a prerequisite for political integration, which in turn is a prerequisite for political stability, especially in democracies.[24] It is also further argued that shared culture may not be a prerequisite for unification, but a requirement that has to be fulfilled before the process can be advanced.

Claude Ake stresses the requirement from the members of the political system to identify with and trust one another. He insinuates that 'without some basic mutual trust among members of a civic body there can be no stable expectations about the modes of acquisition and exercise of political power, no coherence and predictability in political life.'[25] He further argues that if the different cultural entities within the political system are so profoundly dissimilar that they cannot communicate with one another, mutual trust and a sense of collective identity cannot develop. Therefore, one of the essential preliminary requisites for political integration is the broadening and intensifying of *social communication*. The improvement of the communicative facilities of a new state depends, in turn, on social mobilisation, 'the process in which major clusters of old social, economic and psychological commitments are eroded or broken down and people become available for new patterns of socialisation and behaviour.'[26] Social mobilisation involves a massive transformation of an old way of life and, therefore, generates tensions. Claude Ake hypothesised: '[T]he political system driving for integration maximises its chances for achieving a high degree of integration and remain stable, in spite of short-run destabilising effects of the drive for integration, if it is an authoritarian, consensual, "identific", and paternal.'[27] Ake said that the pursuit of integration underscores the need for authoritarianism, as the quest for integration aggravates political instability by attempting to make people relate to national symbols, rather than to tribal ones. Thus, in order to maintain a minimum of political stability, it is crucial that the government be strong enough to deal with the centrifugal forces that the drive for integration will activate, and the government must also be able to decide and act quickly.[28]

For successful political integration, Claude Ake further requires leaders of a new state not to concentrate power in their own hands, but father social transformation and be innovative as they are committed to integration of their culturally pluralistic societies. They must destroy or modify certain habits of mind and undermine certain traditional symbols of collective identity; they must induce the people to accept new norms, new goals, new motivations; they must readjust patterns of social and economic relationship and to this effect they must supply the initiative for realising it. As sociocultural gap between the elite and the masses is one of the most striking features of the newly independent state which poses the threat of mutual alienation between them, the political style and the way of life of the ruling elite must be calculated to dramatise its concern for and identity with the masses so as to lessen this threat. Political leaders need to eschew corruption, conspicuous consumption and social snobbery, and give their politics a distinctly *populistic* one. Ake believes that 'the ultimate cure for the inherent instability of the new states lies mainly in the modification of the political behaviour c f its elites.' He argues that the 'government should be a coalition of the leaders of the major social, religious, professional, and ethnic groups…. Consensus is sought not at the grass-roots level but at the leadership level by enlisting the support of leading personalities from all major social groups.' Political integration is said to occur 'when the linkage consists of joint participation in regularised, ongoing decision-making.'[29]

John Wood criticises Verba and Ake's equation of political integration with the achievement of national identity or a value consensus. He not only acknowledges the importance of these psychological phenomena to the *making whole* that integration connotes, but also argues that they are dependent aspects insofar as the fundamental political process is concerned.[30] Wood further pointed out that Verba and Ake wrongly suggest integration as implying a homogenisation of political values and conformity of political purposes. Etzioni also views that homogeneity of political values among sub-units does not guarantee political integration anymore than heterogeneity precludes it.[31] Political integration cannot be assessed by measuring sameness. Rather, some measures of political interaction and exchange among the integrating units must be devised.

Deutsch's communication theory stresses on communication among persons, cities, ethnic groups, language communities and countries. To him, the success or failure of political integration depends in part upon the compatibility of autonomous responses as well as on the distribution and balance of range of social transaction, and of the streams of experiences to which they give rise.[32] As political integration does not just happen anywhere, a core area of 'larger, stronger, more politically, administratively, economically and educationally advanced' political units is usually present to lead the process.[33] In their study of the North Atlantic area, Deutsch and others found that *mutual compatibility of main values* was an essential condition for both amalgamated and pluralistic security communities.[34] They conclude that political communities occur whenever groups not only exchange a high proportion of communications, but also share a superordinate goal and a *we-feeling*.

Referring to Deutsch's approach as too broad, Ernst Haas excludes transactional and institutional criteria from his initial formulation, though he considers them as potentially helpful factors.[35] Haas specifies that integration is a process which takes place in a period of time 'between the establishment of common economic rules and the possible emergence of a political entity', and which must consist 'of increasing politicisation, of shifting loyalties, of adaptation by the actors to a new process of mutual accommodation.'[36] Thus, the goal of the political community is 'a condition in which specific groups and individuals show more loyalty to their central political institutions than to any other political authority, in a specific period of time and in a definable geographical space',[37] whereas the functional theory of David Mitrany stresses the role of non-political international organisations as promoters of integration whenever experts replace politicians as key actors. Haas refines Mitrany's functionalism by emphasising the need for both political and non-political actors, since technical organisations can only expand in number and in scope so long as they have political support.[38] According to Haas, political integration is a process where the goal is the eventual formation of a political community.

William Riker, on his work on federalism and coalition formation, propounds the *bargain* concept, a tool to analyse the exchange of rewards and loyalties between political actors of the core and the periphery.[39] Political bargains may be public or secret, explicit or undefined, confirmed or anticipated. They may be amicably negotiated or arrived at under stress.

In integrational terms, the bargains forge new links among hitherto separate units and facilitate the building of new loyalties to a larger system. The term *counter-bargain* implies competition among bargain offers and alternative integrational formulae. The later may appear at the onset of the integrational process or at the later stage if, in the view of at least one bargainer, the initial bargain has been debased or broken. Marxists conceive successful political integration as a method of state-building, having performed two critical state functions: provision of the political infrastructure for the expansion of productive forces in protocapitalist and capitalist societies and an appropriate means for legitimating the power necessary to maintain the social relations integral to these societies.[40]

Majority of the integration theorists deal with the contemporary world only. They argue at some length about the appropriate definition of their dependent variable, whether there is more or less integration, how one is to measure it, whether different dimensions of integration change at different speeds and whether some measures are better predictors of the future of the phenomenon than others. Michael Haas summarises the objectives of the various approaches as an:

> attempt to discern preconditions for the achievement of higher levels of integration, variables that account for the maintenance of existing levels of integration and factors that promote increases from present to future levels of integration. Key variables in all three research avenues, when reversed, may tell us about factors accounting for backsliding in integration.[41]

According to Ernst Haas, integration theories are 'becoming obsolete because they are not designed to address the most pressing and important problems on the global agenda of policy.'[42] Rapid changes in technology and communications have thrown the process of integration itself into doubt. Growing international interdependence has created a turbulent world with crucial problems whose solutions are international rather than regional, global rather than European.[43]

Political Integration in Asia and Africa

Most nation-states in Asia and Africa had been under colonial subjugation. In the early post-independence years, these countries had inherited a vast array of problems which needed to be tackled. One among of them which needed to be solved at the outset was the problem of political integration. These countries also inherited from the colonial rule certain features of administrative and legal system, forms of government and fixed territory that help in their efforts to build their state and nation.

Several approaches to the problem of political integration were followed in Asia and Africa. One of them is avoiding the problem altogether by retaining the essential *steel frame* feature of colonialism—open or disguised.[44] This process has been followed in the Belgian and Portuguese territories. A similar result has been achieved in the federation of Rhodesia and Nyasaland by means of the wide devolution of power from imperial government in the United Kingdom to the European settlers in Africa. Another approach is found in the role played by powerful political leaders, nationalist movements and political parties, and territorial political institutions as instruments and new modes of integration. Charismatic leadership exercised by Kwame Nkrumah, Jawaharlal Nehru, Mahatma Gandhi, Sardar Vallabhai Patel, etc., was a factor in the successful transition from a British colony to a stable parliamentary democracy. Political movements of the INC, Northern Rhodesia National Congress and Sierra Leone People's Party have been instrumental in enlarging the scale of political activities. Moreover, territorial assemblies and legislatures, centralised bureaucracies and other territory-wide institutions have been structures that have fostered—indeed forced—progressive integration.[45]

Common language, which is one of the most important factors favouring political integration, is absent in most of the Asian and African countries. Linguistic regionalism remains a formidable obstacle in the path towards integration in Asian countries. Although these countries lack common language, efforts were made to introduce a national language in the interest of integration, and in order to counteract to *linguistic regionalism*.[46] There are instances of the introduction of English as a second language in some countries of Southeast Asia. Language as a key factor in the integration of Southeast Asian societies naturally features prominently in educational policies, which are themselves virtually concerned with integration—political, social and cultural.[47]

The impact of British conquest and occupation has resulted in bringing the issue of minorities into the open, where it has 'left a difficult legacy by accentuating the distinctions and differences between various groups.' They also 'left a valid tradition of effective political hegemony with control' from the centre of administration and 'a sketchy but uniform system of

statewide education and modern communications network which ultimately should prove to outweight the difficulties they created and left.'[48]

Political Integration in India

Even though India is one geographical entity, the subcontinent has never
achieved political homogeneity throughout its history. Even during the
heydays of the Gupta and Mughal empires, the country did not come
under one political umbrella. Having a subcontinental size, characterised
by diversity of race, language, religion and lifestyle, bringing the whole
geographical areas of the Indian subcontinent under one political umbrella
was a gigantic task. It has, however, 'achieved over the millennia some
feeling, however loose ill-defined, that all the diversities had their place
in a single whole.' But this 'amorphous spiritual identity had found no
expression in political unity: the characteristic political condition was a
shifting array of states and principalities, conquest and alliances, lending
colour to the trite comment that India was only a geographical expression.'[49] The British rule considerably brought about an enduring political
consolidation in India. The effect of the British rule, plus modern innova-
tions in transport and communications, in promoting a working sense of
Indian unity was of vital importance. The maintenance of law and order,
administrative unity, the introduction of a common body of social and
political concepts and values, the appearance of English as a lingua franca,
fiscal and economic integration, all served to link together the disparate
elements which made up the Indian society as did the common national
struggle against British rule.[50]

With the end of the Second World War, the withdrawal of the British
from India was imminent. The transfer of power was formulated in the
Cabinet Mission Plan of 16 May 1946, which made suggestions and
recommendations for India's demand for self-government and independence. The most important constitutional issue that emerged in view of
the imminent withdrawal of the British from India was the status and
future of the Indian native states. At the transfer of power, all rights sur-
rendered by the states to the paramount power were to devolve to the
states. Different plans for the autonomy of many princely states began to
emerge. The lapse of the political arrangements between the states and

the crown was to be filled by the states entering into a federal relationship with the new government or enter into a particular political arrangement with or without them.[51] The states were given freedom to associate with another state or to stand alone.

On the eve of British withdrawal from India, two diametric forces were in operation: a pan-Indian nationalism seeking an integrated independent India and the separatists seeking independent existence. At first, the INC leaders were not against giving the right to self-determination and even the right to secession to the aggrieved constituents, and agreed to prepare a constitution 'acceptable to all' and a 'federal one with residuary power vested in the units.'[52] However, alarmed by the rising number of claims, the Congress refused to give any territorial unit the right to secede from the Indian Union. Although the Congress stated that 'it cannot think in terms of compelling the people in any territorial unit to remain in an Indian Union against their declared established will',[53] independent India wanted to inherit as much of British India as possible. However, the Indian subcontinent after the end of Second World War witnessed a different political environment 'where it became difficult to effect this policy as popular will was often suppressed by the ambition of the rulers.'[54] With the impending lapse of paramountcy, some determined rulers still had the desire for sovereignty. In the meantime, there was an upsurge of people in 1947–48 demanding political rights and elective representation in the Constituent Assembly as well as sovereign homelands and states within the Indian federation, and threats of joining Pakistan or Burma. The task of the new nationalist government was to suppress the forces of disintegration and preserve the territory given to them by the British. A States Department, headed by Sardar Vallabhai Patel and V.P. Menon as secretary, was created to carry out the arduous task of integrating the princely states and all dissident groups. Sardar Vallabhai Patel said that the first task of the States Department was to prevent the balkanisation of the country and stop any possible inveiglement of the states by Pakistan, and to bring the states into some form of organic relationship with the Centre.[55]

British India was granted independence on 15 August 1947 as the separate dominions of India and Pakistan. The British government dissolved its treaty relations with over 600 princely states. The states were given freedom whether to join India or Pakistan, or to stand alone. Most of the states acceded to India, and a few to Pakistan. Hyderabad and Manipur opted for independence, although the armed intervention of India brought

Hyderabad into the Indian Union and the Manipur Maharaja was coerced into signing a merger agreement with India.

The integration of Indian states took place in two phases—with a skilful combination of baits and threats of mass pressure in both. The primary 'bait offered was that of very generous privy purses, while some princes were also made Governors or Rajpramukhs.'[56] One of the most arduous tasks in the process of integration was that of the integration of states with the neighbouring provinces or into new units. By 15 August 1947, almost all states had agreed to sign an Instrument of Accession with India, acknowledging central authority over the areas of defence, external affairs and communications. The gaining of independence was 'a culmination of long-drawn, multi stream process of transformation, unification and integration of the Indian people into one political entity.'[57] On 26 January 1950, when the Constitution of the Indian Republic came into force, all the states and all the outlying areas were fully integrated.

Many princely states were merged with the neighbouring governors' provinces of British India to form Part A states under the 1950 Constitution. A large number of princely states which were governed by *rajpramukhs* (appointed governors of certain Indian provinces and states during the British colonial rule) were combined into *states union*; and together with the three biggest principalities—Hyderabad, Jammu and Kashmir and Mysore—they acquired a separate existence as Part B states for a while. For strategic and other reasons, former chief commissioners' provinces and other centrally administered areas, except Andaman and Nicobar Islands, were Part-C states. The Part-C states were Ajmer-Merwara, Bhopal, Bilaspur, Coorg, Delhi, Kutch, Himachal Pradesh, Manipur and Tripura.

With linguistic reorganisation, the distinctions between Parts A, B, and C states ended, and a complex recombination of ex-princely and ex-British territory were carried out. Therefore, the great ideal of geographical, political and economic unification of India: an ideal which for centuries remained a distant dream and which appeared as remote as a difficult of attainment as ever, even after the advent of Indian Independence, was consummated by the policy of integration.[58] Great credit can be given to Sardar Vallabhai Patel for the rapid integration of Indian states. The nationalism evoked by the independence movement was responsible for the integration of people belonging to different religions, languages and cultures into a single political entity.

India's Northeast Scenario

The Northeastern region of India had its first interaction with the British East India Company as early as in 1792 at the request of the king of Assam who sought commercial advantages by a friendly and open intercourse.[59] The persisting internal strife and disorder led to repeated invasion by the Burmese who occupied the plains of Assam from 1817 to 1826 and Manipur from 1819 to 1826. This forced the Ahom King to request assistance from the British East India Company, who responded to the request and defeated the Burmese, and they were forced to surrender their suzerainty over Assam and Manipur by the Treaty of Yandaboo in 1826. By the right of conquest, Assam became a Non-Regulatory Province of the British Indian Empire in October 1838. Eventually, the British rulers annexed the whole region in the subsequent years: the Cachar Plains (1830), Khasi Hills (1833), Jaintia Hills (1835), Karbi Anglong or Mikir Hills (1838), North Cachar Hills (1854), Naga Hills (1866–1904), Garo Hills (1872–73), Lushai Hills (1890) and Kuki Hills (1919).

The whole of the present Northeastern region was part of Bengal province until 1874. Due to the British policy of expanding areas under their control and administrative restructuring after 1857, the Assam province was created and governed by a chief commissioner. In subsequent changes, the Assam province became a distinct unit directly administered by a governor-general. The British administration gave the hill people a paternal government which allowed them the free exercise of their own genius in the management of themselves, with just that amount of control from above.[60] However, these steps were regarded as the policy of *segregation* by mainland Indian scholars.[61] A series of Acts and regulations were passed by the British to protect the people in the hill areas of the Northeastern region. The legal enactments made for the rest of the country cannot be enforced automatically in these areas, except in specific cases. Successive legal and administrative decisions taken between 1874 and 1935, the separation of Burma from British India in 1937 and the partition in 1947 gave Northeast India a distinct region and identity.

All these Acts and regulations discontinued the little interaction that existed between the mainland Indians and the hill people of the region, and allowed the hill people to exist independently as in the pre-colonial period. Therefore, the British policy of non-interference allowed the tribes to conduct their own affairs and imposed a kind of strict neutrality on the British state. This mix of autonomy and neutrality of the British state prevented confrontation and insulated the hill tribes from mainstream political influence.[62] As the politics of mainstream political parties did not have any impact on the hill areas of the Northeastern region, the people waged their own struggles against British expansion arising from the need to protect their freedom and land. The nature and intent of their resistance to British rule was in no way connected to the Indian freedom movement. According to Rupert Emerson:

> ... [The] one common aspect of their lives has been the brief period of subjugation to foreign rule, and this, for the bulk of them, has often meant virtually nothing in the way of common life ... they have been under a common government with its uniform economy and system of law and administration, but in practice they have lingered very largely within the framework of their traditional societies and have perhaps only recently been brought into any significant degree of association with their fellow colonials.[63]

When there was a clear indication that the British rule in India was ending, the hill people were filled with uncertainty and anxiety. The plains people, whom they considered weak and inferior, were going to replace the British as rulers, and they resented it. One of the initial responses of the hill people to this rush of events was political activation and unification of the tribes to safeguard their interests and aspirations. They felt the need to participate in the political process and to be allowed to decide their future themselves.

In order to articulate their political aspirations, the tribals of the Northeast initially formed the Hill Leaders Union in 1945 at Shillong. This union worked for the welfare of the hill areas of Assam. To make the movement stronger and broader, and to unify the hill and plain tribals to this endeavour, another union, the Plains and Hill Tribals and Races Association was formed in the same year. However, both the associations broke down within a few years. The tribal students in Calcutta formed an association called the Indo-Burma Movement in 1946 which aimed:

> ... [T]o unite into one unit all the party of the land lying along the border of India and Burma and other adjacent areas which are inhabited by a similar

kind of people and which can be convinently demarcated into a unit; the unit thus formed (was) designed as 'Indo-Burma' and the people dwelling it be called collectively Indo-Burmans whilst retaining their tribal names separately. The future status of Indo-Burma thus formed will be decided by the representative body of the peoples.[64]

Ever since independence in 1947, the Indian state and its political apparatus have been challenged and questioned by various extremist groups of the region. Arunachal Pradesh, formerly known as the North East Frontier Agency (NEFA) and under the MEA until it attained statehood in 1987, was the only one that did not resist its integration into the Indian Union. The processes of integration of the other Northeastern states are briefly discussed as follows.

Manipur

William Riker's theory of *bargain* under stress may be applied to Manipur's political integration with the Indian Union. The princely state of Manipur staunchly opposed its integration into the Indian Union. There had been much activity in Manipur to restore its past glory and independence before India gained independence. Hijam Irabot, a communist leader of Manipur, was one of the forerunners for the mobilisation of people. In 1946, Irabot, along with Longjam Bimol, formed the Praja Sangh political party. Irabot wanted an independent Manipur with its own parliament, constitution and cabinet. Instead of the monarchical system, he wanted the representatives of the people to administer the state on socialistic principles.[65] Those who did not subscribe to Irabot's ideas, had set up a rival political party, the Manipur Congress, which had no links with the INC.

The Constitution of Manipur was framed in 1947 at the initiative of Pearson, the president of Manipur State Durbar. Under the provisions of the Manipur Constitution Act of 1947, assembly elections were held in 1948. This was the first ever election held in India based on adult franchise. A coalition government was formed by parties other than the Congress. The Manipur Congress, which started working against the Manipur Constitution, also launched a movement for the merger of Manipur with India. Irabot and the Maharajah of Manipur, Bodhachandra, strongly opposed the move to merge Manipur with India. Irabot also opposed the proposal to form the state of *Purbanchal*, consisting of Manipur, Cachar, Lushai Hills and Tripura.

After India's independence, Akbar Hydari, the then governor of Assam, visited Manipur to assess the political situation and also to explore the possibility of the merger of Manipur into India. Through Hydari's visit, the GoI learned the views of the king and its people. Dhabalo Singh, president of the ruling party in Manipur, wrote a memorandum to the king on 17 December 1948, expressing the party's desire that Manipur should remain autonomous with the king of Manipur as the constitutional head and with its sovereignty intact. The ruling party's general secretary, N. Ibomcha Singh, also stated in another memorandum that majority of the people of the state were against integration or merger. Due to its concerns about the prevailing international situation, especially the communist uprising in Burma, the Manipur Congress supported the consolidation of India through integration and merger of native states, especially Manipur.

The maharaja of Manipur was invited to Shillong in September 1949 for talks on integration. An already prepared *Merger Agreement* was placed before the maharaja on the first day of the meeting by Akbar Hydari, whereby Manipur would be merged into the Indian Union. The maharaja stood firm that he could not sign the agreement without prior consultation with the council of ministers. The maharaja was placed under house arrest and debarred from any communication with the outside world. The maharaja was thus forced to sign the *Merger Agreement* with India on 21 September 1949 and Manipur became *Part-C state* of the Indian Union. The Kuki chiefs of Manipur also opposed the Manipur Merger Agreement in 1949, as they regarded the agreement to be threatening the territorial integrity of the Kukis.

In Manipur, the bargaining negotiation for integration or merger was under stress and there were no rewards to the political actors of the periphery, and thus loyalty to the core could not be expected. The manner in which the merger was brought about has left a residual bitterness that the insurgent groups successfully tap into. A number of insurgent groups regarded the merger as illegal and unconstitutional, and many among the Manipuri intelligentsia are bitter about the way it was affected.[66] In principalities, such as Manipur, political integration involved overcoming parochial loyalties and residual loyalties;[67] however, the transitional government's approach failed to overcome these loyalties.

Nagaland

One of the other areas that opposed its integration into the Indian Union was the then Naga Hills District. Due to advancements in education during the first half of the twentieth century, a small middle class emerged among the Nagas. With British patronage, the Naga Club was formed in 1918, perhaps 'the first attempt at organised political opinion in the Naga Hills.'[68] However, the club's activities faded after they submitted their memorandum to the Simon Commission in January 1929.

The inactivity of the Naga Club led Charles Pawsey, the then deputy commissioner of the Naga Hills District, to establish the Naga Hills District Tribal Council with Naga leaders. However, the Naga Hills District Tribal Council did not last long as it was not a representative body of the different tribes. To respond to the fast changing political scene, the Tribal Council was reorganised and rechristened as Naga National Council (NNC) at a meeting held by various Naga tribes at Wokha, in February 1946. The emergence of NNC out of the Naga Hills District Tribal Council heralded the rise of middle-class intellectuals.[69] One of the first activities of the NNC was to call for self-determination and for acquiring fundamental rights. However, the NNC was talking more in terms of full regional autonomy and not in terms of complete independence. The tone and content of Jawaharlal Nehru's letter to NNC leader T. Sakhrie in August 1946 showed that the independent status of the *Naga territory* was accepted by the Indian leadership but it felt that for historical as well as strategic reasons, this territory must have formed part of the Indian Union.[70]

The NNC held another meeting at Wokha on 19 June 1946 and passed a resolution, strongly opposing the grouping of the Naga Hills District into Assam by the Cabinet Mission, and demanded autonomy for the Nagas. Jawaharlal Nehru talked about giving autonomy to the Naga Hills within the province of Assam. But the NNC was divided on this issue, with one section putting forward the idea of an independent Naga homeland and others preferring a mandate status, with Great Britain as the guardian power. However, they were unanimous on one point—that the Nagas never were a part of India, and they must be given the choice to decide on the nature of their relationship with the latter.

Unsatisfied with Nehru's assurance, the NNC had made a demand for a 10-year *interim government* for the Nagas to the Advisory Committee on Aboriginal Tribes, which visited the Naga Hills in May 1947, whereby the Nagas would run their own government under the supervision of a guardian power. The negotiation between the sub-committee and the NNC ended in a deadlock on the question of autonomy and the Nagas relationship with the guardian power. The deadlock was broken by the Hydari Agreement, which recognised the right of the Nagas to develop according to their freely expressed wishes and provided full safeguard to the Naga customary laws. Even though NNC approved the Hydari Agreement by a majority vote, the extremist section within the council refused to accept it by stressing the ninth point of the agreement that the Nagas should be given the right to choose whether to be part of the Indian Union or to be independent.

The moderates within the NNC soon lost ground and declared that the ninth point actually gave the Nagas the right to complete independence. The Indian government's interpretation was that this point (Article) gave the Nagas the freedom only to suggest changes in administration after 10 years, but did not give them the right of secession. The extremist group leader A.Z. Phizo went with a five-member delegation to meet Mahatma Gandhi on 19 July 1947. Gandhi, after unsuccessful argument with the Naga delegation, said: 'The Nagas have every right to become independent.'[71] Phizo declared independence for Nagaland on 14 August 1947. Aliba Imti also met Nehru to press the NNC's view but nothing substantial came out of the meeting, except Nehru asking Imti to accept the Sixth Schedule. Phizo became the president of the NNC in November 1949. With this, the moderates in the council were silenced, and the demand for Naga independence gained momentum.

Being unable to resolve the political demands of the Nagas through dialogue, the GoI cracked down the NNC in 1953. It tried to accommodate the Naga revolt within the ambit of the Indian Constitution by creating the state of Nagaland to draw the Naga people into the democratic process. Yet some of the issues raised by the Nagas remained largely unsettled. Much of the tragedy unleashed on the Naga Hills could have been avoided had serious and consistent efforts been made to understand the Nagas initial demand for 'home rule.' But preconceived notions, arrogance and the heady brew of power prevented the national leaders from seeing things from the other's point of view, even after the NNC's successful boycott of the 1952 elections and plebiscite.[72] As in the case of Gujarat, political integration in stages could have been adopted in Nagaland so as to permit the time and space for adjusting to the constraints and opportunities to the new system and developing a homogeneous political culture.

Assam

The state of Assam has been home to different ethnic communities, and a hotbed of many social and political agitations since the colonial period. It was the centre of British administration and India's political activity after independence for integrating the Northeastern region. The idea of *Swadhin Asom* (independent Assam) came to the fore after the British annexation of Assam and the subsequent peasant uprisings (1857–58) due to rising rates of taxation. It arose after the consolidation of Assamese nationalism based on linguistic lines. The forces of *Swadhin Asom* were to re-read, re-interpret and even re-create history in order to build up the theoretical base that Assam had always been a free nation, and that its amalgamation into British India had been achieved by trickery and fraud.[73] This idea of independent Assam gained momentum after the Assamese public became increasingly agitated by the large-scale migration from East Bengal and the occupation of cultivable lands by migrants.[74]

It was against this background that Assamese middle-class intellectuals put forward the need to defend Assamese homeland against foreign incursions. The Congress' failure to take an unequivocal stand on the issue of continued influx which threatened Assamese identity and its attempt to force Assam to accept the Cabinet Mission Plan were some of the factors that pushed Ambikagiri and Jatiya Mahasabha to raise the demand for an independent Assam. When the Congress government in Assam, after independence, failed to check infiltration from the newly created East Pakistan, Roychoudhury and Jatiya Mahasabha started espousing the cause of an independent Assam. At the meeting held on 1 January 1948, the Jatiya Mahasabha proposed that Assam should come out from the Indian Union and become an independent nation.

The idea of *Swadhin Asom* was propagated by many Assamese intellectuals in the pre-independence period. The leading intellectual of Assam, Jnananath Bora, said:

> Today, Kamrupa, which had always been a separate country, has become a province of India. The history of our country is not the same as that of the other provinces of India and there is no need to reiterate that our culture and society have little in common with them. Till today our people have not been able to accept our country as a province of India.[75]

He maintained that although the British forcibly incorporated Assam into India, the Assamese have always considered Assam to be an independent nation and that Assam cannot become a part of India just because they are brought under a single administrative unit under British India. Bora blamed the educated section among the Assamese for having betrayed Assam's cause:

> The educated section amongst us have been trying to prove for a long time that since Assam has been under British administration for quite sometime, it is naturally a province of British India.... It is these people who are trying in different ways to turn our country into a province of India.[76]

This argument is similar to the United Liberation Front of Asom's (ULFA) present stand regarding the role of intellectuals in Assam who are dubbed as Indian agents. During the initial years, the ULFA was keen on building a strong trans-ethnic solidarity as a bulwark against the *colonialism* of Delhi.[77] Time and again, the ULFA leadership issues warnings to the intellectual class to desist from acting as the agent of New Delhi. Their grievances include loss of self-determination, Indian colonial attitude, exploitation and neglect, cultural anxiety, nativism and illegal immigration, citizenship and irredentism.[78] Even though the radical section of the Assamese people glorifies Assam's past and independence and they succinctly espouses secession from India, Assam is the centre of activity of the Indian government for negotiating and holding the adjoining hill areas and the princely states of Manipur and Tripura.

Mizoram

The political changes during the 1940s generated awakening among the Mizos in the then Lushai Hills. Being apprehensive about their future and their uncertain present, the Mizo intellectuals felt the need to have a political party of their own which would determine the course of their future.[79] The first political party, the Mizo Common People's Union, was formed in April 1946 and was later rechristened as Mizo Union. The Mizo Union was the major political force in the Lushai Hills. It aimed at introducing social reforms in the Mizo society, and was primarily against the tribal chiefs. The Bordoloi Committee accepted the Mizo Union as the sole representative body of the Lushai Hills and the sub-committee invited the Union to be a co-opted member which, after some debate, it accepted.

This implied the Mizos' consent to be part of the Indian Union, since the sub-committee represented the Northeastern region in the Constituent Assembly, framing the Constitution. This triggered a public debate among the Mizo leadership, and they were divided on this issue. The right-wing groups were against the merger with India while the left-wing groups were in favour, provided the interests of the Mizos were safeguarded by the Constitution. However, the Mizo Union adopted a resolution in support of the merger of the Lushai Hills with the Indian Union. In its first General Assembly on 24 September 1946 at Kulikawn, Aizawl, the party resolved that in the event of India attaining independence, the Lushai Hills must be included within the province of Assam.[80]

In July 1947, the United Mizo Freedom Organisation (UMFO) was formed in reaction to the formation of Mizo Union, with the support of the chieftains to oppose the merger with India. One of the main objectives of the UMFO was to officially start a movement for joining Burma during the transfer of power. Their argument was that the Mizos were ethnically and linguistically close to the Burmese and politically it would be more advantageous to join Burma as it was smaller than India, and hence Burma would grant the Mizos a voice in the political affairs.[81]

The poor handling of the famine (mautam) of 1959–60 and inadequate relief measure caused great frustration among the Mizos. This, coupled with the imposition of Assamese as the official language in the state, accelerated the politics of negativism. The Mizo National Famine Front was formed in 1960 to undertake relief operations, and it was converted into a political party—Mizo National Front (MNF) in October 1961—with Laldenga as its president. The objective of the party was to achieve independence of greater Mizoram. The Union Government, in July 1971, offered to make Mizo Hills into a union territory. The Mizo leaders were ready to accept the offer on the condition that the union territory would be upgraded to that of state. As such, the union territory of Mizoram came into being on 21 January 1972. After prolonged negotiations with the Union Government, the MNF agreed to become a state within the Union, and thus the state of Mizoram was created on 20 February 1987. However, the demand for greater Mizoram, comprising Southern Manipur (Churachandpur District) and some areas of Cachar Hills, remains unfulfilled.

Meghalaya

The present state of Meghalaya consisted of 25 Khasi states, Jaintia and Garo Hills during the British rule. The British government recognised these states, and categorised them as semi-independent and dependent. The rise of political activity in these hills in the early part of the twentieth century affected the rulers of the states, who in early 1934 formed the federation of Khasi states. As early as in April 1945, when the tribal people in the Northeastern region were beginning to take a more vocal interest in their own future, the Khasi, Jaintia and Garo people also raised their voices. A meeting in Shillong, which was attended by most of the prominent people, categorically opposed their inclusion either in India or Pakistan.[82]

The Federation of Khasi States on 8 August 1947 agreed to accede into the Indian Union on three terms: defence, communication and foreign policy. On the following day, the Khasi states signed the Standstill Agreement, wherein the states agreed that with effect from 15 August 1947 all existing administrative arrangements between the province of Assam and the Union and Khasi states would continue to be in force for a period of two years, or until new or modified arrangements were arrived at. The GoI faced problems in getting the Khasi states to sign the Instrument of Accession.[83] However, on 2 December 1947, Akbar Hydari, armed with an order from Delhi, asked the Khasi chiefs to sign the Instrument of Accession, which they subsequently did. After executive notifications and the promulgation of the Constitution of India, integration of the Khasi states into the Indian Union was completed.

There was no strong popular support for independence or incorporation into Assam. However, in response to the uneven political developments during the 1940s, the Garos formed the Garo National Council. Three Garos, who represented their people, were filled with dismay to hear the rumours that some British officials in Assam planned to exclude their districts from Assam and India.[84] Mikat Sangma, who had been educated in Calcutta, reacted sharply against independence and partition.[85] He proclaimed himself as the chief of the southern parts of Garo Hills. Even though he failed to get the title recognised, Mikat Sangma gathered a band of followers protesting against the partition of Garo Hills into India and East Pakistan.

Tripura

The state of Tripura was a small tribal kingdom. During the British rule, the kingdom did not come directly under the British rule but the king paid tribute every year, and Tripura was counted among the princely states of British India. During the partition of Bengal in 1897, many Bengali Hindus migrated to the state and occupied mainly the plain areas. The migration of people from Bangladesh continues even after independence. The Tripuri people, for instance, who constituted more than 85 per cent of the population in 1947, constitute just above 30 per cent of the total population of the state.

The last independent king of Tripura, Bir Bikram, died on 17 May 1947. When the British left India, the situation was fluid and a rumour was spread that Muslim refugees from neighbouring East Pakistan were hatching a conspiracy to merge Tripura with East Pakistan. As a condition for India's *help*, the queen of Tripura was made to sign the Tripura Merger Agreement in September 1947, and its final integration with India was effected from 15 October 1949. Thus, Tripura became a *Part-C state* of the Indian Union, administered by a chief commissioner as its administrative head. From 1 November 1956, Tripura remained a union territory until it attained statehood on 21 January 1972. The radical section of the Tripuris question the mode of integration of the state into the Indian Union and the increasing migration from Bangladesh.

Thus, the mode of integration involved negotiations, promises, baits and even force.[86] Some areas, such as the Naga Hills and Manipur, refused to merge with India and desired withdrawal from the Union. Even before the national government could stabilise itself, the fragility of the integration was visible. Secessionist demands and withdrawal declarations were made by several quarters of the region.

The Fallout

In the formation of a new and sovereign India, the integration of more than 600 princely states and other loosely administered areas enjoying varying degrees of autonomy was a great challenge to the new government. It posed a serious obstacle to the unity, cohesion and stability. While some princely states willingly joined the Union, most of them made stiff opposition to the integration process. As hypothesised by Claude Ake, in most of the process the Indian state adopted an authoritarian approach in integrating the Northeastern states, where different techniques were used to coerce the constituent units to come to terms.

Considering the various ethnic communities that are found in the region, there is an inadequate incentive for political integration as its components lacks, what Etzioni calls, the *elements of shared culture*. The failure to understand the political history and cultural uniqueness of the region by the Indian ruling class led to acute *democratic deficiency* in the process of integration of Manipur, Tripura, Naga Hills and Lushai Hills. In most of these processes, the Indian state adopted various methods of assimilation to integrate the diverse ethnic groups in the Northeast.

Like most post-colonial countries, it was the state which came first and the nation later in India. Therefore, India can be categorised as a state-nation rather than nation-state, and the process of nation-building is yet to be completed.[87] The communities in India's Northeast have all the attributes, such as independent historical experience, racial, ethnic and religious peculiarities and geographical isolation, which are integral for the formation of regional forces. Thus, political integration in this particular region involves overcoming parochial loyalties and the problems of ethnic cleavages.

The tribal people in Northeast India have been given limited opportunity for protected political representation during the transition period. The leaders of the ethnic communities of the region were not given identification, as they did not participate in the national politics. This resulted in resentments in various forms from various ethnic communities.

The specific problems in integrating the princely states of Manipur and Tripura into India and the failure of the GoI to adequately address the political aspirations of other ethnic groups in Northeast India resulted in secessionist movements. By emphasising the federal nature of the Union of states, the GoI could not draw strength from a popular sense of national identity. Each state in India developed a sense of sub-national identity. The ethnic criterion of sub-national identity building is also on the rise.

As political integration of the Northeast with India was brought about without the approval of its people, the leaders of the present-day insurgent outfits continue to struggle for independence. The main argument for separation and secession was that tribal people were simply not Indians at all.[88] This mindset of not being Indian at all still dominates the propaganda and ideological setup of most of the secessionist groups of the region. As Rajni Kothari points out, there is 'no easy approach to the development of a manifest and categorical 'national identity'… the Indian identity will continue to evolve in the forms of a complex network of relationships rather than a unit relationship.'[89]

Notes

1. Alexander Mackenzie, *North East Frontier of India,* First published in 1884 as *History of the Government with the Hill Tribes of the North-East Frontier of Bengal.*
2. Amalendu Guha, *Planter-Raj to Swaraj: Freedom Struggle and Electoral Politics in Assam 1826–1947*, p. 73.
3. B. Pakem, 'Introduction', p. 9.
4. Fuller's 'Introduction' written for Major A. Playfair, *The Garos.* London: 1909, p. xiii, quoted in S.K. Chaube, *Hill Politics in Northeast India,* p. 1.
5. Mahadev Chakravarti argues that although Sikkim does not qualify for the inclusion into the Northeast as it does not meet the contiguity criteria, it was due to the insistence of Sikkim Chief Minister Pawan Kumar Chamling that the Centre had agreed for its inclusion into the region. See Mahadev Chakravarti, 'Social Change in North-East India: Partition, Ethnicity, Revivalism, Globalization', p. 11.
6. Udayon Misra, *The Periphery Strikes Back: Challenges to the Nation-State in Assam and Nagaland,* p. 1.

7. Wasbir Hussain, 'India's North-East: The Problem.'

8. Manorama Sharma, 'Socio-Economic History in Pre-colonial North-East India: Trends, Problems and Possibilities', p. 1.

9. B.G. Verghese, *India's Northeast Resurgent: Ethnicity, Insurgency, Governance, Development*, p. 280.

10. Myron Weiner, 'Political Integration and Political Development', p. 52.

11. Gabriel A. Almond and G. Bingham Powell Jr., *Comparative Politics: A Developmental Approach*, p. 36.

12. Myron Weiner, 'Political Integration and Political Development', pp. 53–54.

13. Earns B. Haas, *The Uniting of Europe: Political, Social and Economic Forces*, p. 16.

14. Karl W. Deutsch, *Political Community at the International Level: Problems of Definition and Measurement*, p. 33.

15. Ralph M. Goldman, 'The Politics of Political Integration', p. 28.

16. Arend Lijphart, 'Cultural Diversity and theories of Political Integration', p. 3.

17. Joseph S. Mye Jr., 'Comparative Regional Integration: Concepts and Measurement', p. 871.

18. Leonard binder, 'Crises of Political Development', p. 46.

19. Claude Ake, 'Political Integration and Political Stability: A Hypothesis', p. 487.

20. Rupert Emerson, 'Nationalism and Political Development', p. 96.

21. Myron Weiner, Political Integration and Political Development', p. 52.

22. Sidney Verba, 'Comparative Political Culture', p. 513.

23. Ibid., p. 526.

24. Arend Lijphart, 'Cultural Diversity and theories of Political Integration', pp. 4–5.

25. Claude Ake, 'Political Integration and Political Stability: A Hypothesis', p. 487.

26. Karl W. Deutsch, 'Social Mobilization and Political Development', p. 494.

27. Claude Ake, 'Political Integration and Political Stability: A Hypothesis.'

28. Ibid., p. 489.

29. Lenon N. Lindberg, 'Political Integration as a Multidimensional Phenomenon Requiring Multivariate Measurement', p. 649.

30. John R. Wood, 'British versus Princely Legacies and the Political Integration of Gujarat', p. 68.

31. Amitai Etzioni, *Political Unification: A Comparative Study of Leaders and Forces*, pp. 25–27.

32. Karl W. Deutsch, 'Social Mobilization and Political Development', p. 4.

33. Karl Deutsch et al., *Political Community and the North Atlantic Area*, p. 58.

34. Ibid., pp. 58, 66.

35. Ernst B. Haas, 'International Integration: The European and the Universal Process', p. 20.

36. Ernst B. Haas and Philippe C. Schmitter, 'Economics and Differential Patterns of Political Integration: Projections About Unity in Latin America', p. 266.

37. Earns B. Haas, *The Uniting of Europe: Political, Social and Economic Forces*, p. 5.
38. Ernst B. Haas, *Beyond the Nation State*, Chapter 2.
39. William H. Riker, *Federalism: Origin, Operation, Significance*, p. 42.
40. Peter Cocks, 'Towards a Marxist Theory of European Integration', p. 4.
41. Ernst B. Haas, *The Uniting of Europe: Political, Social and Economic Forces*.
42. Ernst B. Haas, 'Turbulent Fields and the Theory of Regional Integration', p. 178.
43. Ernst B. Haas, *The Obsolescence of Regional Integration Theory*, pp. 18–20.
44. James S. Coleman, 'The Problem of Integration in Emergent Africa', p. 46.
45. Ibid., p. 47.
46. Brian Harrison, 'Problems of Political Integration in Southeast Asia', pp. 143–44.
47. Ibid., p. 144.
48. Kyaw Thet, 'Burma: The Political Integration of Linguistic and Religious Minority Groups', pp. 161–162.
49. Rupert Emerson, 'Nationalism and Political Development', p. 12.
50. Ibid.
51. V.P. Menon, *Integration of Indian States*, p. 476.
52. Resolution of the Working Committee of the Indian national Congress on United India and Self Determination, 12–18 and 21–24 September 1945.
53. Ibid.
54. Sajal Nag, *India and North-East India: Mind, Politics and the Process of Integration 1946–1950*, p. 2.
55. V.P. Menon, *Integration of Indian States*, p. 464.
56. Sumit Sarkar, *Modern India 1885–1947*, p. 451.
57. Sajal Nag, *Nationalism, Separatism and Secessionism*, p. 74.
58. Quoted in V.P. Menon, *Integration of Indian States*, p. 490.
59. S.K. Bhuyan. *Anglo-Assamese Relations, 1772 to 1826*, p. 389.
60. David R. Syiemlieh, 'Response of the North East Hill Tribes of India towards Partition, Independence and Integration: 1946–1950', p. 2.
61. S.K. Chaube, *Hill Politics in Northeast India*, p. 14.
62. Rafiul Ahmed and Prasenajit Biswas, *Political Economy of Underdevelopment of North-East India*, p. 3.
63. Rupert Emerson, 'Nationalism and Political Development', p. 20.
64. Resolution of 'Indo-Burma Movement' at December 1946, quoted in Asoso Yonua, *The Rising Nagas: A Historical and Political Study*, p. 165.
65. Soyam Chatradhari, *Manipur Itihasta Irabot*, p. 34.
66. Sanjib Baruah, 'Generals as Governors: The Parallel political systems of Northeast India'.
67. John R. Wood, 'British versus Princely Legacies and the Political Integration of Gujarat', p. 66.
68. Udayon Misra, *The Periphery Strikes Back: Challenges to the Nation-State in Assam and Nagaland*, p. 29.

69. S.K. Chaube, *Hill Politics in Northeast India,* pp. 153–54.
70. Udayon Misra, *The Periphery Strikes Back: Challenges to the Nation-State in Assam and Nagaland,* p. 31.
71. S.K. Chaube, *Hill Politics in Northeast India,* p. 158.
72. U.A. Shimray, 'Naga Issue and Nehru: A Brief Note', http://www.kanglaonline.com (downloaded on 29.12.2014).
73. Udayon Misra, *The Periphery Strikes Back: Challenges to the Nation-State in Assam and Nagaland,* p. 83.
74. Ibid., pp. 83–84.
75. Jnananath Bora, 'Kamrup Aru Bharat Varsha', p. 88.
76. Jnananath Bora, 'Asom Desh Bharatvarsha Bhitarat Jhakiba Kia?' p. 88.
77. Samir Kumar Das, 'Conflict and Peace in India's Northeast: The Role of Civil Society', p. 13.
78. Swarna Rajagopalan, 'Peace Accords in Northeast India: Journey over Milestones', p. 17.
79. S.K. Chaube, *Hill Politics in Northeast India,* p. 25.
80. Lalchungnunga, *Mizoram: Politics of Regionalism and National Integration,* p. 73.
81. Vanlawma, *Kan Ram le Kei,* p. 217.
82. N. Mensergh (ed.), *The Transfer of Power 1942–1947,* p. 912.
83. D.R. Syiemlieh, 'The Political Integration of the Khasi States', p. 149.
84. D.R. Syiemlieh, 'The Crown Colony Protectorate for North East India: The Tribal Response', pp. 206–11.
85. D.R. Syiemlieh, 'Response of the North East Hill Tribes of India towards Partition, Independence and Integration: 1946–1950', p. 12.
86. Sajal Nag, 'Withdrawal Syndrome: "Secessionism" in Modern North-East India', p. 295.
87. B. Pakem, 'Nationality Question in the Hill Areas of North-East India', p. 324.
88. Paul R. Brass, *The Politics of India Since Independence,* pp. 192–202.
89. Rajni Kothari, *Politics in India,* p. 336.

5

Economic Development in Northeast India

The history of contemporary period is often referred to as the history of development. The term *development* as denoting a process which societies undergo became a focus of concern after the Second World War. Since then the concept and perspectives in which it has been understood have undergone spectacular changes. The term was used interchangeably with *growth*. However, the two terms are now clearly distinguished, where growth has limited connotations and is generally defined in quantifiable indices, such as Gross National Product or per capita income. Development, on the other hand, implies a kind of structural transformation in all aspects of society, from traditional society to modern society, where a society or part of it is transformed in the economic sphere.[1] Therefore, development, as Arndt points out, encompasses almost all facets of the good society, everyman's road to utopia.[2] It has many spheres: economic, social, cultural, political etc. However, the development of a country or a community is usually measured in economic terms.

Economic development is a historical and an evolutionary process, where historical past cannot be ignored since history appears in an essential way in any analysis of the evolutionary process of development.[3] There is no commonly accepted definition of the term *economic development*. The definitions are broad and theoretical, including phrases such as 'the process of improving the standard of living and well-being of the population.' Other definitions focus on activities and projects that are used to achieve economic development goals. Therefore, economic development is better described than defined.[4]

Although different societies within the Northeastern region might have had different levels of development within a given time frame,[5] certain commonly shared features, such as their history and geography, their economic structures and the structural change they have witnessed overtime, and their economic and psychological distances from the mainland India binds them together.[6] In this chapter, the history of economic development in India's Northeast, excluding Sikkim, is analysed from the colonial to the post-independence period, till the late 1980s.

Economic Development during the Colonial Period

Northeast India, which occupies the remote corner of India, is one of the least developed regions of the country. This development begins with the region's initial absorption into the world economy as a marginal periphery, a part of frontier of the British rule and which eventually leads to the region's peripheral position within the Indian nation-state after independence.[7]

As mentioned earlier, the Northeastern region of India had its first interaction with the British East India Company in 1792, which was mainly commercial intercourse. The prevailing internal disorder during the first half of the seventeenth century resulted in frequent Burmese attacks, and occupation of Assam and Manipur. The armed intervention of the British defeated the Burmese, leading to annexation of Assam and Manipur into British India. Eventually, the British rulers annexed the whole region in the subsequent decades. These annexations brought about drastic changes in the polity as well as in the economy of the region, with the gradual decay of feudal institutions and the rise of capitalist economic entities.

The British East India Company had no interest in the Northeastern region until the discovery of tea in 1823. The modern economic development in the Northeastern region became a priority with the increased interest shown by the East India Company on items, such as tea, oil and coal, available plenty in the region. Robert Bruce, a British merchant, who came to Assam in 1823 learnt about the existence of tea plant from a *Singpho* chief.[8] The information provided by Bruce led William Bentinck, the Governor-General of India, to appoint a 12-member committee (Tea Committee) to examine the possibility of introducing tea cultivation in 1834. The Tea Committee reported: 'We have no hesitation in declaring this discovery ... to be by far the most important and valuable that has ever been made on matters connected with the agricultural or commercial resources of this empire.'[9] Subsequently, some European and Indian entrepreneurs formed the Bengal Tea Association in 1838. The Assam Company was also formed in England in 1839, and within a year the Bengal Tea Association merged with the Assam Company.

Through the introduction of tea plantation, the region was drawn into the world economy by the British rulers and all developments in Assam during 1840–59 centred on tea and the Assam Company. The British rulers introduced various wasteland rules, which were revised after a certain period of time to attract investments. Hence, the British became the owner of large tracts of wastelands and other valuable resources in the plains of Assam. It was in the interest of the British to exploit these wastelands for profit. To clear these vast tracts of wastelands, the British rulers encouraged migration of tribals, mainly from Bihar, Orissa, Madhya Pradesh and Andhra Pradesh. To attract migrants, a pull factor was formed by allocating rent-free lands for tea plantation. This was primarily done to meet the interest of the British private capital in tea plantation as the local Assamese were reluctant to join the labour force.[10] Migration, thus, brought about a massive change in the economy of British Assam which resulted in the expansion of tea plantation economy. All this led to a period, often described as *tea mania*. Although tea was under British control, some enterprising Assamese carved out a position for themselves. Maniram Dewan was the first Assamese tea planter who was, as British rulers held, executed for treason in 1858.

Although the goal of wasteland grants did not yield immediate returns in terms of government revenue, the object was to clear the vast tracts of forests and promote immigration, and induce people to bring English capital largely into the market.[11] Lands were cleared without much environmental concern resulting in huge ecological degradation, and the villagers were largely deprived of the use of timber and other forest products. To recover the huge loss of revenue in granting rent-free wastelands, the tax on agricultural lands were increased in the 1890s. The local populations, who mostly depended on agricultural lands, were greatly affected by this hike. It resulted in various resentments by Assamese peasants against the increased taxation. As a result, the land-abundant valley became land scarce, and the labour-shortage economy turned into a labour-surplus one during this period.

Apart from the migrant tribal labourers from Chota Nagpur, there were several migrant communities. The Bengali Muslims from East Bengal settled initially on fallow land along the Brahmaputra, but gradually extended their hold over lands in traditional tribal areas and Assamese villages. The Bengali Hindus took up clerical and other middle class jobs in Assam and Tripura. They also started small businesses after settling in several towns of the region. When the migrant communities started concentrating their hold over land and other sources of livelihood, there was a fairly neat division in respect of economic spoils among the migrant communities from an ethno-economic angle.[12]

Even though the sole interest of the East India Company's annexation of the region was to exploit the rich natural resources, in order to exploit these resources they firstly need to develop transport and communication. From 1859, the East India Company came forward to take up road construction work to facilitate tea industry. Within few decades, various roads linking Bengal and the Northeastern region, as well as roads connecting various towns within the region were constructed. Rail lines were also constructed in the latter part of the nineteenth century. Apart from the colonial interest of developing transport and communication to maximise profits in tea and oil industries, the East India Company laid stress on the improvement of communication both by land and water to control rebellions in the region.[13] Hence, the growth of tea estate, commerce, transport and communication were an interrelated process.

Oil and coal were the other two important discoveries of the British in Assam apart from tea. The formation of Assam Railways and Trading Company in 1881 became the forbearer of economic development in Assam. The company introduced railways, developed petroleum and coal as an object of emergent trade and geared up tea and timber industries. After the Assam Railways and Trading Company gave up its interests in petroleum, the Assam Oil Company was formed in 1899 with its headquarters at Digboi. The Assam Oil Company was engaged in the exploration of oil and setting up of Digboi Refinery in 1901. All these undertakings by the British brought about a new dawn in the field of industry. Yet, these commercial ventures did not leave any scope for native participation.

The Northeastern region came under colonial economic system but except for tea plantation, no strong linkages were established with the outside market. The plantation revolution was not accompanied by agricultural revolution within Assam to raise agricultural productivity and marketable surplus. The local economy was not able to meet the needs of the rising immigrated workforce in the plantation sector. Food grains were imported into the region to meet these rising needs. As such, people were brought into the region to meet labour requirement, their foods imported and their wages remitted back home by the labourers, making the region a resource provider, to be extracted and exploited by outsiders, where the local population have nothing to gain out of it. The limited participation of the local population in the economic activities further restricted their fusion with the main currents of development.

In the hill areas of the Northeastern region, the British rulers followed the policy of minimum interference due to the unique geo-political and historical background of the tribals and with a view to check entry of people into this area, the hills and plains were governed by different laws.[14] As a result, the tribal people remained outside the ambit of the capitalist path of development and continued to lead a life of relative independence with minimum colonial presence.[15] In fact, the hill areas were of little economic value and considered to be a burden by the British rulers.

The people of the hill region mostly lived on subsistence economy. Shifting cultivation was the predominant form of agriculture, although terraced cultivation was practiced by some tribes, such as the Angamis of Nagaland, Apatanis and Monpas of Arunachal Pradesh and the Khasis of Meghalaya. The rice economy was supplemented by food gathering, hunting and fishing.[16] As the main interest of the British was maximisation of profit, the development of transport and communications was mainly concentrated in the resource-rich plains of Assam, and the hill areas were out of the ambit of these developments. Thus, the colonial economy was mainly concentrated in the two valleys of Assam, where most of the natural resources were located and could be exploited because of its easy accessibility as compared to the hills.

Most of these hill areas were brought within the British fold through the introduction of monetised economy in the traditional trade and exchange. The colonial powers introduced manufactured, glamorised and finished products, which attracted the hill people and created a demand for such goods at big fairs. The tribal people became not only frequent visitors to the fairs held in the foothills, but also became more dependent on imported goods. The merchant class introduced opium selling and, in turn, acquired natural products produced by the hill people. The dependence of the tribes in finished imported products and opium led to the destructive mode of acquiring resources which eventually led to the depletion of traditional resource base.[17] During the colonial period, the hill areas were marginally integrated into the colonial politico-economic system and remained isolated from the central political system of Fort William.

The development of railways and waterways, and the establishment of other productive enterprises—such as coal, petroleum, wood manufacturing—were all guided by the sole objective of maximisation of profit from the plantation economy. Whatever little profit the industries and enterprises created were mostly extractive in nature. The economic development of Assam during the colonial period, therefore, was essentially enclave in nature.

From the pattern of economic development in Northeast India during the British rule, it can be seen that: first, unlike the prediction of development theories, the traditional sector did not provide a source of labour supply to the modern sector.[18] Hence, the important link between the two sectors in the labour market was not established. Second, the income generated in the modern sector did not remain within the region. Apart from the profits being remitted outside the region, a substantial portion of the wages earned in this sector was also remitted. Moreover, the immigrants spent their incomes on items which were not locally supplied. Thus, there was huge drain of money from the region. Even after independence, a dual economy ethos is continuing in which the wages of the migrant labourers are remitted to their homes outside the region, and this group of labourers constitute a majority in various construction projects.[19] Thirdly, the rapid growth of workforce in the modern sector raised the demand for agricultural products, and the price of these products too increased. However, the agricultural sector had been not able to keep pace with the increasing demand, as there was a marginal increase in the supply of agricultural products.

In short, it can be said that the coming of the British in the region brought about the growth of modern sector without raising the standard of living of the people due to their limited participation in the economic activities. By the end of the nineteenth century, 'the economy of Assam had developed all the characteristics of a dual economy'[20] with huge investments pouring into the modern sector, the traditional sector being left out of this developmental process. The modern sector flourished on the resources of the region, serving the interests of outsiders through employed capital and labours from outside the region, and served an external market. As a result, the traditional sector and the hill areas of the region remained underdeveloped and untouched by the process of development.

Barrister Pakem summarises the impact of British rule in the economy of Northeast India as follows:

The British after pushing up their administration to Northeast India, did not help the region in bringing about economic development for the benefit of the area. What ever industries they had set up, like tea plantation, oil and other mineral extractions, were done only to further their own interests. Hence during the colonial period limited economic development took place, and that too was confined to the tea and oil producing areas of Assam plains and in some mineral producing areas in the Khasi Hills of Meghalaya. In the rest of the hill areas baring a few pockets the traditional tribal economy of the primitive type of agricultural jhumming and pastoral economy, among others, persisted. This variation in the respective economies of the hills and the plains is the function of different physical features, different social relations, and the neglect and isolation of the region by the colonial masters. This in turn produced a multi-structural economy in the region and this position continued till India's Independence.[21]

Economic Development in the Post-Independence Period

Independent India started with the shockwave of partition in 1947. Partition redrew the political boundary of British India, culminating in the creation of present-day India and Pakistan, and the subsequent creation of the then East Pakistan as independent Bangladesh. It resulted in mass migration of people with serious demographic, socio-political and economic repercussions in the country. The redrawn political boundary had far-reaching consequences for the economy of Northeast India. It created a physical barrier with the mainland, and formed what is now called the *Northeastern region*. Before partition, there was no concept of a separate Northeastern region as every province or hill region that it now constitutes was closely linked for trade, economy, movement and education to the adjoining areas of East Bengal, Burma and Tibet.[22] Many parts of Manipur (Kuki and Tangkhul Naga areas), Lushai and Naga Hills had direct links with Burma, where many of their ethnic kins live. The Khasi, Jaintia and Garo Hills maintained close relations with Sylhet, the Lushai Hills with Chittagong Hill Tracts and Tripura with Comilla, Noakhali and Sylhet. The areas of NEFA (present Arunachal Pradesh) had close contacts with Tibet, Bhutan and also with Burma. All these relations changed suddenly in 1947.

The partition caused disruption of the age-old pre-independence inland water, road and railway communications through erstwhile East Bengal. All of a sudden, the region became isolated from the rest of the country. It became virtually landlocked with a tenuous connection with mainland India through the 21-kilometre-long landmass, often described as the *chicken's neck* or the *Siliguri corridor*, which is less than 2 per cent of the 5,000 kilometre combined perimeter formed by the seven Northeastern states. The Chinese takeover of Tibet resulted in the creation of new international political boundaries, replacing the soft territorial frontiers of South Asia. It also resulted in the disappearance of a crucial buffer and brought the Chinese Army right to the borders of India, and the virtual closure of the border with Burma added to the isolation of the region. The flourishing trade with the plains of adjacent East Bengal/East Pakistan, Tibet, Bhutan and Burma were halted. The separation of communication lines and well-developed markets with the plains of East Bengal thwarted economic growth of the region. It created havoc for the Northeast, making it the most regulated, sensitive border region and the most exposed territory. Using the region's two per cent perimeter as a major linkage point with the rest of India, and, at the same time, checking the inflow of goods and people from across the remaining rest of the 98 per cent has been a gigantic task.[23] B.G. Verghese commented: '[I]f imperial politics distanced the Northeast from its trans-border neighbourhood further east, partition in 1947 all but physically separated the Northeast from the Indian heartland.'[24]

The effect of the partition is large on the contemporary life of Northeast India. Though the new international borders dividing India and Bangladesh are seen as inviolable, the partition could not change the position that the region acquired during the colonial times as a frontier. Partition also did not stop immigration from Bangladesh. These demographic changes, in one way or the other, contributed to the unrest in the region. Social and communal tensions, agitations and disturbances which some parts of the region witnessed during that time had seriously impeded the process of developmental activities right at their take-off stage.[25]

Apart from these, there were popular movements, and the national governments also endeavoured after 1947 to close off and regulate national borders more rigorously than ever before with a goal to defend national territory against foreign threats and to secure national territory against internal disruption that might be fed by forces across the border.[26] The Northeast was closed off to defend India's borders. As a result, the region became the most exposed territory, facing alien states around most of its perimeter. These conditions have not been conducive to the region's economic and political well-being, and have caused extreme geo-political isolation of the Northeast. The loss of connectivity and market access, according to B.G. Verghese, sets its economy back by at least a quarter century.[27] The restriction of the age-old mobility through the regulation of national borders and the partition of India has made Northeast India virtually landlocked and a periphery. Even though the isolation of the region is recognised lately, no adequate study has been done since independence on the exacerbated post-partition effects on the region.

The closing of Northeast India's traditional trading partners—Bhutan, Myanmar and Tibet—during the British colonial rule and continued by independent India was replaced by opening up local barrier to trade, leading to unrestricted flow of migrants into the region. In fact, it was part of the colonial policy to introduce an intermediary class, as the colonial policy discouraged local entrepreneurs.[28] With the improvement of transport and communication and the flourishing extractive enterprises, such as tea, oil, plywood and coal, the flow of migration continued unabated in the region. Capitalists from the mainland acquired mineral rights and timber lands and set up saw mills, coal business and other extractive enterprises in the region. Although some of the enterprises were locally owned, the majority of the resources and a large number of workers were controlled by non-residents. This core–periphery relation made Northeast India an internal periphery. The Northeastern region is converted from a frontier region during the British rule to an internal periphery in the post-independence period. This development in the region can be termed as *internal colonialism*.

Though the term *internal colonialism* has been applied in a variety of contexts, it is widely used to describe the exploitative relationship between the *core* and *periphery* within a nation-state. An internal colony produces wealth for the benefit of the capital area. The members of the internal colonies are distinguished as different by a cultural variable, such as ethnicity, language or religion. They are then excluded from prestigious social and political positions, which are dominated by members of the metropolis.[29]

The conceptualisation of *internal colonialism* to a large extent originated from the research carried out in Latin America by Gonzales-Casanova during the mid-1960s.[30] However, Michael Hechter's *Internal Colonialism: The Celtic Fringe in British National Development* is considered to be one of the most pivotal publications on the subject. Hechter's conceptualisation of *internal colonialism* arose from his study of the Celtic fringe in British national development. Hechter views the process of geo-political integration of Wales and Ireland into the English state, the Union of England and Scotland in 1603 and the passing of the Act of Union in 1707, which left a single Parliament in London as always unequal. When this political integration was compounded by economic exploitation, Scotland, Ireland and Wales were converted into Britain's *internal colonies*. This condition emerged with the spread of industrialisation from English heartland to the peripheries. Capitalist industrialism created a new economic dependence of the periphery on the core. Trade and commerce in the peripheral regions tend to be monopolised by members of the core. Economic development in the periphery is designed to complement and promote economic development of the core. There is relative lack of services, lower standard of living and higher level of frustration among the members of the peripheral groups. There is national discrimination on the basis of language, religion or other cultural forms. Thus, the aggregate economic differences between core and periphery are causally linked to cultural differences.[31]

In Northeast India, the exploitation of resources resulted in the destruction of peripheral modes of production where intermediary sectors of the economy fully gained access and control over the resource base of the peripheral modes of production. This core–periphery relationship does not allow the integration of periphery with the core, which subsequently resulted in a situation where the 'core develops and spreads underdevelopment by way of a direct exploitation of the periphery.'[32] As a result, the hills of the Northeastern region still practice a subsistence form of economy, and the plains which act as an extension of markets of the mainland follows an economy of surplus and abundance. Thus, the hill areas are marked by underdeveloped productive forces, while plains are marked by productive forces of the core and the periphery becomes a market for goods and services brought by the core.

India's economic policy towards the Northeastern region during the initial few decades after independence was not different from that of the

British colonists. Since independence, the region has been looked upon as a place for extracting natural resources—the process which started well in the British era.[33] In the plains of Assam, not much developmental activity took place except the nationalisation of oil and coal industries. Although Assam's tea, oil and jute provided the much needed foreign exchange during the 1960s when foreign exchange crisis had hit India, the benefits of nationalisation of oil and coal industries to Assam's economy was marginal.[34] Neither the Assam government nor the people, except minimal employment, benefited from it.

While most of the trade and commerce in the Northeastern region have been controlled by a growing migrant population, big Indian capitalists enjoy monopoly over oil, tea and plywood industries. Out of about 620 tea gardens in the Brahmaputra valley of Assam, Assamese planters own only about 158 gardens.[35] The tea gardens of Assam account for about 55 per cent of the total tea produced in India and earn an annual ₹500 crore as foreign exchange for the country. Except for the newly formed Assam Tea Corporation, a public sector enterprise owning a few sick and unprofitable tea gardens, the majority of the big gardens are under foreign and Indian companies which are controlled from Kolkata. The main office of the tea board is situated in Kolkata, although most of the gardens are located in Assam. Since major portion of tea was sold in Kolkata, Assam had lost the vital sales tax on tea. Thus, the core-based companies used cheap labour of the internal periphery to reduce their operating cost.

The state of Assam produces about six million tonnes of oil each year, and has an estimated reserve of 70.46 million tonnes of crude oil and 23,000 m³ of natural gas. This crude oil has a very high aromatic content and is rated high in the world market. According to international price standards, Assam crude oil should cost 1.5 times higher than the low grade Organization of the Petroleum Exporting Countries crude oil.[36] Till 1980s, Assam had no refinery and crude oil was sent to Barauni refinery in Bihar. A number of scholars of the Northeast often ask as to why any refinery was not set up in Assam. The simple reason, believed to be, is that the Barauni refinery was set up at a time when Indian president was Dr. Rajendra Prasad, who was from Bihar.[37] The sales tax that Assam derives from her crude oil is ₹54 per ton, whereas India gets ₹991 per ton as sales tax on Assam crude oil.[38] Apart from Assam, crude oil has been discovered in the state of Arunachal Pradesh and a defunct oilfield in Nagaland. In recent years, coal and gas reserves were located in Tripura and Mizoram. This economic exploitation of Assam's resources and the Central Government's apathy towards the people of Assam was also responsible for the Assam Movement of the late 1970s and the eventual formation of the political party, Assam Gana Parishad (AGP) and an insurgent group, ULFA. During the formative stages of the movement, the leaders noted with dismay that although the state of Assam supplied 60 per cent of India's crude oil production at that time, it received less than 3 per cent of its value in the form of royalties from the central government.[39] It was a major producer of tea, but its royalty earning was incredibly low.[40] The same was the case with plywood. Even the regional capitalist class that developed in Assam after independence was composed mainly of *Marwari* entrepreneurs.[41] Assam's enrichment, according to the movement leaders, served the investors from elsewhere rather than the region's population. There is a widespread feeling that the pattern of development to which Assam, and the Northeast in general, has been exposed is purely extractive, exploitative, colonial and profits transferred outside the state with little re-investment. Many scholars of the Northeast blame that the colonial economic structure is largely retained only to make the region a periphery of the Indian capitalist system. The British had invested in tea plantation, in timber, in oil, in railways and river transports, since then no major industries have come up in Assam. As such, there are good reasons for the people of the Northeast to have the feeling of being neglected.

In the post-war years, national governments attempted to improve their economy by using various institutions and policies. Planning was adopted as a mechanism to attain balanced growth and to ensure minimum standard of living in the relatively impoverished places. A formal model of planning was adopted in India after independence. Accordingly, the Planning Commission was set up on 15 March 1950 with Prime Minister Jawaharlal Nehru as the chairman. The main aim of planned development in India has been to attain balanced economic growth by transforming the backward colonial economic system into a developed modern industrial one. The five year plans have undertaken this challenge and most regions in the country have felt their long-term impact. The main approach to planning for development of the tribal villages has been to break their isolation and build rural infrastructure, and raise their standard of living through the adoption of improved technology of production, that is, replacement of shifting cultivation by settled cultivation.[42]

In the early 1970s, the Indian government began to recognise that the people of Northeast India have been left behind in economic development. Thereafter, various schemes for development of infrastructure and economy of the Northeastern region were formulated since the 1970s. These schemes include the Hill Area Development Projects, Tribal Area Sub-Plan, Tribal Development Agency Projects, Border Area Development Programme and formation of the NEC. The whole of the Northeastern region, except Assam, was declared as *backward* for the purpose of industrial assistance. It was realised that the path of development adopted by the GoI in the past had resulted in uneven distribution of the benefits of economic growth between geographical areas and also between socio-economic groups. Recognising the topographical, socio-cultural and other peculiar problems as the main factors contributing to the backwardness of the region, the Hill Area Development Programme was launched which started receiving special attention since the Fifth Five Year Plan (1974–79). In the subsequent years, several committees were set up by the Planning Commission, such as the Tiwari Committee (1980), Sivaraman Committee (1981), Swaminathan Committee (1982), Trivedi Committee (1985), Bhupender Singh Committee (1985), which reviewed the programmes and suggest measures for the development of the Northeastern region.

The GoI's approach to development planning since the 1970s involved special support for geographically backward areas. The *Gadgil Formula* for allocation of central plan assistance to states was evolved in 1969. The criteria used to define these states include: (a) remoteness and hilly terrain, (b) large populations of indigenous (tribal) peoples, (c) inadequate economic and social infrastructure and (d) inadequate capacity to raise resources on their own. Most of the Northeastern states fall under this category. The Gadgil Formula was revised in 1980 and other similar states were added to this *special category states*. For this special category states, assistance was provided on the basis of 90 per cent grant and 10 per cent loan. In the state of Assam, the pattern of central assistance is 70 per cent loan and 30 per cent grant.

To bring about an integrated development of the Northeastern region, the central government set up the NEC in 1971 by an Act of Parliament— the NEC Act, 1971. The council started functioning from 1972, and it acts as an advisory body and development wing of the Ministry of Home Affairs. The NEC (Amendment) Act, 2002, put Sikkim into the NEC fold. Since its inception, the NEC has been functioning as a regional planning body for the Northeastern region, formulating specific projects and schemes to benefit two or more states and reviewing the implementation, and recommending measures for the effective coordination in the implementation of such projects and schemes. It has taken up several projects for the development of infrastructure in the region. The policies of industrial licensing, concessional finance and investment subsidy, growth centres as well as freight equalisation of some major industrial inputs have also been used towards economic development.[43] To bring about balanced socio-economic development in the region, the NEC supplements the efforts of the states by rendering them such balancing and infrastructural support as they need. A significant development of this period was that the region drew special attention of the planners. The share of the Northeastern region in the total national plan steadily increased from 2.29 per cent in the First Five Year Plan to 5.35 per cent in the Fifth Five Year Plan, 5.58 per cent in the Sixth Five Year Plan and 6.10 per cent in the Seventh Five Year Plan.

However, critics have pointed out that the NEC has worked only up to a point and is no longer greatly favoured by the constituent states. On the formation of the NEC, M.S. Prabhakar observes:

> ... [I]t is difficult to see the rational behind the formation of the North Eastern Council.... North Eastern Council seeks not merely to usurp the limited powers of the states, but to totally replace the authority of the states by the Centre, especially by the most active repressive organs of the Centre.... What is sought to be achieved is not so much the whittling down of the powers of the states of the region but their reduction to a state of total impotence.[44]

He further asserted that the whole idea of an integrated and coordinated development of specific areas is faulty, and the council is merely a decorative body. The NEC is blamed for adopting a highly bureaucratic and technical approach in its quest for finding regional policies for the region, and spends a major portion of its plan outlay in developing infrastructure and assumes that by taking care of infrastructural development it can achieve regional development.[45] Munshi, Guha and Chaube have shown that infrastructural indices associated with modernisation have no correlation with the actual growth indices in the units of Northeast India.[46] With its overemphasis on infrastructure with a half-hearted concern, the NEC failed to create human capacity formation for a balanced regional development. With the establishment of the Ministry of Development of North Eastern Region (MDoNER) in September 2001, the NEC now functions under this nodal department of the central government.

The failure in building the local forces of production and human capacity development has made the region increasingly dependent on the mainland. Although the region has rich mineral, water and forest resources, the absence of industrialisation makes the region a market ground for manufactured products from industrialised regions of India, and more new industries and jobs created outside the region. A vast chunk of the money earned is spent on buying consumable items imported from industrial parts of mainland India. The Shukla Commission in its report submitted to the GoI in March 1997 titled *Transforming the Northeast* estimated that about ₹2,500 crore worth of consumable items are imported from outside the region every year.[47] Therefore, the questions of being neglected, the geo-political and economic situation after independence, the colonial economy still retained and the government approaches to development in the Northeastern region are often being raised.

The mainstream economic thinkers generally blame economic backwardness or neglect as the main source of political turmoil in the Northeastern region and that once this problem is taken care of, the main source of political turmoil will go away.[48] It is true that militant groups, political parties and public opinion in Northeastern states do complain about the region's economic underdevelopment and this has resulted in alienation of the people. Once developmental efforts begin to generate, a host of opportunities will penetrate into the lower strata of society and people will cease to resort to insurgency. As the mainstream analysts believe, one of the main reasons for the rise, growth and sustenance of insurgency in the region is lack of development, and the region as a whole suffers from lack of developmental initiative. It is also true that insurgent groups in the region have been successful in exploiting the prevailing sense of general deprivation among people to further embolden their position. However, the belief that initiation of developmental efforts would automatically end insurgency is just a wishful thinking. Such a line of thought fails to analyse the problem in its entirety.[49] Although the insurgent groups complain about economic backwardness or neglect, their primary complain is perceived injustices grounded in the history of how the Indian post-colonial constitutional order came into being.[50] What is striking is that the bureaucrats, politicians and military officers who make *Northeast policy* are either oblivious of the historical issues that insurgencies raise, or consider them too trivial to merit substantive engagement.[51]

Of late, the central government has recognised the economic backwardness of the region, and that economic backwardness and under-development generate the feeling of alienation and relative deprivation among the people. Hence, it pumped in crores of rupees as developmental funds with the intention of stimulating economic growth and development in the region.[52] The general notion is that by bringing about development, people of the region will put aside problems of identity, ethnic assertion and immigration from neighbouring countries, and finally result in the abatement of insurgency. Thus, successive central governments announced developmental packages. In 1996, the then Prime Minister H.D. Deve Gowda announced an economic package of ₹6,100 crores, following his visit to the region. His successor I.K. Gujral endorsed this package. To boost economic development of the region, the BJP led National Democratic Alliance (NDA) government under Atal Bihari Vajpayee also announced another package of ₹10,217 crore in 1998. In October 1996, under the *New Initiatives for North Eastern Region*, it was stipulated that at least 10 per cent of the budgets of the central ministries/departments should be earmarked for the development of Northeastern states. As the expenditure on the Northeast by some union ministries during 1997–98 fell short of the stipulated 10 per cent target, the NDA government created a Non-lapsable Central Pool of Resources to support infrastructure development projects in the region. Between 1990 and 1991 and 2002–03, the region received about ₹1,08,504 crores.[53] As such, underdevelopment in the region cannot be due to lack of funds. It can be said that there is some sort of political or psychological neglect, but definitely not in terms of devolution and transfer of resources from the Centre. In fact, as Congress leader Jairam Ramesh has argued, this kind of public expenditure has become very much part of the problem of the Northeast.[54]

After pouring in a large sum of money as developmental funds, the region still has problems of underdevelopment. The large non-implementation of the developmental packages neutralise the intended impact. This occurs because of poor monitoring, lack of accountability and non-adherence to the set time frame for project implementation. What is needed is not just periodic developmental packages, but also proper utilisation and monitoring of funds. Some believe that pumping in money without proper streamlining and utilisation has opium-like effects. The bureaucrats, who are arms of the government, must be reoriented to meet the requirements of the day. Wasbir Hussain listed two main reasons why pumping of funds into the region by the Centre have not had the intended impact:

1. Leakage of funds at various levels of the government machinery. Development funds making their way into the coffers of the insurgent groups are common knowledge.
2. Lack of capacity by the states in the region to absorb the huge quantity of funds in the absence of training and expertise to successfully come up with implementable location-specific projects and the infrastructure to get some of these projects off the drawing board stage.[55]

With the gaining of independence, organised developmental activities started in India. In more than six decades, the GoI has tried different developmental approaches in the Northeastern region where some of them have achieved success, more or less, but others have not been able to show the expected results. The policy framework for the Northeastern region is guided by a combination of political, economy and culture,[56] and these policies are implemented mainly through the Planning Commission and the NEC. As a result of this, the combined approach to the process of economic development, the role of bureaucrats has been given undue importance resulting in red tapism and resultant delays in implementation of projects. Despite massive financial investments, this has failed to produce the desired results.[57] Though development as a concept took formal shape in the post-independence period, it is actually a continuation of the colonial policy whose basic objective is to maximise production (profit) through the optimum utilisation of natural resources.[58] Therefore, it is being argued that the presence of *outsiders* either privately or through corporate houses into the region provided short-term benefits, but the process, as a whole, has permanently scarred the tribal economy and undermined their knowledge systems and intangible heritage acquired through centuries of intimate interaction with nature.

The Northeastern region is marked by diversity in economic pursuits, but geopolitical hindrances have prevented the area to develop economically at par with many other parts of the country. The lack of development and industrialisation has resulted in the growing economic disparity of the region vis-à-vis the national average, and this rising disparity has further led to the growing sense of alienation among the people.[59] Economic deprivation, disparity, exploitation, lack of development and a growing sense of alienation, en masse, created congenial condition for the rise of ethnic conflicts leading to insurgency in the region.[60] Approval of the objectives of these movements in certain cases had further deteriorated the situation, and, as a result, a sense of integration with the national mainstream faced a serious setback. For this reason it is felt that 'the region is heading towards a paradoxical state of external integration and internal disintegration and thereby frustrating the developmental efforts.'[61] Though underdevelopment is not the only reason for the rise of insurgency, yet it still remains the prime factor for the prevailing insurgency in the region. Due to widespread insurgency, political turmoil and social tensions, developmental funds are being diverted for the maintenance of law and order which only makes the situation worse. The operation of banking activities, laying of railway tracks, operations of the oil and tea companies, etc., constitute a major challenge for the developmental process. Most importantly, the continuation of insurgency provides the corrupt political establishment with a smokescreen for its non-performance. Therefore, there is a vicious cycle of underdevelopment, political and social tensions, and insurgency in the region since independence.

Notes

1. V. Xaxa, 'Tribal Development in the North-East: Trends and Perspectives', p. 25.
2. H.N. Arndt, *Economic Development: The History of an Idea*, p. 1.

3. Alokesh Barua, 'Introduction', p. 29.
4. United States General Accounting Office, Report to Congressional Committee, p. 7.
5. Manorama Sharma, 'Socio-Economic History in Pre-Colonial North-East India: Trends, Problems and Possibilities', p. 16.
6. Alokesh Barua, 'Introduction', pp. 14–15.
7. Rafiul Ahmed and Prasenjit Biswas, *Political Economy of Underdevelopment of North-East India*, p. 50.
8. Rajen Saikia, *Social and Economic History of Assam*, p. 146.
9. Tea Committee's Report cited in William Robinson, *A Descriptive Account of Assam*, pp. 137–38.
10. Edward Gait, *A History of Assam*, p. 413.
11. Moffatt Mills, Report on the Province of Assam, 191, quoted in Sanjib Baruah, 'A Nineteenth Century Puzzle Revisited: Clash of Land Use Regimes in Colonial Assam', p. 172.
12. B.P. Singh, 'North-East India: Demography, Culture and Identity Crisis', p. 265.
13. H.K. Barpujari, *The Comprehensive History of Assam*, p. 294.
14. N.L. Dutta, 'Tribal Situation and its Implication on Development in North-East India', p. 77.
15. M.N. Karna, 'Aspects of Tribal Development in North-Eastern India', p. 14.
16. Amalendu Guha, *Medieval and Early Colonial Assam: Society, Polity, Economy*, p. 3.
17. Rafiul Ahmed and Prasenjit Biswas, *Political Economy of Underdevelopment of North-East India*, p. 52.
18. H.K. Nath, 'The Rise of an Enclave Economy', p. 135.
19. B.P. Singh, 'North-East India: Demography, Culture and Identity Crisis', p. 267.
20. Amalendu Guha, *Medieval and Early Colonial Assam: Society, Polity, Economy*, p. 197.
21. B. Pakem, 'The Economic Structure of North Eastern Region of India', p. 179.
22. Subir Bhaumik, 'Insurgency in North East.'
23. Gulshan Sachdeva, 'Demystifying Northeast.'
24. B.G. Verghese, *India's Northeast Resurgent: Ethnicity, Insurgency, Governance, Development*, p. 2.
25. Anand Kumar Yogi, *Development of the North East Region: Problems and Prospects*, p. 67.
26. David Ludden, *Where is Assam? Using Geographical History to Locate Current Social Realities*.
27. B.G. Verghese, 'Unfinished Business in the Northeast: Priorities towards Restructuring, Reform, Reconciliation and Resurgence.'
28. Rafiul Ahmed and Prasenjit Biswas, *Political Economy of Underdevelopment of North-East India*, p. 53.

29. Nicholas Abercrombie, Stephan Hill and Bryan S. Turner. *The Penguin Dictionary of Sociology*, p. 183.
30. P. Gonzales-Casanova, 'Internal Colonialism and National Development', pp. 27–37.
31. Michael Hechter. *Internal Colonialism: The Celtic Fringe in British National Development, 1536–1966*, pp. 33–34.
32. Rafiul Ahmed and Prasenjit Biswas. *Political Economy of Underdevelopment of North-East India*, p. 134.
33. Nabendu Pal, 'India's North-Eastern Region: Towards a more humane approach', pp.1–38.
34. J.N. Roy, 'The North-East needs New Approach', p. 65.
35. Tilottoma Misra, 'Assam: A Colonial Hinterland', p. 1359.
36. Ibid.
37. Nabendu Pal, 'India's North-Eastern Region: Towards a more humane approach.'
38. Tilottoma Misra, 'Assam: A Colonial Hinterland.'
39. Jyotirindra Dasgupta, 'Community, Authenticity, and Autonomy: Insurgence and Institutional Development in India's Northeast', p. 355.
40. Jyotirindra Dasgupta, 'Ethnicity, Democracy and Development', pp. 165–167.
41. J.B. Bhattacharya, *Studies in the Economic History of Northeast India*, pp. 349–63.
42. J.B. Ganguly, 'Economics of Development of the Tribal Villages of North East India.'
43. M.S. Prabhakar, 'The North Eastern Council: Some Political Perspectives', pp. 1823–26.
44. Ibid.
45. Rafiul Ahmed and Prasenjit Biswas, *Political Economy of Underdevelopment of North-East India*, p. 55.
46. S. Munshi, A. Guha and S. Chaube, 'Regionalisation and Integrated Economic Development in North-East India.'
47. S.P. Shukla, Commission Report, p. 19.
48. Sanjib Baruah, 'Governor as Generals: The Parallel Political Systems of Northeast India.'
49. Bihu Prasad Routray, 'Is Development a Riposte to Insurgency?'
50. Sanjib Baruah, 'Governor as Generals: The Parallel Political Systems of Northeast India.'
51. Sanjib Baruah, *Durable Disorder: Understanding the Politics of Northeast India*, p. 78.
52. Zarin Ahmad, 'India: Package for the North East.'
53. Gulshan Sachdeva, 'Demystifying Northeast.'
54. Jairam Ramesh, 'Northeast India in New Asia.'
55. Wasbir Hussain, 'Interaction on the North East.'
56. Gulshan Sachdeva, *Economy of the North-East: Policy, Present Conditions and Future Possibilities*, p. 6.

57. Gulshan Sachdeva, India's Northeast: Rejuvenating a conflict-riven Economy.'

58. Tiplut Nongbri, *Development, Ethnicity and Gender*, p. 63.

59. Alokesh Barua and Arindam Bandyopadhyay, 'Structural Change, Economic Growth and Regional Disparity in the North-East: Regional and National Perspective', p. 239.

60. P.C. Dutta, 'Problems of Ethnicity and Insurgency in North East India', p. 112.

61. Gurudas Das, 'Understanding the Underdevelopment of North-Eastern region of India.'

6

India's Northeast Policy

Since independence, the Indian government has adopted several policies towards the Northeastern region and many of these policies have changed in the past decades. Scholars of the region often question as to how a country have a policy towards its own. In Mrinal Miri's words:

> To whom, or for whom, do you have a policy? What is the object of a policy? ... The Northeast is a part of this country and at the same time we think that the people of the Northeast should be made the object of a policy.[1]

He reiterated that human beings do not have a policy towards family members or friends. To be made an object of policy implies that the peoples of the region are not in a relationship of human concerns, such as love, friendship, understanding of the other, but in a relationship of the manager and the managed, where the idea of management and the idea of a policy are almost the same.[2] Policies are made to derive some advantage and manipulate for benefit.

However, it is true that the Indian government has adopted several policies towards the region since independence, and many of these policies have changed in the past decades. Such policies were measures to solve the complex problems of alienation, insurgency and ethnic identity, and to bring about economic development in the region.

Nehru–Elwin Period

With the birth of the Indian Union, a debate on the future of the hill areas of the Northeastern region and their politico-administrative character began. The relative isolation of the tribals has been considered as one of the problems of nation-building. The attitude of the new political leadership has been the same as the early colonial mind, that of an amused bewilderment—seeing something so exotic and so far so remote.[3] In response to the worldwide debate as to what should be the approach of the developed complex societies towards the simple tribal structures coexisting within the same political boundary, two different alternatives to the policy of isolation, that is, either assimilation or integration, have been discussed. The main question is whether to establish unity by integration or by assimilation. In view of the fact that tribal socio-economic structures, culture and value systems, ways of life are totally different from that of the non-tribal complex societies, any attempt to forced assimilation may be counter-productive in the long run—the policy of integration instead of assimilation got world-over recognition from both the academic as well as administrative circles.[4] Independent India also adopted this integrational approach towards tribal minorities. While assimilation means a total loss of cultural life and identity for the group that is being assimilated,[5] its absorption into the dominant group would lead to 'antagonism, tension and increasing alienation of each from the other.'[6] The latter calls for political, economic and administrative integration within a framework of cultural plurality, where minorities can join the majorities, without losing their linguistic, religious and cultural identities. Since independence, the GoI has adopted several policies and measures to solve the problems of alienation, insurgency, ethnicity and cultural identity and to bring about economic development in the Northeastern region.

The policies of the GoI towards the Northeastern region have changed over the years. The first one and half decades of India's policy towards the Northeastern region can be described as the *Nehruvian policy framework* or *Nehru–Elwin policy* where quick administrative expansion associated with the revivalist-protectionist approach towards tribal development in the hill areas was followed. In the early 1950s, Jawaharlal Nehru had realised the necessity of a tribal policy to go beyond the political integration of the Northeastern people with India. Verrier Elwin took an active part in the process of formulation of India's tribal policy. For Elwin, 'it was not the question of reviving anything. It is more a problem of introducing change without being destructive of the best values of old life' in Northeast India.[7] He said:

The old controversy about zoos and museums has long been dead.... [W]e do not want to preserve the tribesmen as museum specimen but equally we do not want to turn them to clowns in a circus. We do not want to stop the clock of progress, but we do not want to see that it keeps the right time. We do not accept the myth of Noble Savage; but we do not want to create a class of Ignoble serfs.[8]

The anthropological approach of the government views Northeast India as a 'phenomenally diverse mosaic of cultures which have to be preserved and enriched.'[9] It has accepted the rights of tribals to retain their way of life and identity, and has sought to integrate them through democratic means into the federal frame of the Constitution of India.[10] Therefore, the post-colonial Indian state continued with the British policy of Inner Line Regulation within the Nehruvian policy framework, which ensures non-interference from the people of the plains, and also carved out an area of unimpeded self-development for the tribes of the region.[11] Through the various Acts and regulations, it was viewed that protection of the tribal identity and culture was already assured and the important problem was how to give the tribes the good things without destroying the good things of theirs. However, due to special constitutional arrangements, historical background as well as geographical location, the central government has been trying to integrate the Northeastern region with the national economy through a special policy framework.

Jawaharlal Nehru was not against the modernisation of tribes, but wanted the process to be gradual. In 1960, he wrote:

> Political and economic forces impinged upon them and it was not possible or desirable to isolate them. Equally undesirable, it seems to me, was to allow these forces to function freely and upset their whole life and culture, which had so much good in them.[12]

In the foreword to the second edition of Verrier Elwin's book, *A Philosophy for NEFA*, in 1959, Nehru spelt out *Panch Sheel* or five cardinal principles concerning the government's attitude towards the tribals in order to prevent the loss of identity and culture, and also for their development.

1. People should develop along the lines of their own genius and we should avoid imposing anything on them. We should try to encourage in every way their own traditional arts and culture.
2. Tribal rights in land and forests should be respected.
3. We should try to train and build up a team of their own people to do the work of administration and development. Some technical personnel from outside will, no doubt, be needed, especially in the beginning. But we should avoid introducing too many outsiders into tribal territory.

4. We should not over administer these areas or overwhelm them with multiplicity of schemes. We should rather work through, and not in rivalry to, their social and cultural institutions.
5. We should judge results, not by statistics of the amount of money spent, but by the quality of human character that is involved.

Nehru was totally against the assimilation of tribals with the mainstream Indian culture. He felt that this would have disastrous effects on the tribals of Northeast India who would ultimately lose their own culture and tradition, and would put an end of their arts and craft, dance and music and their ways of living.[13] He stated: 'We may well succeed in uprooting them from their way of life with its standards and disciplines and give them nothing in its place.'[14] Verrier Elwin was also against making the tribals of Northeast India *a second rate copy* of the mainland Indians. He felt that two extreme courses should be avoided: one was to treat them as anthropological specimens for study and the other was to allow them to be engulfed by the masses of Indian humanity.

It can, thus, be seen that there has been recognition of specific tribal and ethnic identities through the policy of the state, but such a policy was not complemented with adequate support of capability-building in the region.[15] The Nehruvian policy of leaving them alone did not ensure appropriate self-development. Rather, the policy of pursuing development through political concessions and funding from the centre have drawn the region into the fold of nation-building process that sharpened the difference and unevenness between levels of progress as obtained at the national and regional plane.

Aftermath of the Chinese Aggression in 1962

There was a drastic change in India's policy towards the Northeastern region in the early 1960s. During the first decade of India's independence, Jawaharlal Nehru wanted India to be a leading proponent of decolonisation and acted as a neutral mediator on global issues, which gave him recognition by the Afro-Asian countries as one of the Third World leaders. However, the defeat against Chinese Aggression in 1962 was the first setback in India's foreign policy. It was an eye opener for the national government and leaders that such a neglected area could shake the whole country, and subsequently it changed the course of India's security and even foreign policy.

The Nehru–Elwin policy, which was followed during the first one and half decades since independence, came under sharp criticism. There was a wide recognition that administrative penetration into the hill areas of the Northeastern states was negligible or unsatisfactory. The revivalist–protectionist approach was dominated by an isolationist insinuation which is believed to sharpen the wedge between the tribals and non-tribals, as well as the hills and plains. The policy began to change from 1963 and was largely abandoned after the death of both the proponents—Nehru and Elwin—in 1964. All developmental efforts by the government, henceforth, were guided by the security-related approach. To tighten its grip of control on even the remotest corner of the Northeast, the GoI created more administrative machineries. The Indian Frontier Administrative Service (IFAS) was formed in 1953 to meet the problem of technical personnel and trained staff shortage. This special service administers the people of NEFA, Manipur and Tripura, who were living in difficult terrains with cultural sensitivities. Even though this service was doing a commendable job in difficult and dangerous circumstances, it was abolished in the latter half of the 1960s and was merged with the Indian Administrative Service (IAS) as 'the expedient of providing a separate cadre for an extremely limited service proved inexpedient as practically no avenues of proportion which is an inactive for work, existed in the new cadre.'[16] Hence, there was some sort of administrative and political development in the region. However, this political and administrative development was not accompanied by corresponding economic development of the region.

The new policy pursued since the 1960s was centred on the assumption that the tribals face problems that are by no means peculiar to themselves. The corollary to this assumption is that they do not require any special design of development other than the one applicable to other parts of India. Thus, two major shifts in the policy pursued can be seen. First, instead of developing a tribe by keeping its linguistic and cultural identity, the focus was on developing a territorial unit inhabited, mostly though not exclusively, by the tribals. Secondly, there was a perceptible shift from a culture-sensitive design of development to massive investment and greater reliance on technology as the universal panacea whether they are detrimental to tribal identity. Thus, the Nehru–Elwin policy of gradual integration was largely abandoned after 1962 in favour of progressive politico-economic and cultural integration of the tribal people in order to speed up their socio-economic development.[17] The advocators of the isolationist policy during the British rule, namely, Hutton, Parry, Grigson, Robert Reid and Verrier Elwin were severely criticised.

Politics of Political Representation

In the aftermath of independence, many tribes of Northeast India started demanding either autonomy or statehood or independent nationhood. As a result, there was a conception in the early 1970s that the region 'required political representation; the diverse tribal cultures and diverse sub-nationalities required participation in "mainstream" democratic process.'[18] Apart from the external threats across the border, new states were formed in the region during this period to fulfil certain ethnic, cultural and political aspirations for self-government among various tribal groups. The premise was that they require a voice—representation in the democratic process—that once they have voice and representation in the pluralistic parliamentary democracy, many of the problems associated with this region would be minimised. As such, the GoI reorganised the political boundary of undivided Assam through a series of parliamentary Acts enacted during 1962–72, without considering financial and economic viability. It started with the creation of Nagaland in 1963, comprising of the then Naga Hills District of Assam and Tuensang division of NEFA. The North-Eastern Areas (Reorganisation) Act, 1971, gave birth to three more full-fledged states, that is, Meghalaya, Manipur and Tripura and two Union Territories, that is, Mizoram and Arunachal Pradesh (NEFA). Although the people of Arunachal hardly voiced for a separate state, the strategic importance of this territory, the growing unrest among the tribal minorities elsewhere in the region and the failure of Assamese sub-nationalism in accommodating the tribal aspirations were instrumental in delinking Arunachal from Assam.[19] The reorganisation of Northeast India has given the tribals a sense of pride in their separate political status, and the local elite and dominant sections of the middle class have greatly benefited in economic and political terms. The benefits of reorganisation, however, are yet to penetrate down the masses in a satisfactory manner. The liberal allocation of finance by the central government and the growing deviousness of political life have led to the flow of black money in the region and political defections.[20]

Despite the creation of several new states, the basic problem of integration, insurgency and balanced economic development still remain. The creation of several new states, instead of solving problems at large, acted as a model for smaller ethnic communities of the region to aspire for greater autonomy, and hence rising insurgent and autonomy movements in the region. Such carving out of states was a restatement of self-development for the tribes, but the machinery and the governance could not fully attain such goals.[21] Although quick politico-administrative and cultural integration, rapid economic development was viewed as the necessary pre-conditions for the security of the Northeastern borders, most of the resources for the region during this period were directed towards defence needs and little could be achieved in the field of economic development.

Efforts towards rapid politico-administrative and cultural integration were associated with programmes for rapid modernisation of stagnant traditional tribal economies. For rapid economic integration, the region was brought under the sphere of banking activities during this phase. Following the recommendations of the Gadgil Study Group of the National Credit Council and of the Nariman Committee, the Reserve Bank of India formulated the Lead Bank Scheme in 1969 where the State Bank of India was decided to be the lead bank for the hill states of the region. Thus, the policy of progressive integration adopted during the transitional phase was pursued fervently after 1972, and this policy of progressive integration has been implemented on such a massive scale that the line of demarcation between assimilation and integration got blurred.

The Development Syndrome

In the 1980s, the GoI developed a new policy for the Northeastern region, which can be termed as the *development paradigm*. This policy assumes that if institutions of development were created and money poured into this region, the problems of politics, of society, of ethnic strife and of integration will get abated. Thus, the 1980s saw a remarkable increase in public expenditure in the region. Several developmental packages were announced by various prime ministers on their visits to the region.

In 1996, the then prime minister of India, H.D. Deve Gowda, announced an economic package of ₹6,100 crores, following his visit to the region. His successor, I.K. Gujral, endorsed this package. To boost the economic development of the region, the NDA government led by Prime Minister Atal Bihari Vajpayee also announced another package of ₹10,217 crores in 1998. In October 1996, under the *New Initiatives for Northeastern Region*, it was stipulated that at least 10 per cent of the budgets of the central ministries/departments should be earmarked for the development of the Northeastern states. As the expenditure on the Northeast by some Union ministries during 1997–98 fell short of the stipulated 10 per cent target, the NDA government created a Non-lapsable Central Pool of Resources to support infrastructure development projects in the region. Between 1990–91 and 2002–03, the region received about ₹1,08,504 crores.[22]

Of late, there is a wide recognition among policy-makers and economists of the region that the main stumbling block for economic development of the Northeastern region is the disadvantageous geographical location.[23] A new policy developed among intellectuals and politicians that one direction the Northeastern region must be looking to as a new way of development lies with political integration with the rest of India and economic integration with the rest of Asia, with East and Southeast Asia in particular, as the policy of economic integration with the rest of India did not yield much dividends.[24]

With the development of this new policy, the GoI directed its Look East policy towards developing the Northeastern region. This policy is reflected in the *Year End Review 2004* of the MEA, which stated:

> India's Look East Policy has now been given a new dimension by the UPA Government. India is now looking towards a partnership with the ASEAN countries, both within BIMSTEC and the India–ASEAN Summit dialogue as integrally linked to economic and security interests, particularly for India's East and North East region.[25]

Notes

1. Mrinal Miri, 'North-East: A Point of View'.
2. Mrinal Miri, *Identity and the Moral life*, p. 920.
3. Binayak Dutta, 'Constructing India's North Eastern Tribal Policy and Verrier Elwin—A Review', p. 290.
4. Gurudas Das, *The Tribes of Arunachal Pradesh in Transition*, p. 76.
5. M.N. Srinivas and R.D. Sanwal, 'Some Aspects of Political Development in North-Eastern Hill Areas of India', p. 120.
6. V. Venkata Rao, *A Century of tribal Politics in North-East India, 1874–1974*, p. 546.
7. Verrier Elwin, *The Tribal World of Verrier Elwin–An Autobiography*, p. 295.
8. Verrier Elwin, 'A Philosophy for NEFA: The Fundamental Problem', p. 246.
9. Jairam Ramesh, 'Northeast India in a New Asia'.
10. Gulshan Sachdeva, 'Fiscal Governance in the Northeast', p. 54.
11. Rafiul Ahmed and Prasenjit Biswas, *Political Economy of Underdevelopment of North-East India*, p. 3.
12. Quoted in M.K. Raha, 'North-East India and Nehru', pp. 123–24.
13. Ibid., p. 125.
14. Jawaharlal Nehru quoted in Verrier Elwin, *A Philosophy for NEFA*, p. 54.
15. Rafiul Ahmed and Prasenjit Biswas, *Political Economy of Underdevelopment of North-East India*.
16. Manilal Bose, *History of Arunachal Pradesh*, p. 238. In recent years the Congress Minister Jairam Ramesh mooted about a separate administrative cadre for tribal regions, like the IFAS, which Jawaharlal Nehru created for some states of the Northeast with the advice from Verrier Elwin.
17. Samir Kumar Das, 'Tribal politics in Contemporary India', p. 348.
18. Jairam Ramesh, 'Northeast India in a New Asia'.
19. Gurudas Das, *The Tribes of Arunachal Pradesh in Transition*, p. 87.
20. B.P. Singh, *The Problem of Change: A Study of North-East India*, p. 139.
21. Rafiul Ahmed and Prasenjit Biswas, *Political Economy of Underdevelopment of North-East India*, p. 4.
22. Gulshan Sachdeva, 'Demystifying Northeast', p. 77.
23. Gulshan Sachdeva, *Economy of the North-East: Policy, Present Conditions and Future Possibilities*, p. 145.
24. Ibid.
25. Government of India, 'Year End Review 2004', *Ministry of External Affairs*.

7

Political Impact of the Look East Policy

In the second phase, which was launched in 2003, the Look East Policy was given a new dimension wherein India started looking towards partnership with the ASEAN countries, integrally linked to the economic and security interests of the Northeastern region.[1] With this reorientation, there has been rippling effects not only among the state governments of the Northeast, but also among the media, bureaucrats, academicians and even the common people. The Look East policy has enormous potentials; however, there are also equally challenging hurdles for the Northeastern region. There is a growing concern that there may be more rhetoric than substance in the policy.

Although there is a huge potential for economic cooperation between India's Northeast and its neighbouring countries in the East, which can be a step towards bailing out the region from its economic problems, such a proposal for closer ties needs to be examined in the context of persisting assertions of ethnic nationalism and the problems of ethnic integration with mainland India. As Swarna Rajagopalan puts: 'Integration without consent, colonial attitudes, nativism, legal and illegal migration, relative deprivation, cultural nationalism, irredentism, and, increasing in some places, criminalisation have sparked violent conflict in the region over more than five decades.'[2] This situation is exacerbated by a deep sense of antagonism and mistrust among various communities, lack of a sense of belonging and the continuing communication gap. As a result, there exists a high degree of alienation among the people of the Northeast. Such problems persist together with other transborder menaces, such as migration, insurgency and drug trafficking, and the nexus between the latter two. In the like of this situation, this chapter examines the four persisting issues of the region, that is, integration, migration, insurgency and drug trafficking, and explores the extent of *sovereignty bargains* that the Indian state will be willing to engage with.

Ethnic Integration

Many nation-states today are characterised by multi-ethnic populace. Most of them become multi-ethnic 'as a result of long histories of changing borders, occupation by foreign powers and regional migration' or 'as a result of deliberate policies encouraging migration or by way of colonial or imperial legacies.'[3] Ethnic aspirations and conflicts continue to rage around the world, threatening disintegration of some multiethnic states. These aspirations are 'not the product of isolation, but rather the result of increasing interaction among ethnic groups.'[4] Such concomitant problems continue to confront nation-states today. India has also been saddled with the problems of ethnic integration since independence. In order to analyse the process of ethnic integration in Northeast India, it is pertinent to briefly look into how ethnic diversity is accommodated in multiethnic societies and suggest policy measures in the light of the Look East policy.

Ethnic Integration in the United States, Europe and Africa

In the United States, the *melting pot* model, where immigrants are completely assimilated to the Anglo-American norm, is the process of cultural development. Although the Anglo-American culture has remained the pre-eminent one, its character in some parts reflects the impact of different ethnic groups that now compose the American population. The term *melting pot* is also applied to countries such as France, Brazil and Bangladesh, mostly referring to the increased level of mixed race and culture. The United States and many European countries are pluralistic in many senses. In such pluralistic countries, ethnic groups are separate but equal, as is demonstrated by Switzerland, where French, German and Italian groups coexist in the same society. The leaders of most ethnic minority groups in such countries increasingly emphasise the path of pluralism.

In East Africa, the institutions inherited from colonialism in the 1960s did not work satisfactorily. The trend of nation-building and integration of ethnic communities in Uganda, Kenya, Zaire, Sierra Leone, Nigeria and elsewhere in Africa failed. The main reason is that the parliamentary system 'failed to deal adequately with the problem of sub-cultural nationalism.'⁵ The same is the case with Sri Lankan Tamil minorities and various ethnic groups in Myanmar continuing their struggle.

Ethnic Integration in the Northeast

Integration of the ethnic communities in India's Northeast with the national mainstream is one of the arduous tasks faced by the Indian government since independence. Ethnicity or ethnic consciousness rose steadily since the beginning of the twentieth century with renewed vigour in the post-independence period. It culminated during the late 1980s and early 1990s, which found its expression in the rise of various insurgent movements demanding ethnic homelands, ranging from different levels of autonomy within the Indian state to secession from India. A combination of historical, cultural and economic factors was responsible in shaping such ethnic consciousness.

India's Northeastern region is a home to numerous ethnic nationalities. Their 'plot of history', as Clive Christie points out, 'has been written retrospectively by the winners (the British).'⁶ The British was perceived to have laid the foundation for the emergence of ethnicity as a political force among the tribes. Ethnographic studies along with administrative and military accounts of the region were done by various British administrators and military officers. Different Acts and regulations were passed by the colonial government to protect the tribes. The Bengal Eastern Frontier Regulation of 1873 was the first among them which allowed the colonial state to create an Inner Line along the Assam foothill tracts.⁷ This regulation was supplemented by the Scheduled Districts Act of 1874 and the Frontier Tract Regulation Act of 1880 which permitted the exclusion of the territories under their purview from the codes of civil and criminal procedures; the rules on property legislation and transfer and any other laws were considered unsuitable for them. With the same purpose, the GoI (Excluded and Partially Excluded Areas) Act of 1935 was passed, which declared the Naga Hills District, the Lushai Hills District, the North Cachar Subdivision of Cachar District and the frontier tracts as excluded. The Garo Hills District, the Khasi and Jaintia Hills District (excluding Shillong) and the Mikir Hill Tracts of Nowgong and Sibsagar District as partially excluded areas. Such measures, according to Sanjib Baruah, instituted the move from 'soft to hard boundaries.'[8]

On the pretext of protecting the tribal people, colonial rulers practised the policy of non-interference in their administration, and separate treatment was given to them. However, such Acts and regulations were largely designed to serve the administrative, economic, strategic interests of the imperial government, rather than in the overall interest of the tribal people. Although the colonial rule integrated the Northeastern region with mainland India territorially their policies, which were enacted in various acts and regulations, acted as a barrier and prevented socio-cultural and political interactions between the hill areas with the plains within the region. These distinctions and isolation continued to have impact on the people, and they continued to think in terms of racial difference and conflict situations between the core and the fringe.[9] During the colonial period, ethnic movements were in the rudimentary stage and more concerned with the preservation of their distinct ethnic identities. They were not prepared to merge their culture completely with the national mainstream and wanted to maintain their distinct identity.[10]

Hunter and Phillip conceive that ethnic minorities which are often subjected to discrimination or even outright repression by the dominant group(s) in their society, may respond either by seeking to blur the distinctions between themselves and others or by emphasising their distinctions and demanding recognition and tolerance for their own group.[11] In Northeast India, the ethnic communities emphasise their distinctions in their relationship with the dominant mainland communities and which, in turn, leads to growing ethnic consciousness and identity expansion.

On the eve of independence, various ethnic communities of the Northeastern region demanded autonomy, stating that they have never been subjected under any rule before the British and they belong to an entirely different ethnic entity. After independence, such demands for autonomy were invariably looked upon with distrust by the GoI, which saw it as attempts to break-up of the country. Ashok Kumar Ray considers the official view of such autonomy demands in Northeast India as 'quite narrow', where '(t)he conflict in the northeast was interpreted as essentially toward the crisis of law and order. Eventually the political aspects of such demands were largely ignored.'[12] The opposition to accession to the

Indian Union by ethnic communities in the Northeast was not a political question. As Tiplut Nongbri observes:

> The resistance reflected a deep rooted fear in the minds of the tribes, fear of losing control over their territory and, hence, being politically, economically and culturally subjugated by the more numerically and economically dominant population of the plains that explains the uncertainties and doubts that pervaded the political climate in the hills.[13]

According to Paul Brass, the centre has been following pluralist policies in relation to the various linguistic, religious and other minorities in the country, and consequently developed a workable means of maintaining political unity in the world's most culturally diverse country.[14] However, such policies, as argued by Nabendu Pal, were followed half heartedly and such a half-hearted approach bears fruits in the form of ethnic strife.[15] India has track records of suppressing ethnic aspirations ruthlessly. Scholars of the region often question the *unequal* and *forced* integration of the Northeastern region into the Indian *mainstream*.[16] In attempting to turn itself into a nation, the Indian state did not respect the cultural and ethnic identities of different groups or recognise that the tribals have a culture and religion of their own.[17] Coupled with this was the tendency of national leaders towards homogenisation. What has in fact emerged during the second half of the last century in India is the extension and generalisation of the cultural model of the Hindu majority, rather than a true synthesis of ethnic diversities. This has not only taken India away from the social ideal, but also has created new conditions for the mobilisation of ethnic minorities with a view to forestall an inundation by the majority.[18] The tribals reacted against the efforts to homogenise cultures.

Walker Connor's thesis that increases social mobilisation also increases ethnic tensions and is conducive to separatist demands fits into this situation.[19] These ethnic minorities started posing a problem as 'arbitrarily defined national boundaries have included diverse and sometimes mutually antagonistic groups.'[20] Such a failure of the national leaders to understand and solve the aspirations of the ethnic communities alienated them. Sunanda K. Datta Ray considers the overall ethnic situation in India as a sort of challenge of diversity. According to him, the ethnic movements of Northeast India are primarily a result of the 'feelings of fringe people's being out in the cold.'[21] After more than six decades of India's independence, the

Northeastern region is yet to be brought to the *mainstream*, thus, fostering *national integration*. Many scholars believe that the cultural gap between the people in the Northeast and those of the mainland is so deep that the region is unlikely to be psychologically integrated with India in the near future. As a result, it is alleged that the people of the Northeast are alienated from the rest of India.

In the contemporary world, the 'new metaphor of integration, multiculturalism, has replaced the assimilationist model exemplified by the classical American conception of the assimilationist "melting pot". Inspired by trends in modern ethnology and literary studies, politicians have shown in recent years a welcome sensitivity to subaltern cultures.'[22] Such is also the case of Indian leaders with regard to their homogenising efforts. The tremors of the 1960s and 1970s, and the turbulence of the 1980s have compelled frequent reiteration of emphasising cultural diversity and maintaining individual identity.

If the Look East policy is to be pursued fervently, it should involve deepening of India's cooperation in trade and investment, technology, transport and communications, energy and tourism with its eastern neighbours. Sanjib Baruah, a staunch proponent of a continental Look East policy, advocated that 'India should take more advantage of Northeast India's history and culture as a soft power resource.'[23] This involves the reviving of shared historical and cultural ties between the people of Northeast India and Southeast Asia. Thus, the Look East policy implies looking towards the East in every sphere. So, the question arises whether looking east would further compound the problem of ethnic integration and ethnic alienation in the Northeast. In fact, the region has several constraints in the political, economic and ethnic integration not only with mainland India, but also within the region as well. These constraints make it extremely difficult to formulate any concrete policy for the region and promote concerted efforts towards development.

Ethnic integration needs to be seen not only as a problem of integrating the ethnic communities of the Northeast with the mainland cultural domain, which has always been resisted. It also needs to be understood and seen from both the perspectives of the legacy of colonial geo-politics and the present globalised world where there is much propagation for a borderless world and formation of economic zones. Due to geographical constraints and British policies, there was hardly any cultural interaction between mainland India and communities of the Northeast during the colonial period. Even after independence, various colonial policies of non-interference continued. Many of the ethnic communities, such as the Kukis, Mizos and Nagas, were divided into two halves by the separation of Burma and British India in 1937. The partition of India in 1947 by the British also alienated numerous ethnic communities of the region. The imaginary political boundary drawn by Cyril Radcliffe in Delhi before the partition divided the Garos, Khasis and Kuki-Chin groups between India and Bangladesh. These borders forced the ethnic communities to live in different countries. It also disrupted the old trade routes and deprived the communities in Northeast India of their trading activities with the other side of the international boundary. These have caused discomfort and, to a large extent, have been responsible for the discontentment of such separated ethnic communities.

It is advocated that, as a frontier, the Northeast can develop into a new region. Sharing 98 per cent of its borders with other countries, which are described as extended neighbours, India's Northeast can not only be a bridge, but also be an impetus for regional cooperation and development in an era of globalisation. The coming of globalisation has brought forth a new global culture. This new global culture is the expression of deterritorialisation and a borderless world. While the term *global culture* is a politics of inclusion, the Indian youth is embracing the global culture and have become more endearing to their way of customs by losing their culture.[24] The elite and middle class in India share similar values and lifestyles with similar social classes in the western countries. There has emerged, thus, a new breed of identities based on mobility,[25] and mobility within and across borders is considered good for economy. The emerging global culture and mass embracement of this culture by the Indian youth have started blurring the line of cultural distinctions, and this will continue in the coming days. This underlying circumstance reveals that there is no question about ethnic integration of the Northeast people with the mainstream culture. What we find is the progressive integration of not only the ethnic communities of the Northeast, but also the Indian youth as a whole to the global culture.

The propagation of *borderless world* is often associated with economic integration under the banner of globalisation.[26] De-emphasising the political borders and formation of an economic zone or what Keniche Ohmae termed as *region states*,[27] which may fall within a country or they may overlap the borders of two or more countries, would be another way round for a solution. In doing this, the transborder ethnic communities can revive their age-old relations and practices by reducing the *forced border* created by the British which, to some extent, generates sub-nationalist tendencies. The Look East policy should also include rekindling the age-old ties between the transborder communities of the region. This could reduce the sense of alienation created by colonial geo-politics. The formation of sub-regional economic groupings, such as BIMSTEC and BCIM Forum, is a way forward. B.G. Verghese observes, 'Northeast cannot ignore its immediate neighborhood, which is far more international than national.' However, the country's diplomatic and trade policies in relation to the region and emerging opportunities therein remain wedded to past shibboleths and there is a continuing inwardness of approach. B.G. Verghese extols the recognition of transborder ties, which was indeed the lifeblood, between the communities of the Northeastern region with the countries beyond and the improving relations with neighbours.[28]

The steady technological advancement and the forces of globalisation since the late 1970s changed the economic system of the world. These forces enabled multinational companies to do more with less, as such, outsourcing services anywhere around the world became the trend. The onslaught of globalisation, communication revolution and the opening and liberalisation of Indian economy have transformed major cities in India into a global city with the proliferation of multinational companies, leading to the burgeoning of business process outsourcing, which now contributes about 2.5 per cent of India's GDP. The focal point of these changes is the emergence of an economic system which thrives on the mobility of resources, services and products. It is even asserted that increasing mobility is good for democracy and vice versa.[29]

This transformation has created new opportunities for migrants from Northeast India where the talented youth of the Northeast increasingly find jobs in such openings. Employment opportunities in the neo-liberal spaces of the global city are fuelling a rapid increase in migration from the Northeast, the very limit of India's geographical and cultural imaginary. In this space of economic inclusion, the Northeast migrants continue to live as exceptional citizens. The experiences of the Northeast migrants in global cities reveal how neo-liberal transformation is connecting heartland cities to frontier regions in ways previously unimagined.[30] As a result, the hearts and minds of their relatives way back in the remote corners of the Northeast are always on such global cities in India. Thus, the global forces have brought about an automatic emotional integration than the conscious efforts of the GoI in the past decades.

One political initiative the GoI needs to pursue is to frame policies which may involve some kind of constitutional reforms so that not only the voice of the Northeastern people is heard at the Centre, but also their unique cultures and their participation in the struggle for independence are recognised. B.K. Roy Burman recommends a Scandinavian *Sami Council*—like multilayered parliamentary system in which ethnic communities will have the right to represent themselves instead of being bound by the majoritarian commands of Indian parliamentary system.[31] The Kukis and Meiteis of Manipur joined the Imperial Japanese Army, and Subhash Chandra Bose led the Indian National Army and fought the British colonial rule. However, such participation did not receive national recognition and did not even figure in the history of India's struggle for independence. An average *mainland* Indian has no clue about the location of the Northeastern states, whether it is a part of India, Bangladesh or Myanmar. This ignorance about the region, and the people and local culture has accumulated over the years and is creating havoc in this region.[32] It has sidelined the people of this region and compounded their ethnic alienation. Looking east should not only look into the eastern neighbours. The Look East policy should also include looking towards the Northeast, its needs and problems first, vis-à-vis the current globalised world.

The *politics of recognition* has been one of the effective tools in redressing the grievances of the sidelined people. Such groups demand recognition of their distinctiveness—their distinct identity, history and culture. The premise is that it is the distinctiveness that has been ignored, glossed over, assimilated to a dominant or majority identity.[33] Citing the success model of how the transborder communities in Europe are accommodated within the EU, Sanjib Baruah calls for *transnational politics of recognition* of the geographical and ethnic identities that cut across international borders with the objective of making the Look East policy beneficial to the Northeastern region.[34] In Europe, ethnic groups that straddle inter-state boundaries were seen as threats by European nation-states. The Maastricht Treaty of 1993 gives such groups influence in the EU decision making and an opportunity to pool resources and pursue a transnational politics of recognition that has been able to compensate for their marginalisation within nation-states. Coupled with this is the call for revival of the ancient trade routes under the Look East policy. The Mizo Accord promised to promote Indo-Myanmar border trade. Such a recognition and revival of ancient trade has the potential of abating the numerous insurgencies in Northeast India through regional and sub-regional cooperations. B.G. Verghese also argues that the path to closer integration of the Northeast lies in opening up the region to its external neighbourhood, including Southeast Asia, China and Bangladesh.[35]

Migration

One of the other major issues that the Northeastern region confronts is the unabated in-migration. Migration into Northeast India and Assam, in particular, is of two types—migration from other parts of India and migration from outside India, which is generally termed as *influx* and the immigrants often called *foreigners*, and has taken place in two time periods—colonial and post-colonial. The large inflow of immigrants resulted in huge demographic changes in the last century. Thus, as Myron Weiner pointed out, in a multiethnic developing country like India, migration tends to have destabilising effects and can arise intense conflict.[36]

During the British period, the colonial state encouraged large-scale migration from different parts of British India and Nepal into the Northeastern region. Raising land revenue was the motive behind this state-sponsored migration. Tribal people were brought by the British capitalists mainly from Bihar, Orissa, Chottanagpur, Madhya Pradesh and Andhra Pradesh to labour in tea gardens consequent upon the development of tea gardens in Assam, as the local supply of labour was too small.[37] The Bengali Muslim peasants from East Bengal, who were pressurised by the shortage of cultivable land, were encouraged to migrate to the vast tracts of fertile lands in Assam. The Hindu Bengali migration was in the service sector and Marwari migration in trade, business and industry. These four separate spheres where migration was large in numbers had long-run implications for the process of nationality formation in Assam and had intensified the competition for resources.

The new Muslim League government of Assam formed in 1921 under the leadership of Sayed Mohammad Abdullah gave political impetus to migration in the name *grow more food* by easing land holding regulations for immigrants from Bengal Province.[38] Due to such political impetus and driven by land scarcity, there was large-scale migration of Bengali Muslims from East Bengal during the 1920s.

Migration provided the much needed labour force in exploiting the sparsely populated fertile lands of the Northeast frontier. However, large-scale migration since the 1920s began to undermine the initial benefits that migrants brought along with them. The new migrants created acute economic problems from the mid-1930s as they began to settle down in forest lands, particularly in the tribal areas. Forceful occupation, purchase, mortgage, etc. paved way for land alienation of the indigenous population.[39] Alarmed by the rate of immigration, the Census Superintendent of Assam S.C. Mullan wrote in 1931:

> Probably the most important event in the province during the last twenty five years - an event, moreover, which seems likely to alter permanently the whole future of Assam and to destroy more surely than did the Burmese invaders of 1829, the whole structure of Assamese culture and civilisation— has been the invasion of a vast horde of land hungry Bengali immigrants; mostly Muslims, from the districts of Eastern Bengal sometime before 1911 and the census report of that is the first report which makes mention of the advancing host ... in another thirty years Sibsagar district will be the only part of Assam in which an Assamese will find himself at home.[40]

Thus, migration brought enormous changes in the ethnic composition of the population as well as in the economy of British Assam. The land-abundant valley became land scarce. The labour-shortage economy turned into labour-surplus one. The relatively ethnic homogeneity of the society was replaced by ethnic heterogeneity.[41]

The partition of British India in August 1947 resulted in quick and large-scale mass migration. Although the partition had established a political boundary between East Pakistan and India, immigration into the Northeastern region still remained unabated in the post-independence period. The unchecked immigration and government's indifferent attitude towards illegal influx into Assam resulted in a student movement, which is popularly known as the *Assam Movement*, towards the end of 1970s. The popular Assamese sentiment is reflected in the words of

Myron Weiner: '[T]he Assamese often think of themselves as a "forgotten" and "neglected" state within the Indian union, and as a neglected people in danger of being overwhelmed by migrant peoples and absorbed by neighbouring state.'[42] In 1978, the Chief Election Commissioner S.L. Shakdher observed:

> I would like to refer to the alarming situation in some states, especially in the North-Eastern Region where from disturbing reports are coming regarding large scale incursions of foreign nationals in the electoral rolls. In one case, the population in the 1971 census records an increase as high as 34.98 percent over the 1961 figures and this increase was attributed to the influx of a very large number of persons from the neighbouring countries. The influx has become a regular feature ... the increase that is likely to be recorded in the 1991 census would be more than 100 percent over the 1961 census. In other words, a stage would be reached when the state may have to reckon with the foreign nationals who may, in all probability constitute a sizable percentage, if not the majority of the population in the state.[43]

Many scholars of India believe that leading Bangladesh strategic analysts and intelligentsias introduced the theory of *lebensraum* (living space) in their country during the 1980s to further encourage Muslim infiltration into India. Sanjoy Hazarika firmly believes that this *lebensraum* is India's Northeast and other eastern states, setting up areas of potential political conflict over natural resources, such as water, food, land and competition for jobs in government programmes and private enterprises.[44] Sadeq Khan, a former diplomat of Bangladesh, wrote in Deccan Weekly, *Holiday*, on 18 October 1991:

> All projections, however, clearly indicate that by the next decade, that is to say by the first decade of the 21st century, Bangladesh will face a serious crisis of lebensraum ... if consumer benefit is considered to be better served by borderless competitive trade of labour, there is no reason why regional and international co-operation could not be worked out to plan and execute population movements and settlements to avoid critical demographic pressure in pockets of high concentration.... A natural overflow of population pressure is there very much on the cards and will not be restrainable by barbed wire or border patrol measures. The natural trend of population over-flow from Bangladesh is towards the sparsely populated lands in the South East in the Arakan side and of the North East in the Seven Sisters side of the Indian sub-continent.[45]

Apart from Muslim Bengali immigration into Assam, the partition had resulted in large-scale migration of Bengali Hindus from East Bengal to Tripura. Even in the post-independence period, influx continues into Tripura which alter the demographic composition of the state. The tribals who share two-third of the population are now reduced to a minority, sharing a little more than 30 per cent of the state's population. It is assumed that most of the Hindus from Bangladesh have been forced to move to India primarily due to discriminatory practices against them, and, secondarily, fear of persecution both by the state and the majority religious community of Bangladesh.[46] As a result, '[s]ettlement of an alien population leads to battle over resources, particularly land.'[47]

The Nepalese constitute one of the largest immigrant communities in Northeast India. The flow of Nepalese immigrants into the region started with the British occupation of Assam when the British administration recruited them in the army. After retirement from the imperial services, many of them preferred to stay back in Assam and different parts of the region, and settle permanently. In the subsequent years, fresh batch of Nepalese migrants began to move into the region in large numbers as graziers, cultivators and herdsmen in the hill slopes. They were more or less unnoticed because they preferred to settle in the forest areas near the foothills and occupied large areas of the forest land.[48] Starting with mean business, the Nepalese began to occupy large chunks of grassland and paddy fields in due course of time. This had incited the feeling of uneasiness among the local population and resulted in land alienation in some parts of the region.

In the last few decades, since the liberation of Bangladesh in 1971, there are powerful economic and environmental push factors in Bangladesh which have been combined with politically and economically motivated pull factors in India, leading to an unending influx of Bangladeshis into the border states of the Northeast. Due to the atrocities committed by the majority Muslims, displacement by the Kaptai Dam reservoir in 1964 and failure of payment of compensation by the erstwhile East Pakistan government in Chittagong Hill Tracts, thousands of displaced Chakma refugees sought refuge in India. In 1964, the GoI temporarily resettled about 35,000 Chakmas in Lohit, Changlang and Papumpare districts of the then NEFA (present Arunachal Pradesh). Others were dispersed in Cachar, Mizoram and Tripura. The recipient communities, especially the students' unions, in Arunachal Pradesh and Mizoram have often expressed their resentment and protested over the demographic changes. Apart from the Chakmas, there is an estimated one lakh Chin refugees in Mizoram who fled there to escape abuses from the violent crackdown of pro-democracy movement by the Myanmarese government since 1988. There are also recent instances of the Meiteis of Manipur being concerned about the immigration of Chin refugees in different parts of the hill districts, especially Churachandpur, the Bangladeshi Muslims in Jiribam sub-division bordering Cachar and the migrant labourers in Imphal valley who are mainly from Bihar, Uttar Pradesh and Gujarat. In Meghalaya, the Khasi Students' Union, from time to time, expressed their resentment over the influx of migrants from Bangladesh and Nepal.

Although Nepali and Chakma migration stopped after a certain period of time, migration of Muslims from Bangladesh continues till date. After an environmental and demographic study of Bangladesh, Santanu Roy believes that Assam will continue to look like a greener pasture for Bangladeshis for decades to come. And if decisive steps are not taken to curb the incentives for further migration, a significant flow of illegal immigration is likely to continue in the future.[49] In their studies on migration of population in South Asia, Patil and Trivedi made an observation that migration:

> ...has contributed directly towards high levels of instability in the region. One of its more unavoidable long-term legacies has been the creation of circumstances in which ethnic tension has been the hallmark of the relationship between the original population of the region and the new comers. Throughout the Indian subcontinent, migration has led to substantial levels of ethnic conflict, usually provoking resentment on the part of the locals against the new comers who are seen to be upsetting the existing balance of interests in the region or state.[50]

Such conflict was observed in the Bodoland Autonomous Territorial Districts (BATD) of Assam in the months of July and August 2012 between Muslims and Bodos.

Due to massive immigration of Bangladeshis into India, the bilateral relationship between India and Bangladesh has never been cordial. Attempts of detection and deportation of foreigners from Assam have always been mired by the politics of *vote bank*. As a result of the conspiracy of silence of all political parties the issue, in spite of its serious social, political, economic, security and law and order implications, has not been permitted to come to the national agenda, if at all, it is viewed as a regional problem affecting the Northeast and a few states.[51] The efforts of the Assamese to nationalise infiltration often failed, leading to the feeling of alienation from the rest of the country. As such, Udayon Misra entreats the need for a 'major change in the attitude of the centre', and calls upon the issue of illegal influx to be 'fought at the national level and must not be viewed as a problem faced by the Assamese alone.'[52]

There has been a wide variety of suggestions ranging from issuing temporary work permits to fencing the borders. While border crossing cannot be stopped totally by fencing borders, the 'concept of border management is undergoing rapid transformation with the increasing acceptance of globalisation. Nations are coming closer. Barriers are being lowered. Trade and commerce are bonding people across the international borders. The restrictions along the borders are no longer as stringent as they were in the past.'[53] Issuing of work permits has been widely propagated and practiced in a number of western countries, and even in the West Asian countries. The scheme of issuing work permits will allow migrants to come legally into the region. Work permits are intended to discourage illegal migration, and promote healthy economic cooperation at a sub-regional and local level of both sides.[54] The other step would be to enact a law, prohibiting employment of Bangladeshis other than who has a work permit. It has also been suggested that a massive programme of infrastructural building by focusing on inland waterways, roads and railway lines would generate huge capacity for employment and a vast range of ancillary industries.[55]

The end this stalemate, as pointed out by Sanjib Baruah, is not to look for unilateral solutions, but to build cooperation with the source country.[56] He regarded India as not the only country facing the problem of large-scale illegal immigration from a neighbouring country. But unlike some other countries, India has not realised the value of cooperation with the source country, and has mostly struck to a unilateral course of action. Nevertheless, bilateral cooperation has produced good results in other parts of the world.[57] The Indo-Bangladeshi bilateral relation has hardly been cordial except the few initial years after Bangladeshi liberation.

The proponents of economic cooperation argue that economic integration can be promoted even among states in conflict, and can eventually overcome political antagonism.[58] This is also expected to work in India's Northeast and its neighbouring countries. C. Raja Mohan views: 'Borders in the subcontinent need not necessarily remain political barriers. They need to be transformed into zones of economic cooperation among regions that once were part of the same cultural and political space.'[59]

In the case of Bangladesh, the country is considered to be a stubborn, difficult opponent to deal with at the diplomatic level. This difficulty is admitted by some of the main proponents of sub-regional cooperation, such as Jairam Ramesh, Rajiv Sikri and C.V. Ranganathan. Diplomats have expressed pessimism about improving relationships with Bangladesh although they also believe that the sub-regional framework, rather than bilateral negotiations, will ease the attitude of Bangladesh towards India.[60] The proposal of creating a BCIM free trade and the Framework Agreement on the BIMSTEC Free Trade Area signed on 8 February 2004 at Phuket is expected to develop closer sub-regional cooperation through the development of transnational trade. Acharna Upadhayay believes that the development of infrastructure and sector-specific cooperation, transnational tourism among the neighbouring areas could grow manifold. She observes:

> With gradual integration of capital, output and input markets in the region, thickly populated countries like Bangladesh would have to have formal access to the Indian labour market. Given the difficulties in prohibiting illegal migration and the need for developing a mutually beneficial framework for economic cooperation, it would be in India's long term interest to establish effective institutional mechanisms to regulate and control cross-border population migration.[61]

The coming into power of the Awami League, under the leadership of Sheikh Hasina, on 6 January 2009 in Bangladesh initiated an accommodating and cooperative relationship with India.

As the main focus of the Look East policy is to forge economic ties and build the necessary infrastructure and investment for such cooperation in the Northeast and its neighbouring countries, the policy is also expected to result in building-up economic infrastructure and thereby reducing push factor for immigration. As the central government is blamed for not handling this problem effectively,[62] the Look East policy must include such policies as discussed earlier, which involves sub-regional cooperation.

Insurgency

The growing ethnic consciousness and insecurity among various ethnic groups in Northeast India on the eve of independence led to various demands for autonomy. These movements did not start as a militant one at the outset. When the grievances of the ethnic communities were not redressed, this discontentment manifested in the form of unrest. In the words of Subir Ghosh, 'either frustration or sheer conviction that might is right pave the way for violence.'[63] Ethnic consciousness and insecurity and the menace of migration, among several factors, were the major roots that led to the spurt of enormous insurgent groups in the Northeast during the initial period of independence. In Assam, illegal migration was, in the words of Myron Weiner, 'the prime contributory factor behind the outbreak of insurgency in the State. There is a tendency to view illegal migration into Assam as a regional matter, affecting only the people of Assam. Its more dangerous dimension of greatly undermining our national security is ignored.'[64] On the eve of Indian independence, there were two opposite forces operating in the region—one, a pan-Indian sentiment seeking to integrate and be a part of a single Indian nation-state; two, another regional, religious or ethnicity-based sentiment which sought to secede from the prospective Indian nation-state and seek its national destiny independently.[65]

The Naga insurgency was the first to rise and be followed by similar movements in Manipur and the then Lushai Hills district. From the late 1980s, almost every ethnic group in the region formed their own insurgent group. In the Naga Hills, the unsatisfactory responses of the British and post-independence Indian government to the autonomy demand of the NNC paved the way to Naga insurgency. Though the Indian government tried to accommodate the aspirations of the Nagas in the subsequent years, the Naga insurgency already had diversified ideologies among its leaders and negotiations always produced dissenters, continuing the movement. Paul R. Brass views that the state governments in India often pursued assimilative and discriminatory policies in relation to minority groups within their jurisdiction.[66] In the undivided Assam, the Assamese political elites played vital roles in the integration of various hill areas in the post-independence period, and they wanted to assert dominance in the form of language in the region. Girin Phukon made a succinct observation:

> Strange enough it may seem, while the Assamese elite wanted to protect themselves from Bengali dominance, they at the same time wanted to see the emergence of the whole North Eastern Zone as a single political unit having a common culture. Somehow, they did not see that their idea of Assamese becoming the language of the whole of the North-Eastern region was in some ways similar to the Bengali idea of enforcing the legitimacy of the Bengali as the language of this area.[67]

This language chauvinism was mainly responsible in instilling a sense of insecurity among the Mizos and other tribal communities of Assam. The failure of the Indian government to tackle the outbreak of famine in the Lushai Hills, subsequently, resulted in the outbreak of insurgency in the Lushai Hills district of Assam. Mizo insurgency ended with the signing of Mizo Accord in 1986, which created the present Mizoram from the Lushai Hills district of Assam.

In the princely state of Manipur, the Indian state adopted different tactics of coercion to integrate Manipur with the Indian Union, which had left deep scars in the minds of a section of the Meiteis. On 21 September 1949, the maharaja of Manipur was forced to sign the *Merger Agreement* in Shillong, which merged Manipur as Part-C State of the Union and the democratically elected state assembly was dissolved. Following the dissolution of the Assembly, Hijam Irabot, a member of the dissolved council, went underground. Although Irabot died six years later, in 1955, the seeds of protest that he had shown germinated into a full-blown militancy by the early 1960s.[68] Many *Meitei* revolutionary groups were formed later, seeking a pan-Mongoloid movement against what they termed as *Indian colonial rule*. The Kuki communities in the hills of Manipur also protested against the integration of Kuki areas in Manipur, emphasising the independent existence of the Kukis in the pre-colonial period and even during the British rule till 1919. They demanded a separate state for the Kukis within the Indian Union. In this regard, the Kuki National Assembly had submitted several memoranda to the central government since 1961, and stated that they were accidentally brought under the territory of Manipur by the British and that they have the right for a separate territory.

Insurgency in Tripura is mainly the offshoot of massive migration of Bengali Hindus from the then East Bengal, which was driven by the fear of religious persecution in the wake of the Partition of Bengal in 1947, and later by the Bangladesh Liberation War in 1971. As a result of this large-scale migration, the state witnessed a major demographic change, reducing the tribals into minority. The unabated influx from Bangladesh, increasing marginalisation of tribals in their own land and the dependence of New Delhi almost wholly on the Bengali-dominated bureaucracy alienated them. Subir Bhaumik pointed out that the tribals had good reasons to feel marginalised as foreigners in their own land, as the successive Congress governments showed little concern for tribal sensitivities.[69] Thus, insurgency in Tripura, adds Bhaumik, is the inevitable manifestation of a socio-psychological paranoia of outsiders, resulting from a process of marginalisation that saw the tribal peoples of Tripura deprived of the bulk of their lands and excluded from the state's economic and political decision-making.[70] Since its formation, the Tripura National Volunteers has been engaged in attacking non-tribals. The Bengalis had struck back by forming the United Bengal Liberation Front and engaged in anti-tribal violent activities. This ethnic conflict between the Bengali settlers and the indigenous tribals has only intensified over the years. Due to the constant engagement of the Tripura government to bring insurgent groups to a negotiating table and their efforts to reduce discontentment among the tribals through developmental programmes and other public policies, insurgent activities have now reduced to a minimal level.

Like Tripura, the ultimate cause of insurgency in Assam was migration, in addition to the longstanding disenchantment of the exploitation of Assam's economic resources. Tilottoma Misra gives an illustrative explanation of the exploitation of Assam's resources in his essay titled *Assam: A Colonial Hinterland*.[71] During the transition period, there was a strong sense of secessionism articulated in the minds of a section of Assamese elite as they believe that, '[w]ithin the framework of the Indian federation the "legitimate" Assamese interest would not be protected.'[72] But the secessionist tendency developed among a section of Assamese elite was not sufficient to press for their demands, as the INC in Assam was strong enough to check the centrifugal urges developed among a section of Assamese. As Assam began to occupy a central position in the Northeastern region after independence, most of the Assamese elites engaged themselves in consolidating the region.

In the post-independence period, the Congress-led ruling elites in Assam encouraged the migration of Muslim Bengalis from East Pakistan, as the migrant Muslim Bengalis readily adopted Assamese as their mother tongue and their ethnic identity.[73] They not only became a *safe vote bank* for the Congress, but also strengthened the majority claim of the Assamese in the undivided Assam. Thus, at one stage, the migration of Muslim Bengalis from across the border was seen as part of a larger political strategy which had enabled the ethnic Assamese political elites to stake majority claim in order to justify the realisation of the goal of nation-province.[74] As the number of migrants reached an alarming proportion in the mid-1970s, the growing apprehension on the part of the Assamese elites that they would be swamped by the continuous flow of migrants into Assam, the resentment resulted in the anti-foreigners movement of the late 1970s and early 1980s. This movement revived the dormant Assamese nationalism and secessionist urge among a section of Assamese elites. In spite of sensitising some of the security concerns arising out of fresh illegal migration from Bangladesh, the Assam Movement had failed in realising its goal as far as the deportation of migrant Muslims was concerned.[75] The discontentment resulted in the formation of ULFA. Sanjib Baruah observed:

> Assam Movement transformed the state's political landscape. The prolonged civil disobedience campaign marginalised national political parties and when the movement ended in 1985, the leaders formed the AGP that has twice formed the government in Assam. A radical fringe of the Assam movement became the ULFA and six years of campaigning on the foreigner's issue brought to the surface cracks in Assam social fabric.[76]

However, ULFA later on moved away from the migration issue to secessionism and economic exploitation of Assam resources.

Insurgency in India's Northeast is the manifestation of angst in the minds of the people which is fomented by dissatisfactions of handling the aspirations of various ethnic groups. Such movements mushroomed in the past two decades that 'almost all the letters of the alphabet have been exhausted in the abbreviations of the names of various militant outfits there.' Insurgency flourishes in the region as 'the people have a feeling of separate identity on the basis of ethnicity, culture or history. This is compounded by a sense of neglect, exploitation and discrimination, and immensely aggravated by bad governance, corruption and economic backwardness.'[77]

The government's policy towards recurring ethnic and minority problems in Northeast India since independence has been repressive, treating it as purely *law and order* situation. The state apparatus mainly followed a 'repressive policy towards ethnic conflicts',[78] by adopting an overwhelming military response, justifying such policies as 'the necessary cost of fighting ethnic insurgencies resulting in serious deterioration of law and order.'[79] Due to the significant strategic location of the region,

> any aberrations in normal political behaviour was taken as a national security threat. In many occasion central and state governments were insensitive towards the genuine development priorities and democratic representation of the ethnic minorities in Northeast which has ultimately resulted in alienation and cultural exclusion.[80]

Though the *law and order* approach is necessary and effective in the short run, it cannot be an answer to the region's ethnic and minority conflicts. It has been realised that winning the hearts and minds of the people is necessary for which genuine socio-economic changes in the living conditions of the people have to be effected to retrogress insurgency.[81] It has also been viewed that as long as 'insurgency remains a part of the region's political landscape and India's relations with some of its neighbours remain adversarial or rancorous, counter-insurgency operations and security-driven restrictions are likely to continue.'[82] As a result, the government initiated a few political negotiations which have been largely unproductive, supported by hefty financial packages hijacked by a corrupt and/or inefficient administration.[83]

There has been a change in the nature of most of the insurgent groups of the region since the mid-1990s. They now assume a more urban character and are 'fully organised to harvest easy money (through abduction, extortion, robbery, trafficking, etc.), threatening both the government and the population.' As 'most of the insurgents groups have given up their lofty ideals and their fight for a noble "identity" cause and adopted a more pragmatic and unscrupulous strategy to gain power and control over the parallel economy', Renaud Egreteau opines that 'insurgency in the Northeast needs to be addressed by other means.'[84]

Sanjib Baruah views that reconciling the demands of a globalising economy that relies on greater opening with security concerns is a policy dilemma that many governments, including India, face today.

'If Northeast India is to live up to the promise of becoming India's gateway to Southeast Asia we must imagine a world where border-crossings are not thought of primarily as sites for security checks. In that sense security is tied to better border management, better governance inside the country as well as in the countries of the transnational neighbourhood, deepening relations with our neighbours and developing multilateral institutions of governance.[85]

In response to the shift in Chinese policy of opening its southwestern border for trade and investment to the neighbouring Southeast Asian countries, India too has opened up to its eastern neighbours in what it calls the *Look East* policy. Sushil Khanna views that:

Indian policy makers have used this 'opening-up' to strengthen ties with the military regimes in Bangladesh and Myanmar and launch counter insurgency movements against the groups from North Eastern India. More than the development of backward northeastern states and ending their isolation through re-establishing their historical cultural and economic ties, the military and security establishment has high-jacked the policy to fight insurgents from the region.[86]

Since their inception, most of the insurgent groups were trained and operated from foreign soils bordering the Northeast. The external linkage and support of most of the insurgent groups is one of the main factors responsible for instability in the region. The insurgent outfits pay hefty amounts of money to the host government for providing safe haven. Though the Indian government sought cooperation from the neighbouring countries for dismantling Northeast rebels camps, poor neighbours, especially, Myanmar and Bangladesh, are lured by the hefty amounts of money offered to them, and India's policy often failed. As such, the Indian government often complained that it has not been able to intervene beyond its borders to solve transborder insurgency and trafficking. What can be seen in the last decades is that India has not even managed to solve the issue internally. Since the region suffers from 'negligence by the political elite in addition to lack of trust, criminalisation and increasing dispari-ties', there is every chance that it will 'remain unstable unless New Delhi makes an all out effort to solve the problem internally. If the "external factor" has a considerable weight, the internal dynamics (degeneration of the insurgency coupled with the inefficiency of the Central government) might doom the Northeast.'[87] Rather than blaming neighbouring countries for backing and sheltering Indian rebel groups, India must find ways to cooperate with them.

Sanjib Baruah conceives that 'giving substance to the Northeast Indian thrust of our Look East policy would require settling the region's numerous conflicts through a comprehensive approach that goes beyond the unstable peace that policies shaped by today's counter-insurgency mindset can bring about.'[88] This comprehensive approach of the Look East policy must seek long-term vision of developing the Northeastern region as well as its neighbours, especially Myanmar and Bangladesh, through regional cooperation. Such joint efforts of economic development in the sub-region must involve cooperation in trade and investment, infrastructural development, communication and transport. Without joint efforts to achieve economic development any efforts by India to solve transborder insurgency will not produce any result. Simultaneously, the government should start sincere political dialogue with the insurgent groups. Otherwise, the lofty ideals of the Look East policy will only be a pipe dream.

Drug Trafficking

Drug trafficking is another rampant illicit activity prevailing in the Northeastern region, often incited by insurgency. The problem of drugs is as old as history itself. In Northeast India, drugs were cultivated traditionally for local consumption. The British colonial government did not prohibit such production and consumption although with some control and restriction, and hence the problem during those days was limited to addiction. The reforms introduced as a part of the colonial drug policy in 1893 resulted in an 'appreciable increase of revenue', and ganja formed the principal source of hemp drugs revenue.[89]

The problem of drug use and trafficking, and the arms–drug nexus in the region assumed significant magnitude and came to the limelight only after independence, especially in the past three decades. At present, ganja and poppy are cultivated mainly for commercial purposes in the most inaccessible parts of the region, such as the Indo-Myanmar border. In recent years the region witnessed persistent drug trafficking and drug abuse. The prevalence of drug trafficking in the region is mainly attributed to porous borders, proximity to the Golden Triangle, constant ethnic conflict, unemployment, poverty and transit to international market.[90] Compounded with this is the use of this business by insurgent groups to finance themselves. Recent studies reveal that most of the armed violence and militancy in many parts of the world is often confined to areas contiguous to international borders;[91] most of the drug trafficking takes place along the border areas. As the Indo-Myanmar border area is inhabited by the same ethnic groups on both sides of the border, it makes smuggling of drugs and arms easy. Drug trafficking and production in Northeast India feature the following dimensions:

1. The illicit cultivation of opium and cannabis;
2. The smuggling of heroin and amphetamines from Myanmar in moderate quantities;
3. The trafficking of pharmaceuticals such as dextropropoxyphene and codeine-containing cough syrups from other parts of the country; and
4. The trafficking of ephedrine and pseudo-ephedrine precursors for the manufacture of amphetamines from India to Myanmar.[92]

The Northeastern region is located near the world's second largest drug producing area known as the *Golden Triangle*, a border area comprising Laos, Myanmar and Thailand. Of late, the *Golden Triangle* came to be known as the *Golden Pentagon* with the expansion of this drug producing area to Vietnam–Cambodia and Nagaland–Manipur borders. Myanmar is now one of the world's major heroin producers, and heroin is one of the most valuable export commodities of the country. Despite the claims made by the military junta that they are actively combating drug production and distribution, Myanmar's Shan state has been the centre of opium production and conversion. The official economy of Myanmar offers few alternatives to the heroin trade.[93] India's Northeast has been affected by this flourishing global drug trafficking, and the nexus between insurgency and drug trafficking.

Since their formation, major insurgent outfits in the region depended on China and Pakistan for their training and arms supply. With the liberation of Bangladesh (East Pakistan) in 1971, Pakistan was too distant for any direct support; the rapprochement of Sino-India relations during the Rajiv Gandhi regime gradually stopped Chinese backing these rebel groups since the mid-1980s. The rebel groups of Northeast India turned to the black markets of Southeast Asia for arms supply. It is believed that unless these insurgent groups resorted to smuggling and drug trafficking, they could not have mobilised resources for purchase of weapons and maintenance of their cadres.[94] Although some Manipur insurgent outfits, such as the United National Liberation Front and Peoples' Liberation Army, continue to resist drug trafficking and addiction, other groups, such as the National Socialist Council of Nagaland (NSCN), have taken to drug trade. Ajay Sahni believes that drug trafficking from Myanmar is a major source of income for the NSCN(IM), and both the factions of NSCN—NSCN(IM) and NSCN(K)—run parallel structures of *taxation* (extortion) throughout the regions that they dominate.[95] The Ministry of Home Affairs reported that:

> ... [s]o far as the Northeast states of India are concerned there are clear intelligence reports to indicate that the Naga underground organisations ... are involved in trafficking of drugs and precious stones since 1981. The insurgent group [real name withheld] of Manipur is also involved in the trafficking of drugs.[96]

However, it is clear that although insurgent groups do not engage in narco-production or narco-trafficking, it has nevertheless been found that all of them have regularly taxed and extorted money from the traffickers, while providing protection to the latter for conducting trafficking in drugs.[97] The bitter struggle to control drug trafficking and smuggling through Moreh, the border town of Manipur, resulted in fierce rivalry between the Kuki National Army (KNA) and NSCN(IM) in 1992, which was one of the reasons responsible for inciting ethnic conflict between the Kukis and Nagas, where about a thousand innocent lives from both the communities were lost. With regard to the involvement of insurgent groups in drug trafficking, Barry Rubin observes:

> Firstly, the trans-national narco-networks, now backed by armed insurgents, make anti-narco-production or narco-trafficking drive immensely difficult. And taking into consideration the geographical and topographical conditions in which the insurgents and the traffickers operate, there is now all the more reason to believe that the nationally organised military or coercive solutions may not be the correct way of overcoming the menace of narco-terrorism. Secondly, weapons, particularly small arms in the hands of both the insurgents and traffickers, become more rampant, to the point

of threatening the law and order situation in the vicinity. A large portion of the money received from taxing and extorting the narco-traffickers goes towards purchase of small, at times sophisticated, arms for the insurgents.[98]

Subir Bhaumik listed the threefold threat posed by the increased drug trafficking to the sensitive Northeastern region:

1. Trafficking through the northeast has led to a rise in local consumption. Many addicts use intravenous injections to push drugs and become HIV positive. The number of HIV positive cases in the Northeast has risen to around 20,000 in the last two decades.
2. Several military and paramilitary officials have been arrested for smuggling heroin or lesser drugs in Northeast India. The drug cartel has sucked in several politicians, bureaucrats and even security force officials to carry on their illicit trade. Unless checked firmly, this trend is dangerous for the morale of Indian security forces.
3. Ethnic separatists in India's Northeast are taking to protection of drug mafias as a quick way to raise funds. The Burmese druglords are also encouraging tribal farmers to plant poppy. Unless these new plantations are promptly destroyed and gainful agricultural alternatives provided to the farmers, the India-Burma border will soon be dotted with poppy fields feeding the processing plants in western Burma. A rebel-drug lord-officialdom nexus is emerging in India's Northeast in a repeat of the Colombian scenario.[99]

In the recent years, the *Golden Triangle* is said to increase eight-times in the production of amphetamines from an estimated 100 million tablets in 1993 to 800 million tablets in 2002. Many of the drugs produced there are in great demand in various metropolitan cities of India and London. Recent huge seizures of drugs in the Northeastern region indicate that India has more to worry about Myanmar than just insurgency. Besides the Indo-Myanmar border, a recent study by Central Intelligence Agency confirmed the involvement of 20–25 per cent of the people residing in border areas in the Tripura–Bangladesh border in illicit human trafficking and smuggling. Such illegal activities may surely include small arms and narcotics too.[100] The problem of drugs is a transnational phenomenon associated with high level of violence at every stage of the product which poses serious problems of law and order.

During the NDA government, military-to-military relations between India and Myanmar improved spectacularly. The Myanmarese military chief, General Maung Aye visited India twice, once to meet the regional commanders in Shillong and then to meet his counterpart in New Delhi. The former Indian Army chief, General V.P. Malik visited Rangoon twice in January and July 2000. During Maung Aye's second visit to Delhi, India and Myanmar signed an agreement for increased cooperation to tackle cross-border terrorism and drug trafficking.

If the problem of drugs, HIV/AIDS and trafficking in the region is not curtailed first, the development benefits expected in the Northeastern states from India's Look East policy could be adversely affected. Gopen Moses suggested that this problem has to be fought on a war footing if the development trend is not to be endangered.[101] Since the menace of drug trafficking has a linkage with insurgency and transborder in nature, it requires a comprehensive action plan to tackle these issues. The transborder nature of this problem demands regional cooperation for an enduring solution. Trafficking is run by the transborder communities, which is often difficult to track or handle. While the strategy today should aim at a cooperative solution on the one hand involving other state governments, it must also involve sharing of information not only between governments but also regional and sub-regional organisations, academics, researchers and civil society.[102]

Sovereignty Bargains

The protracted conflicts and unrests in the Northeastern region have been a serious setback in the process of integration with the national mainstream. As such it has been felt that the region is moving towards a paradoxical state of *external integration and internal disintegration* during the latter part of the twentieth century. Earlier in this chapter, the issue has been examined in the light of rapid global changes in the new millennium, and it has been observed that the liberalisation and opening up of the Indian economy have, to a certain extent, integrated the ethnic groups in the Northeast with the rest of India. Rather than the perceived fear of ethnic alienation of the communities of the Northeast with the rest of Indian states on the question of opening the cul-de-sac region and the possible *internal disintegration*, it has also been established that the global forces rather reduce ethnic alienation. The problems of ethnicity, migration, insurgency and drug trafficking are all transnational in nature.

On the economy of the Northeast, if one draws from the pre-colonial and colonial experiences, the region had been thriving on trade not only within the region but also with different areas bordering the region. This demands, especially in the age of globalisation, the restoration of such traditional economic systems through modern trading arrangements, and also preparing the region for such transborder trade and commerce. On the question of migration into the region the system of issuing work permits appears to be the only panacea, or near to it, to this persisting problem. These two situations raise the extent in which India is willing to open this largely insular region. Together with other problems of the region, such as insurgency, ethnification, arms and drug trafficking, its solution largely lies with the extent to which India engages itself with countries neighbouring the Northeast.

On the problems of cross-border insurgency and drug trafficking, apart from the issue of migration along the Indo-Bangladesh and Indo-Myanmar borders, Isidro Morales highlighted the need for a 'comprehensive security regime' between the three countries and cautions that unless such security regime is brought about 'the Bangladeshi–Myanmarese borderline will remain fragile and unsafe.'[103] Therefore, the economic, social, political and strategic concerns in the Northeast call for a comprehensive regional cooperation between India and countries neighbouring its Northeastern region. This necessitates an examination of how much India is willing to engage in regional cooperation.

In the Westphalian state system, political authority is exercised over a defined territory with no role for external actors within the borders of the state. The increasing trend towards the creation of regional political and economic unions frequently violates the Westphalian model and is generally seen as posing an enduring challenge to state's sovereignty. For instance, the EU's concept of shared sovereignty is considered to be contrary to the historical views of Westphalian sovereignty, as it provides for external agents to interfere in nations' internal affairs. Thus, there are breaches of the Westphalian system through conventions, contract, coercion, or imposition, and have been an emerging feature of the international milieu.

The driving force behind regional integration is the postulation that the benefit of integration is worth the cost in terms of diminished national autonomy and power. This argument was expressed by British Prime Minister James Callaghan on the debate whether the United Kingdom should become a member of the European Monetary System (EMS) in the House of Commons on 10 July 1978. Mr Spearing questioned whether the scheme of EMS would be done so at the expense of the Britain's autonomy in internal finances, despite the fact that it would promote stability. James Callaghan replied:

> ... [W]hen we joined NATO, we removed some powers from ourselves but it was the general view of the House, continued for a quarter of a century, that in removing these powers we increased our security. That is surely the test that one needs to apply to this sort of proposal. If it meant lessening powers in order to increase prosperity, the House would have to take a decision whether it wished to remain poor and independent or whether it was willing to sacrifice some powers and be more prosperous.[104]

Increasing prosperity is the only benefit of joining regional unions; it can also increase the bargaining power and influence of a member over others and, thereby, pursue certain goals more directly. This brings in the relevance of Karen Litfin's study on how and why states engage in what she refers to as *sovereignty bargains*—a voluntary agreement to accept some limitations on national autonomy in exchange for certain benefits. 'It is more accurate to say that states engage in sovereignty bargains ... than cede some monolithic principle of sovereignty.'[105] Litfin's key argument calls for a need to disaggregate sovereignty into its constitutive elements of autonomy, control and legitimacy, each of which operates upon the tangible dimensions of territory and population. Autonomy refers to independence in policy making and action; control is the ability to produce an effect; and legitimacy refers to the recognised right to make rules. In a sovereignty bargain, control may be enhanced by sacrificing autonomy, or increased control may undercut a state's legitimacy.[106]

In sum, Litfin's argument is that sovereignty has been reconfigured over time and that this process, induced by pressure from both below and above the state, can only be grasped by disaggregating the key elements that constitute the term. While sovereignty bargains to reconfigure sovereignty, they do not necessarily diminish it; reduced autonomy, for example, may be the price to pay for enhanced control or legitimacy. Nation-states are very cautious about being involved in any *sovereignty bargain*. Walter Mattli goes further by extending Litfin's *sovereignty bargain* in regional integration by carefully specifying the background conditions of sovereignty bargains, 'the factors that affect states' assessment of the costs and benefits of membership.'

In the context of India's policy towards countries neighbouring its Northeastern region, the first visible signs of sovereignty bargains can be seen on its policy towards Myanmar. Despite an overwhelming support for democracy, India took a u-turn in its policy by the turn of the twenty-first century and chose to forge economic cooperation with Myanmar. This can be considered as the first trade-off in India's sovereignty bargains with Myanmar. The Indo-Myanmar Trade Agreement signed on 31 January 1994 for the establishment of trade was based on equality and mutual benefit. The agreement specified that trade should be conducted through the designated custom posts, namely, (a) Moreh in Manipur and Tamu in Myanmar, (b) Champhai in Mizoram and Rih in Myanmar and (c) other places that may be notified by mutual agreement between the two countries. This was followed by several bilateral and multilateral projects, aimed to facilitate trade and enhance connectivity between the Northeast and Southeast Asia. In this regard India built the 165-kilometre-long Indo-Myanmar Friendship Road connecting Tamu and Kalaymyo-Kalewa, and there are other important ongoing and potential infrastructure projects such as India–Myanmar–Thailand Trilateral Highway, Trans-Asian Highway, India–Myanmar rail linkages, Kaladan Multimodal project and Tamanthi Hydroelectricity project. The optical fibre network between Northeast India and Southeast Asia has been operationalised in 2009. Apart from developing road links, efforts are underway to have a rail link from Jiribam in Manipur to Hanoi in Vietnam passing through Myanmar. Besides Myanmar, the border trade between India and China at Nathula in Sikkim was reopened after a gap of 44 years on 6 July 2006. Several border *haats* (rural markets) have been opened in the Meghalaya–Bangladesh sector of India–Bangladesh border, and plans are also in the pipeline to set up border *haats* in the Tripura and Mizoram sectors.

Besides trade agreements and infrastructure development projects, the location and decades of armed rebellions in the Northeast need a grand strategic scheme to resolve the conundrums of unabated transborder migration, and narco-insurgency. In North America, there are proposals that United States, Canada and Mexico engage in a shared governance of *continental perimeter*. This continental perimeter encompasses the defence of a continental space, including its territory, the borderlines, and airborne, sea-borne and cyber-borne mobility and flows.[107] In the line of the proposed North American *continental perimeter*, and what Isidro Morales calls *comprehensive security regime*, a strategic, economic and other cooperations can be initiated with India's Northeast and its neighbouring countries. Within that regional union, issues, such as work permits, can be negotiated, the defence of regional space including territory, borderlines, the flow of illegal arms and drugs.

Border fencing and cordoning the region has only increased dissatisfaction with Delhi and alienate them more than ever before. The increasing presence of security forces in the region for defending external aggression and controlling armed rebellions by giving them special powers through the promulgation of Armed Forces (Special Powers) Act, 1958 have over the years resulted in innumerable human rights abuses which cause more damage than controlling the people. New Delhi needs to admit its failures in dealing with the problems associated with the northeast. Instead of the competitive and antagonistic approach with neighbours cooperative endeavours can not only resolve the age old problems, but also usher in an era of peace and development. The success of India's Look East policy vis-à-vis addressing the problems of the northeastern region depends on the extent of *sovereignty bargains* that India is willing to engage.

Notes

1. Government of India, 'Year End Review 2004', *Ministry of External Affairs*.
2. Swarna Rajagopalan, *Peace Accords in Northeast India: Journey over Milestones*, p. 9.
3. Anthony Giddens and Simon Griffiths, *Sociology*, p. 497.
4. N.H. Owen, 'Land, Politics and Ethnicity in a Carib Indian Community', p. 385.
5. Nathan M. Shamuyarisa, 'Political Development and Political Planning in New African States', p. 244.
6. Clive J. Christie, *A Modern History of Southeast Asia: Decolonialization, Nationalism and Separatism*, p. 1.

7. Alexander Mackenzie, pp. 89–90. First published in 1984 as 'History of the Government with the Hill Tribes of the North-East Frontier of Bengal.'

8. Sanjib Baruah, *India Against Itself: Assam and the Politics of Nationality*, p. 31.

9. B.B. Kumar, 'North-East India: Need for a Fresh Look', p. 17.

10. Girin Phukon, *Politics of Regionalism in Northeast India*, p. 1.

11. E. Hunter and Whitten Phillip. *Encyclopedia of Anthropology*.

12. Ashok Kumar Ray, *Revisiting North East India in the Era of Globalisation*, p. 40.

13. Tiplut Nongbri, 'Ethnicity and Political Activism in North East: Tribal Identity and State Policy', p. 48.

14. Paul R. Brass, *Language, Religion and Politics in North India*.

15. Nabendu Pal, 'India's North-Eastern Region: Towards a more humane approach'.

16. P.S. Datta, 'Roots of Insurgency'.

17. A.K. Ranjit Singh, 'Emergent Ethnic Processes in Manipur: A Reappraisal', p. 234.

18. Vijendra Singh Jafa, 'Administrative Policies and Ethnic Disintegration: Engineering Conflicts in India's North East'.

19. Walker Connon, 'Nation-Building or Nation-destroying', p. 332.

20. D. Saikia and D.N. Majumdar, 'Some Characteristics of Ethno-Cultural Identity of North-East India', p. 28.

21. Sunanda K. Datta Ray, 'Challenge of Diversity: Fringe Peoples Out in Cold'.

22. Stetson Eric Kurlander, 'Multicultural and Assimilationist Models of Ethnopolitical Integration in the Context of the German *Nordmark*, 1890–1933', p. 49.

23. Sanjib Baruah, *Between South and Southeast Asia: Northeast India and the Look East Policy*, p. 33.

24. *Deccan Herald*, 24 June 2008.

25. Sangeeta Rao, 'Otherwise? The Selling of Global Cultural Difference'.

26. Kenichi Ohmae, *The Borderless World: Power and Strategy in the Interlinked Economy*, 1990.

27. Kenichi Ohmae, 'The Rise of the Region State', pp. 78–87.

28. B.G. Verghese, 'Unfinished Business in Northeast', p. 30.

29. Remarks by the President on Economic Mobility, press released on 4 December 2013.

30. Duncan McDuie-Ra, 'Beyond the "Exclusionary City": North-east Migrants in Neo-liberal Delhi', p. 1625.

31. Quoted in Bibhu Prasad Routray, 'Analyzing an insurgency: On the trail of Nagalim'.

32. Nabendu Pal, 'India's North-Eastern Region: Towards a More Humane Approach'.

33. Charles Taylor, 'The Politics of Recognition', p. 105.

34. Sanjib Baruah, 'Between South and Southeast Asia: Northeast India and the Look East Policy', p. 11.

35. B.G. Verghese, 'Unfinished Business in Northeast', p. 30.

36. Myron Weiner, *Sons of the Soil: Migration and Ethnic Conflict in India*, p. 3.
37. Edward A. Gait, *A History of Assam*, p. 413.
38. H.K. Barpujari, *North-East India: Problems, Policies and Prospects*, pp. 37–38.
39. Sreeradha Datta, 'Northeast Turmoil: Vital Determinants', http://www.idsa-india.org/an-mar00-8.ht (downloaded on 29.12.2014).
40. *Census of India* (Assam), pp. 49–50.
41. Gurudas Das, 'Migration, Ethnicity and Competition for State Resources: An Explanation of the Social Tension in the North-East India', p. 309.
42. Myron Weiner, *Sons of the Soil: Migration and Ethnic Conflict in India*, p. 83.
43. Quoted in B.G. Verghese, B. Ahmed, G. Deshpande, N. Desai and R. Upadhyaya, 'Situation in Assam'.
44. Sanjoy Hazarika, *Strangers of the Mist: The Tales of War and Peace from India's Northeast*, p. 29.
45. Quoted in the 'Report on Illegal Migration into Assam', submitted to the president of India by the governor of Assam in November 1998.
46. V.T. Patil and P.R. Trivedi, *Migration, Refugees and Security in the 21st Century*, p. 399.
47. Sanjoy Hazarika, 'Insurgency in Northeast India', p. 118.
48. Jayanta Kumar Gogoi, 'The Migration Problem in Assam: An Analysis', p. 361.
49. Santanu Roy, 'Why do they come? Economic incentives for Immigration to Assam', pp. 390–91.
50. V.T. Patil and P.R. Trivedi, *Migration, Refugees and Security in the 21st Century*, p. 81.
51. Madhav Godbole, 'Illegal Migration from Bangladesh', January–March 2006.
52. Udayon Misra, *The Periphery Strikes Back: Challenges to the Nation-State in Assam and Nagaland*, pp. 174–75.
53. Prakash Singh, 'India's Border Management Challenges'.
54. Paula Banerjee et al., 'Indo-Bangladesh Cross-Border Migration and Trade', p. 2550.
55. Archana Upadhyay, 'Assam: The Infiltrators Issue'.
56. Sanjib Baruah, 'The Shadow of the Foreigner'.
57. Sanjib Baruah, 'Unfriendly Neighbourhood'.
58. Mayumi Murayama, 'Borders, Migration and Sub-Regional Cooperation in Eastern South Asia', p. 1251.
59. C. Raja Mohan, *Crossing the Rubicon: The Shaping of India's New Foreign Policy*, p. 269.
60. Mayumi Murayama, 'Borders, Migration and Sub-Regional Cooperation in Eastern South Asia', p. 12.
61. Archana Upadhyay, 'Assam: The Infiltrators Issue'.
62. B.B. Kumar, 'North-East India: Need for a Fresh Look', p. 21.
63. Subir Ghosh, *Frontier Travails-Northeast: The Politics of Mess*, p. 141.
64. Myron Weiner, *Sons of the Soil: Migration and Ethnic Conflict in India*.
65. Sajal Nag, *Nationalism, Separatism, Secessionism*, pp. 160–220.
66. Paul R. Brass, *Language, Religion and Politics in North India*.

67. Girin Phukon, *Politics of Regionalism in Northeast India*, pp. 26–27.
68. Binalakshmi Nepram, 'The Origins of Manipuri Insurrection', p. 36.
69. Subir Bhaumik, 'Disaster in Tripura'.
70. Subir Bhaumik, *Insurgent Crossfire: North-East India*, p. 77.
71. Tilotoma Misra, 'Assam: A Colonial Hinterland'.
72. Girin Phukon, *Politics of Regionalisn in Northeast India*, pp. 70–71.
73. Udayon Misra, 'Immigration and Identity Transformation in Assam', pp. 1264–71.
74. Gurudas Das, 'Probable Options: Commenting the Faultlines in Assam'.
75. Ibid.
76. Sanjib Baruah, 'The Shadow of Foreigner'.
77. S.K. Sinha, 'Violence and Hope in India's Northeast', 2002.
78. Sudha Menon, 'Northeast India and Globalization: The Way Ahead', http://dlc.dlib.indiana.edu/archive/00002194/01/Northeast_the_way_ahead.pdf (downloaded on 22.12.2014).
79. Samir Kumar Das, 'State against Minorities: State-Building Challenges in Contemporary North Eastern India', p. 50.
80. Sudha Menon, 'Northeast India and Globalization: The Way Ahead'.
81. K.S. Brar, 'India's Turbulent North East: Over Five Decade of Isolation, Neglect and Alienation', p. 203.
82. Sanjib Baruah, 'The Problem'.
83. Renaud Egreteau, 'Instability at the Gate: India's Troubled Northeast and Its External Connections', p. 6.
84. Ibid.
85. Sanjib Baruah, 'The Problem'.
86. Sushil Khanna, 'Look East, Look South: Backward Border Regions in India and China', www.burmalibrary.org/docs4/LookEast-LookSouth-08REVISED.pdf.
87. Renaud Egreteau, 'Instability at the Gate: India's Troubled Northeast and Its External Connections'.
88. Sanjib Baruah, 'The Problem', *Seminar*.
89. Soma Ghosal, *The Politics of Drugs and India's Northeast*, p. 15.
90. Nihar Ranjan Nayak, 'Narco-trafficking: Non-military Threat in India's Eastern Border'.
91. Jasjit Singh, ed., *Light Weapons and International Security*, pp. 50–62.
92. Gopen Moses, 'Drug Use, HIV/AIDS and Human Trafficking in the North-East', July–September 2007.
93. Mary H. Cooper, *The Business of Drugs*, 1990.
94. Mahendra P. Lama, 'India's North-East States: Narcotics, Small Arms and Misgovernance', p. 253.
95. Ajay Sahni, 'Survey of Conflicts and Resolution in India's Northeast'.
96. Cited in Binalakshmi Nepram Mentschel, 'Armed Conflict, Small Arms Proliferation and Women's Responses to Armed Violence in India's Northeast', p. 15.

97. Aparajita Biswas, 'Small Arms and Drug Trafficking in the Indian Ocean Region'.
98. Barry Rubin, ed., *Terrorism and Politics*.
99. Subir Bhaumik, 'Guns, Drugs and Rebels'.
100. Binalakshmi Nepram, *South Asia's Fractured Frontier: Armed Conflict, Narcotics and Small Arms Proliferation in India's North East*, p. 158.
101. Gopen Moses, 'Drug Use, HIV/AIDS and Human Trafficking in the North-East'.
102. Sarah Meek, ed., *Controlling Small Arms Proliferation and Reversing Cultures of Violence in Africa and the Indian Ocean*, p. 39.
103. Isidro Morales, 'Post-NAFTA North America: Three Scenarios for the Near Future', p. 10.
104. Available online at http://www.margaretthatcher.org/document/103727 (downloaded on 30.07.2013).
105. Karen T. Litfin, 'Sovereignty in World Ecopolitics', p. 169.
106. Walter Mattli, 'Sovereignty bargains in regional integration', p. 150.
107. Isidro Morales, 'Post-NAFTA North America: Three Scenarios for the Near Future'.

8

Conclusion

Regional integration/cooperation has been a strategy for economic development through international trade in the post-war period and with renewed vigour since the late 1980s. With huge range of potential benefits, regional integration is regarded as a panacea for solving multiple predicaments. The formation of regional integration has also been greatly successful in bringing historically hostile countries together. In some countries, it has been a tool to cement peace on the borders and create a network of solidarity to preserve young democracies.

The Indian predicament of the early 1990s, the slow pace of economic integration within South Asia, the focus on economic content of international relations, emergence of regional economic groupings, forces of globalisation coupled with the fears of being marginalised in the post-Cold War international system made India liberalise its economy and tread on the path of regionalism. The Look East policy has, thus, become India's effort to regionally integrate its economy with the fast growing East and Southeast Asian economies. The policy marked a strategic shift in India's perspective of the world, and a late recognition of the strategic and economic importance of East and Southeast Asia to India's national interests. Thus, the policy aims for greater economic alignment and an enhanced political role in the dynamic Asia-Pacific region in general and Southeast Asia in particular. The current phase of the Look East policy marks the beginning of a vibrant relationship on the economic, political and strategic fronts. The economic potentials of this policy emphasises a link with the economic interests of the Northeastern region as a whole.

The Northeastern region is beset with persisting assertions of ethnic nationalism against the Indian state since independence. In the context of the history of integration in Northeast India, it is found that the integration with the Indian Union politically remained a serious issue of concern for the people. The mode of integration of the Northeastern states has been sought through negotiations, promises, baits and force. These attempts at assimilation of the region and its people with the Indian mainstream have caused resentment among different ethnic communities. Even before the national government could stabilise itself, the fragility of the integration was visible. Secessionist demands and withdrawal declarations were made in several parts of the region.

The specific problems in integrating the princely states of Manipur and Tripura into India and the failure of the government of India to adequately address the political aspirations of other ethnic groups in the Northeastern region resulted in secessionist movements. The late realisation that the integrationist policy adopted was flawed led the government to concede the autonomy demands of ethnic groups, which has led to the creation of separate states. However, the formation of new states had a cascading effect, leading to new demands from other smaller ethnic groups vying for different levels of autonomy.

Since the eve of India's independence, smaller ethnic groups in the hills of Northeast India had too been asserting their desire for separated administrative units. The Kukis were fully aware of the various aspects of the vexing problems of the hills and the valleys, and therefore pledged to be under Manipur if only conditions are satisfactory. After independence, the KNA demanded a separate state for the Kukis within India. In this regard, the KNA submitted several memoranda to the central government in the early 1960s. The dormant political demands were revived as an insurgent movement in the late 1980s.

After long years of association with the Indian culture and political system, tribal people in Northeast India developed some forms of Indianness. The onslaught of globalisation, rapid changes in technology and communications created a turbulent world with crucial problems whose solutions are international. With the growing emphasis on regional integration and interdependence among countries development, the people of Northeast India and the underground outfits began to develop a feeling that they are in a better position in being part of India, provided if their unique history and culture is recognised.

The Northeastern region had been exposed to international trade during the pre-colonial and colonial period. It had negligible impact on the local economy as tea plantation was developed into enclave production without having any linkage with the hinterland. In the post-independence period, the exploitative nature of the British colonial rule continued in the region with just a change in the stakeholders from British to Indian capitalists.

The main component of the Look East policy is to bring development in the Northeastern region through the expansion of regional trade linkage with the economies of its eastern neighbours. The proposed development of the Northeastern region is to be brought in through increased trade and investment, and engaging the people of the region in productive and profitable activities to end their alienation.

While tracing the evolution of India's Look East policy, it has been found that the policy emerged out of the changed international system in the early 1990s, and economic stagnation and political turmoil within the country. The policy is primarily the product of various compulsions in the post-Cold War era. The changed focus on the economic content of international relations, the emergence of regional economic groupings, rise in the forces of globalisation and slow process of economic integration within South Asia and China's growing assertiveness in the Asia–Pacific region has compelled India to rethink the basic parameters of its foreign policy. The growing trends towards regionalism and India's apprehension of being marginalised and isolated in the post-Cold War international system are the main reasons for paying more attention to the rapidly growing economies of Southeast Asia.

India's Northeast has more geographical proximity and contact with other countries than the Indian mainland. It is connected to mainland India by a mere 21-kilometre-long landmass called the Siliguri Corridor, which is less than 2 per cent of the 5,000 kilometre combined perimeter formed by the seven Northeastern states, while the remaining borders China, Myanmar, Bhutan, Bangladesh and Nepal. The partition of India in 1947 caused this extreme geo-political isolation of the Northeast, making it the most regulated, a sensitive border region and the most exposed territory. In addition, the partition also caused the severance of the inland water, road and railway communications through erstwhile East Pakistan and access to the Chittagong port was lost. The Chinese takeover of Tibet and the virtual closure of the border with Burma added to the isolation of the region.

The coming of globalisation, regional integration and India's outward looking economy since the early 1990s brought forth the conception that economic integration with the rest of the world would foster political integration of Northeast with the mainland. Thus, the second phase of the Look East policy was launched to end economic isolation of the

Northeastern region. Within this policy framework, there is an added prospect for reviving the ancient trade routes in Northeast India, including the *Southern Ancient Silk Road*, and to ably explore the rich resources through regional cooperation with its eastern neighbours. The main focus of the Look East policy is to bring about economic development in the region through regional cooperation. In order to achieve such cooperation in the Northeastern region, the policy has focused on solving the problems that have plagued the region.

The Look East policy rightly aims for the creation of an enabling environment so as to end the landlocked situation and isolation of the Northeastern region by opening up the borders and reintegrating the region's economy through improved trade and connectivity between Northeast India and Southeast Asian countries. However, when we consider the existing ground realities, the growth of border trade between the Northeastern region and neighbouring countries is slow. Except the opening of border trade between India and Myanmar at Moreh and Champhai, and between India and China at Nathula, and the much hyped 165-kilometre-long Indo-Myanmar Friendship Road connecting Tamu and Kalaymyo-Kalewa, which was inaugurated by the then External Affairs Minister Jaswant Singh on 13 February 2001, nothing significant has happened on the ground. Thus, the Look East policy needs a reorientation to suit the development interests of the Northeastern region.

Despite the enormous potentials of the Look East policy, India's border trade with the countries neighbouring the Northeastern region is declining. Border fencing is followed fervently to check drug trafficking and narco-terrorism along the Indo-Myanmar and Indo-Bangladesh borders. Recently, India has sanctioned to raise the iron fencing, along Mizoram's 404-kilometre border with Myanmar. It has also ordered the fencing of the 14 kilometres of the porous international boundary at Moreh in Manipur. This may insulate the age-old ties existing between the ethnic kins living in the border despite the separation between two different nations and further alienate them.

The Look East policy can usher in a new era of development for the Northeast through network of pipelines, road, rail and air connectivity, communication and trade. Though the main focus of the Look East policy is to bring about development through regional economic cooperation, in order that such cooperation flourishes in the Northeastern region the policy also needs to focus on solving the problems that confront the region. While ethnicity and immigration were the main roots of insurgency, insurgency and drug trafficking flourished together. The external linkage of insurgency has been fuelled by trafficking and external support. These four interrelated problems have been the main causes of turmoil in the Northeastern region for the past six decades. All these problems are transnational in nature and can be solved by enhanced cooperation with the neighbouring countries. Apart from such problems prevalent in Northeast India, the people of the region are saddled with unbelief to any policies of the government, rampant corruption, nexus between politicians, contractors, bureaucrats and insurgents, development funds never reaching the intended people.

The Look East policy by addressing the peculiarity of the area and the problems involved with it can bring lasting peace and development in the region. But being underdeveloped with tremendous resource constraints, the Northeastern states are not in a position to execute this task on their own. Therefore, much effort by the central government is required with meaningful regional cooperation with the surrounding countries. These issues have to be tackled at the political level through bilateral and sub-regional cooperation with the neighbouring countries so that meaningful economic cooperation may persist. The Look East policy rightly seeks cooperation from the neighbouring countries in tackling the recurrent problems of insurgency, migration and drug trafficking, besides enhancing economic cooperation. However, such a policy of strengthening ties with eastern neighbours should not be limited to counter insurgency efforts as seen in Bhutan, Bangladesh and Myanmar. The economic potentials existing in the sub-region can surely be exploited with the setting up of trade and communication facilities at the borders in the region. With such improved transport and communication systems, illicit activities in the border areas can be controlled to a great extent.

The Indian government and the Northeastern states have to adopt proactive roles and provide not only infrastructures, but also political stability and good governance. India's Look East policy should include goals, such as combating corruption, cultivating the spirit of intellectual and cultural openness, which can encourage public debate and participation and improve the quality of governance in the region. In this regard, the creation of Public Diplomacy Division of the MEA and the opening of its branch office in Guwahati is a welcome move which would assist in addressing the aspirations of the people of this region in having better liaison with the External Affairs Ministry on issues concerning foreign trade, FDI and cultural exchanges.

There is no easy approach to achieve the goals of any policy pursued which need time and efforts. However, more than a decade has lapsed since the Northeastern region has been given a special place in the Look East policy. The law and order situation in the region may be considered to be one of the main obstacles to the implementation of this policy. Nevertheless, there seems to be lack of political will to implement the policy. Looking into the ongoing peace processes in the region, settlement with most of the insurgent groups would take another two–three decades. Therefore, the government of India needs a strong political will in the form of a robust policy which also involves the people of the northeastern region. Without the participation of the people of the region the policy would falter into another failed lexicon of *India's Northeast policy*.

Bibliography

Primary Sources

Address by Mr Rajiv Sikri, Secretary (East). Ministry of External Affairs. The Sixth Bangladesh–China–India–Myanmar Forum. New Delhi.
————. Ministry of External Affairs. The Sixth Bangladesh–China–India–Myanmar Forum. New Delhi.
Declaration on the Establishment of BIST-EC. Bangkok; 6 June 1997.
Dhaka Statement 2007. Seventh BCIM Forum on Regional Economic Cooperation, Dhaka, 31 March–1 April 2007.
Framework Agreement on Comprehensive Economic Cooperation between the Republic of India and the Association of South East Asian Nations.
Framework Agreement on the BIMST-EC Free Trade Area.
Ha Noi Programme of Action for Mekong–Ganga Cooperation, 28 July 2001, Hanoi, Vietnam.
MCG. 20 June 2003. *Report of the Third Ministerial Meeting on Mekong-Ganga Cooperation,* Phnom Penh, Kingdom of Cambodia.
Ministry of Defence. 1990. *Annual Report, 1989–90,* Government of India, New Delhi.
Ministry of External Affairs. 1992. *Annual Report, 1991–92,* Government of India, New Delhi.
————. 1993. *Annual Report, 1992–93,* Government of India, New Delhi.
————. 1996. *Annual Report, 1995–96,* Government of India, New Delhi.
————. 2004. *Year End Review 2004,* Government of India, New Delhi.
Ministry of Home Affairs (MHA). 1931. *Census of India* (Assam) *1931,* Vol. 3, Part I, New Delhi.
————. 1990. *Economic Survey, 1989–90,* New Delhi.
————. 1991. *Economic Survey, 1990–91,* New Delhi.
Parliament of India, House of the People. 1966. *Foreign Policy of India: Texts of Documents.* New Delhi: Lok Sabha Secretariat.
Prime Minister Manmohan Singh's address at the inauguration of New Capital Complex of Assam, Dispur, 21 November 2004.
Prime Minister Atal Bihari Vajpayee's address to the Institute of Diplomatic and Foreign Relations on 'India and ASEAN—Shared Perspectives', at Kuala Lumpur Today, 16 May 2001.
Prime Minister Manmohan Singh's address delivered at the 5th India–ASEAN Summit Cebu, Philippines, 14 January 2007.

Prime Minister Manmohan Singh's keynote address at special leaders' dialogue of ASEAN Business Advisory Council, Kuala Lumpur, 12 December 2005.

Prime Minister Manmohan Singh's speech at the Asian Corporate Conference 'Driving Global Business: India's New Priorities, Asia's New Realities', Mumbai, 18 March 2006.

Publications Division. 1949. *Jawaharlal Nehru Speeches, 1946–49.* Delhi: The Publications Division, Government of India.

Report of the First Meeting of Inter-Governmental Group (IGG) under the aegis of BIMST-EC, 5–6 February 2001.

Resolution of the Working Committee of the Indian National Congress on United India and Self Determination, 12–18 and 21–24 September 1945.

Shukla Commission Report on Transforming the Northeast-High Level Commission Report to the Prime Minister, 7 March 1997, New Delhi.

Sinha, Srinivas Kumar. November 1998. Report on Illegal Migration into Assam submitted to the President of India by the Governor of Assam, Guwahati.

Sinha, Yashwant. 29 September 2003. 'Resurgent India in Asia'. Speech at Harvard University, Ministry of External Affairs, Government of India, New Delhi.

Severino, H.E. Rodolfo C. 6 July 1999. 'The Greater Mekong Sub-Regional and Regional Peace and Security', Address at the International Conference on the Greater Mekong Sub-region. Available online at http://www.aseansec.org/3317.htm (downloaded on 27.07.2006).

Statement by I.K. Gujral. 1996. Minister of External Affairs and Water Resources, Government of India, Singapore. Available online at http://www.asean.org/4338htm (downloaded on 10.07.2009).

———. 20–21 July 1996. Minister of External Affairs of India, in ASEAN Post-Ministerial Conference, Jakarta. Available online at http://www.aseansec.org/4308.htm (downloaded on 10.07.2009).

United States General Accounting Office. September 2000. *Economic Development: Multiple Federal Programs Fund Similar Economic Development Activities.* Report to Congressional Committee, Washington DC.

Vientiane Declaration on Mekong–Ganga Cooperation,Vientiane, Lao PDR, 10 November 2000.

Secondary Sources

Books

Abercrombie, Nicholas, Stephan Hill and Bryan S. Turner. 2000. *The Penguin Dictionary of Sociology* (4th edition). London: Penguin Books.

Agnihotri, S.K. and B. Datta Ray (eds). 2005. *Perspective of Security and Development in North East India*. New Delhi: Concept Publishing Company.

Ahmed, Rafiul and Prasenajit Biswas. 2004. *Political Economy of Underdevelopment of North-East India*. New Delhi: Akansha.

Almond, Gabriel A. and G. Bingham Powell Jr. 1966. *Comparative Politics: A Developmental Approach*. Boston: Little, Brown & Co.

Arndt, H.N. 1987. *Economic Development: The History of an Idea*. Chicago: University of Chicago Press.

Asher, Mukul G., Rahul Sen and Sadhana Srivastava. 2003. 'ASEAN-India: Emergin Economic Opportunities', in Frederic Grare and Amitabh Matoo (eds), *Beyond the Rhetoric: The Economics of India's Look East Policy*, pp. 59–60. New Delhi: CSH-Manohar.

Barpujari, H.K. 1992. *The Comprehensive History of Assam* (Vol. 4). Guwahati, Assam: Publication Board.

———. 1998. *North-East India: Problems, Policies and Prospects*. Delhi: Spectrum Publications.

Barua, Alokesh (ed.). 2005. *India's North-East: Developmental Issues in a Historical Perspective*. New Delhi: CSH-Manohar.

———. 2005. 'Introduction', in Alokesh Barua (ed.), *India's North-East: Developmental Issues in a Historical Perspective*, p. 29. New Delhi: CSH-Manohar.

Barua, Alokesh and Arindam Bandyopadhyay. 2005. 'Structural Change, Economic Growth and Regional Disparity in the North-East: Regional and National Perspective', in Alokesh Barua (ed.), *India's North-East: Developmental Issues in a Historical Perspective*, p. 239. New Delhi: CSH-Manohar.

Baruah, Sanjib. 1999. *India Against Itself: Assam and the Politics of Nationality*. Pennsylvania: University of Pennsylvania Press.

———. 2005. *Durable Disorder: Understanding the Politics of Northeast India*. New Delhi: Oxford University Press.

———. 2005. 'A Nineteenth Century Puzzle Revisited: Clash of Land Use Regimes in Colonial Assam', in Alokesh Barua (ed.), *India's North-East: Developmental Issues in a Historical Perspective*, p. 172. New Delhi: CSH-Manohar.

Bhattacharya, B.B. 1992. *India's Economic Crises: Debt Burden and Specialisation*. New Delhi: B.R.Publishing.

Bhattacharya, J.B. *Studies in the Economic History of Northeast India*. New Delhi: Har-Anand, 1994.

Bhaumik, Subir. 1996. *Insurgent Crossfire: North-East India*. New Delhi: Lancer.

Bhuyan, S.K. 1949. *Anglo-Assamese Relations, 1772–1826*. Gauhati: Department of Historical and Antiquarian Studies in Assam.

Binder, Leonard. 1971. *Crises and Sequences in Political Development*. Princeton, New Jersey: Princeton University Press.

———. 1971. 'Crises of Political Development', in Leonard Binder (ed.), *Crises and Sequences in Political Development*, p. 46. Princeton, New Jersey: Princeton University Press.

Bose, Ashish, Tiplut Nongbri and Nikhlesh Kumar (eds). 1990. *Tribal Demography and Development in North-East India.* Delhi: B.R. Publishing.

Bose, Manilal. 1997. *History of Arunachal Pradesh.* New Delhi: Concept Publishing Company.

Brass, Paul R. 1990. *The Politics of India Since Independence.* 2nd edition. Cambridge: Cambridge University Press.

————. 1974. *Language, Religion and Politics in North India.* Delhi: Vikas.

Brar, K.S. 2006. 'India's Turbulent North East: Over Five Decade of Isolation, Neglect and Alienation', in Shekhar Basu Roy (ed.) XI (I & II), *New Approach: Our East and North East,* p. 203. Kolkata: Sekhar Basu Roy.

Carl, E.H. 1946. *The Twenty Years' Crisis: 1919–1939.* London: Macmillan.

Chatterji, Rakhahari (ed.). 2001. *Politics India: The State Society Interface.* New Delhi: South Asian Publishers.

Chaube, S.K. 1999. *Hill Politics in Northeast India.* Patna: Orient Longman Limited.

Christie, Clive J. 1996. *A Modern History of Southeast Asia: Decolonialization, Nationalism and Separatism.* London: I.B. Tauris.

Cooper, Mary H. 1990. *The Business of Drugs,* Washington D.C.: Congressional Quarterly Inc.

Couloumbis, Theodore A. and H. Wolfe James. 1978. *Introduction to International Relations: Power and Justice.* Englewood Cliffs, NJ: Prentice-Hall.

Das, Gurudas and Purkayastha, R.K. (eds). 2000. *Border trade: North-East India and Neighbouring Countries.* New Delhi: Akansha.

Das, Gurudas. 1995. *The Tribes of Arunachal Pradesh in Transition.* Delhi: Vikas Publishing House.

————. 1998. 'Migration, Ethnicity and Competition for State Resources: An Explanation of the Social Tension in the North-East India', in M.K. Raha and A.K. Ghosh (eds), *North-East India: The Human Interface,* p. 309. New Delhi: Gyan.

Das, Samir Kumar. 2001. 'Tribal politics in Contemporary India', in Rakhahari Chatterji (ed.), *Politics in India: The State Society Interface,* p. 348. New Delhi: South Asian Publishers.

Dasgupta, Jyotirindra. 1990. 'Ethnicity, Democracy and Development', in A. Kohli (ed.), *Democracy in India* (2nd edition), pp. 165–67. Princeton: Princeton University Press.

Datta, P.S. (ed.). 1995. *The North-East and the India State: Paradox of a Periphery.* New Delhi: Vikas.

Deutsch, Karl W. 1954. *Political Community at the International Level: Problems of Definition and Measurement.* Garden City, New York: Doubleday.

Deutsch, Karl W., Sidney A. Burrell and Robert A. Kann. 1957. *Political Community and the North Atlantic Area.* Princeton: Princeton University Press.

Dixit, J.N. 1996. *My South Block Years: Memoirs of a Foreign Secretary.* New Delhi: UBSPD.

Dutta, N.L. 1994. 'Tribal Situation and its Implication on Development in North-East India', in R.K. Samanta (ed.), *India's North-East: The Process of Change and Development,* p. 77. Delhi: B.R. Publication.

Dutta, P.C. 2005. 'Problems of Ethnicity and Insurgency in North East India', in S.K. Agnihotri and B. Datta Ray (eds), *Perspective of Security and Development in North East India*, p. 112. New Delhi: Concept Publishing Company.

Egreteau, Renaud. 2003. *Wooing the Generals: India's New Burma Policy*. Delhi: CSH-Authors Press.

Elwin, Verrier. 1959. *A Philosophy for NEFA*. Advisor to the Government of Assam, Shillong: S. Roy on behalf of the North-East Frontier Agency (NEFA).

———. 1988. *The Tribal World of Verrier Elwin: An Autobiography*. New Delhi: Oxford University Press.

———. 1989. 'A Philosophy for NEFA: The Fundamental Problem', in Nari Rustomji (ed.), *Verrier Elwin, Philanthropist, Selected Writings*, p. 246. Shillong: Oxford University Press.

Emerson, Rupert. 1966. 'Nationalism and Political Development', in J.L. Finkle and R.W. Gable (eds), *Political Development and Social Change*, p. 96. New York: John Wiley & Sons Inc.

Etzioni, Amitai (ed.). 1965. *Political Unification: A Comparative Study of Leaders and Forces*. New York: Holt, Rinehart and Winston.

———. 1966. *International Political Communities*. Garden City, New York: Doubleday Anchor Books.

Finkle, J.L., and R.W. Gable (eds). 1966. *Political Development and Social Change*. New York: John Wiley & Sons Inc.

Foreign Service Institute. 1997. *Indian Foreign Policy: Agenda for the 21st Century* (Vol. 1). New Delhi: FSI & Konark Publishers.

Grare, Frederic. 2001. 'In Search of a Role: India and the ASEAN Regional Forum', in Frederic Grare and Amitabh Mattoo (eds), *India and ASEAN: The Politics of India's Look East Policy*, p. 120. New Delhi: CSH-Manohar-ISAS.

Gait, Edward. 2008. *A History of Assam* (2nd edition, Indian reprint). Guwahati: Eastern Publishers.

Ghoshal, Baladas. 1999. 'India, ASEAN and APEC', in Nancy Jetley (ed.), *India's Foreign Policy Challenges and Prospects*, p. 151. New Delhi: Sangam Books.

Ghosal, Soma. 2003. *The Politics of Drugs and India's Northeast*. New Delhi: Anamika.

Ghosh, Subir. 2001. *Frontier Travails-Northeast: The Politics of Mess*. Delhi: Macmillan.

Giddens, Anthony and Simon Griffiths. 2006. *Sociology* (5th edition, revised). Cambridge: Polity.

Gogoi, Jayanta Kumar. 2005. 'The Migration Problem in Assam: An Analysis', in Alokesh Barua (ed.), *India's North-East: Developmental Issues in a Historical Perspective*, p. 361. New Delhi: CSH-Manohar.

Gonsalves, Eric (ed.). 1991. *Asian Relations*. New Delhi: Lancer International.

Gordon, Sandy. 1995. *India's Rise to Power in the Twentieth Century and Beyond*. New York: St. Martin's Press, Inc.

Grare, Frederic and Amitabh Mattoo (eds). 2001. *India and ASEAN: The Politics of India's Look East Policy*. New Delhi: CSH-Manohar-ISAS.

Grare, Frederic and Amitabh Mattoo. 2003. *Beyond the Rhetoric: The Economics of India's Look East Policy*. New Delhi: CSH-Manohar.

Guha, Amalendu. 1977/1988. *Planter-Raj to Swaraj: Freedom Struggle and Electoral Politics in Assam 1826–1947*. New Delhi: People's Publishing House.

———. 1991. *Medieval and Early Colonial Assam: Society, Polity, Economy*. Calcutta: K.P. Bagchi, University of California Press.

Gupta, Sisir. 1964. *India and Regional Integration in Asia*. Bombay: Asia Publishing House.

Haas, Earns B. 1958. *The Uniting of Europe: Political, Social and Economic Forces*. Stanford, California: Stanford University Press.

———. 1964. *Beyond the Nation State*. Stanford: Stanford University Press.

———. 1966. 'International Integration: The European and the Universal Process', in Amitai Etzioni (ed.), *International Political Communities*, p. 20. Garden City, New York: Doubleday Anchor Books.

———. 1975. *The Obsolescence of Regional Integration Theory*. Berkeley: Institute for International Studies.

Haas, Ernst B. and Philippe C. Schmitter. 1966. 'Economics and Differential Patterns of Political Integration: Projections about Unity in Latin America', in Amitai Etzioni (ed.), *International Political Communities*. New York: Anchor.

Harrison, Brian. 1956. 'Problems of Political Integration in Southeast Asia', in Philip W. Tayer (ed.), *Nationalism and Progress in Free Asia*, pp. 143–44. Baltimore: The John Hopkins Press.

Hazarika, Sanjoy. 1995. *Strangers of the Mist: The Tales of War and Peace from India's Northeast*. New Delhi: Penguin Books.

———. 1997. 'Insurgency in Northeast India', in B. Pakem (ed.), *Insurgency in North-East India*, p. 118. New Delhi: Omsons Publications.

Heble, Ajay, Dona Palmatur and J.R. Struthers (eds). 1997. *New Contexts of Canadian Criticism*. Peterborough: Broadview Press.

Hechter, Michael. 1975. *Internal Colonialism: The Celtic Fringe in British National Development, 1536–1966*. London: Routledge and Kegan Paul.

Hrem, H. 2000. 'Explaining the regional phenomenon in an era of globalization', in R. Stubbs and G.R.D. Underhill (eds), *Political Economy and the Changing Global Order* (2nd edition), p. 70. Canada: Oxford University Press.

Hunter, E. and Whitten Phillip. 1976. *Encyclopedia of Anthropology*. New York: Harper & Row.

Jetley, Nancy (ed.). 1999. *India's Foreign Policy Challenges and Prospects*. New Delhi: Sangam Books.

Joshi, V. and I.M.D. Little. 1994. *India: Macroeconomics and Political Economy, 1964–1991*. Washington D.C.: World Bank.

Karna, M.N. 1990. 'Aspects of tribal Development in North-Eastern India', in Ashish Bose (ed.), *Tribal Demography and Development in North-East India*, p. 14. Delhi: B.R. Publishing.

Kohli, A. (ed.). 1990. *Democracy in India* (2nd edition). Princeton: Princeton University Press.

Kothari, Rajni. 1970. *Politics in India*. New Delhi: Orient Longman Ltd.

————. (ed.). 1974. *State and Nation Building*. Bombay: Allied Publishers.

Kumar, B.B. 2000. 1995. 'North-East India: Need for a Fresh Look', in P.S. Datta (ed.), *The North-East and the Indian State: Paradoxes of a Periphery*, p. 17. New Delhi: Vikas.

————. 2000. 'The Border Trade in North-East India: The Historical Perspective', in Gurudas Das and R.K. Purkayastha (eds), *Border trade: North-East India and Neighbouring Countries*, p. 6. New Delhi: Akansha.

Lalchungnunga. 1994. *Mizoram: Politics of Regionalism and National Integration*. New Delhi: Reliance Publishing House.

Lawrence, R.Z. 1996. *Regionalism, Multilateralism, and Deeper Integration*, p. 6. Washington, D.C.: Brookings Institution.

Levi, Werner. 1954. *Free India in Asia*. Minneapolis: University of Minnesota Press.

Maadan, Devinder Kumar. 2000. 'SAARC: Origin and Development', in B.C. Upreti (ed.), *SAARC: Dynamics of Regional Cooperation in South Asia*, p. 165. New Delhi: Kalinga Publications.

Mackenzie, Alexander. 2001. *North East Frontier of India*. New Delhi: Mittal Publications. First published in 1884 entitled *History of the Government with the Hill Tribes of the North-East Frontier of Bengal*.

Malik, P.M.S. 1997. 'The Changing Face of India's Economic Diplomacy: The Role of Ministry of External Affairs'. Foreign Service Institute. *Indian Foreign Policy: Agenda for the 21st Century*, 234. Vol. 1. New Delhi: FSI & Konark Publishers.

Mann, Poonam. 2000. *India's Foreign Policy in the Post Cold War Era*. New Delhi: Harman Publishers.

Manserch, Nicholas (ed.). 1953. *Documents and Speeches on British Commonwealth Affairs, 1931–1952*. London: Oxford University Press.

Mattli, Walter. 1999. *The Logic of Regional Integration: Europe and Beyond*. Cambridge: Cambridge University Press.

Melo, Jaime de and Arvind Panagariya. 1996. *New Dimensions in Regional Integration*. Cambridge: Cambridge University Press.

Menon, V.P. 1956. *Integration of Indian States*. Hyderabad: Orient Longman.

Mensergh, N. (ed.). 1974. *The Transfer of Power 1942–1947* (Vol. 5), p. 397. London: Nicholas Publication.

Misra, Udayon. 2000. *The Periphery Strikes Back: Challenges to the Nation-State in Assam and Nagaland*. Shimla: Indian Institute of Advance Studies.

Miri, Mrinal. 2002. *Identity and the Moral life*, p. 920. New Delhi: Oxford University Press.

Mohan, C. Raja. 2003. *Crossing the Rubicon: The Shaping of India's New Foreign Policy*. New Delhi: Penguin.

Momin, Mignonette and Cecile Mawlong (eds). 2004. *Society and Economy in North-East India* (Vol. 1). New Delhi: Regency Publications.

Munshi, S., A. Guha and S. Chaube. 1978. 'Regionalisation and Integrated Economic Development in North-East India', in B. Datta Ray (ed.), *Social and Economic Profile of North-East India*. New Delhi: B.R. Publishing.

Nag, Sajal. 1994. 'Withdrawal Syndrome: "Secessionism" in Modern North-East India', in Milton Sangma (ed.), *Essays in North-East India*, p. 295. New Delhi: Indus Publishing Company.

————. 1998. *India and North-East India: Mind, Politics and the Process of Integration 1946–1950*. New Delhi: Regency Publications.

————. 1999. *Nationalism, Separatism and Secessionism*. New Delhi: Rawat Publications.

Nanda, Prakash. 2003. *Rediscovering Asia: Evolution of India's Look-East Policy*. New Delhi: Lancer.

Nath, H.K. 2005. 'The Rise of an Enclave Economy', in Alokesh Barua (ed.), *India's North-East: Developmental Issues in a Historical Perspective*, p. 135. New Delhi: CSH-Manohar.

Nathan, M. Shamuyarisa. 1974. 'Political Development and Political Planning in New African States', in Rajni Kothari (ed.), *State and Nation Building*, p. 244. Bombay: Allied Publishers.

Nehru, Jawaharlal. 1945. *Discovery of India*. Calcutta: Signet Press.

Nepram, Binalakshmi. 2002. *South Asia's Fractured Frontier: Armed Conflict, Narcotics and Small Arms Proliferation in India's North East*. New Delhi: Mittal.

Nepram, Binalakshmi. 2007. 'The Origins of Manipuri Insurrection', in Jaideep Saikia (ed.), *Frontier in Flames: North East India in Turmoil*, p. 36. New Delhi: Viking.

Nongbri, Tiplut. 2003. *Development, Ethnicity and Gender*. Jaipur: Rawat.

Ohmae, Kenichi. 1990. *The Borderless World: Power and Strategy in the Interlinked Economy*. London: HarperCollins.

Pakem, B. 1982. 'The Economic Structure of North Eastern Region of India', in P. Thakur (ed.), *India's North East*, p. 179. Ludhiania: Gyan Publishers.

———— (ed.). 1997. *Insurgency in North-East India*. New Delhi: Omsons Publications.

———— (ed.). 1990. *Nationality, Ethnicity and Cultural Identity in North-East India*. New Delhi: Omsons Publications.

———— (ed.). 1985. *Regionalism in India: With Special Reference to North-East India*. New Delhi: Har-Anand Publications.

Palmer, Norman D. and Howard C. Perkins. 1953. *International Relations: The World Community in Transition* (3rd edition). Boston: Houghton Mifflin Company.

Patil, V.T. and P.R. Trivedi. 2000. *Migration, Refugees and Security in the 21st Century*. Delhi: Authors Press.

Phukon, Girin. 1996. *Politics of Regionalism in Northeast India*. Guwahati/Delhi: Spectrum.

Pye, Lucian and Sydney Verba (eds). 1965. *Political Culture and Political Development*. Princeton, Princeton University Press.

Raha, M.K. and A.K. Ghosh (eds). 1998. *North-East India: The Human Interface*. New Delhi: Gyan Publishing.

Raha, M.K. Raha. 1998. 'North-East India and Nehru', in M.K. Raha and A.K. Ghosh (eds), *North-East India: The Human Interface*, pp. 123–24. New Delhi: Gyan Publishing.

Ramakant and P.L. Bhola (eds). 1995. *Post Cold War Developments in South Asia.* Jaipur: RBSA Publishers.

Rao, P.V. 2000. 'Globalisation and Regional Cooperation: The South Asian Experience', in B.C. Upreti (ed.), *SAARC: Dynamics of Regional Cooperation in South Asia*, p. 34. New Delhi: Kalinga Publications.

Rao, V. Venkata. 1976. *A Century of tribal Politics in North-East India, 1874–1974.* New Delhi: S. Chand.

Ray, Ashok Kumar. 2007. *Revisiting North East India in the Era of Globalisation.* New Delhi: OM Publications.

Ray, B. Datta (ed.). 1978. *Social and Economic Profile of North-East India.* New Delhi: B.R. Publishing.

Ray, Shekhar Basu (ed.). 2006. *New Approach: Our East and North East* XI (I & II), p. 203. Kolkata: Sekhar Basu Roy.

Riker, William H. 1964. *Federalism: Origin, Operation, Significance.* Boston: Little, Brown & Co.

Richard Stubbs, Richard. 1999. 'Regionalisation and Globalisation', in Richard Stubbs and Geoffrey R. D. Underhill (eds), *Political Economy and the Changing Global Order* (2nd edition), p. 231. Canada: Oxford University Press.

Robinson, William. 1975. *A Descriptive Account of Assam.* Delhi: Sanakaran Prakashak.

Roy, Santanu. 2005. 'Why Do They Come? Economic Incentives for Immigration to Assam', in Alokesh Barua (ed.), *India's North-East: Developmental Issues in a Historical Perspective*, pp. 390–91. New Delhi: CSH-Manohar.

Rubin, Barry (ed.). 1991. *Terrorism and Politics.* London: Macmillan.

Rustomji, Nari (ed.). 1989. *Verrier Elwin, Philantrophist: Selected Writings.* Shillong: Oxford University Press.

Sachdeva, Gulshan. 2000. *Economy of the North-East: Policy, Present Conditions and Future Possibilities.* New Delhi: Konark Publishers.

Saikia, D. and D.N. Majumdar. 1997. 'Some Characteristics of Ethno-Cultural Identity of North-East India', in B. Pakem (ed.), *Insurgency in North-East India*, p. 28. New Delhi: Omsons Publications.

Saikia, Jaideep. 2007. *Frontier in Flames: North East India in Turmoil.* New Delhi: Viking.

Saikia, Rajen. 2001. *Social and Economic History of Assam (1853–1921).* New Delhi: Manohar.

Saint-Mezard, Isabelle. 2003. 'The Look East policy; An Economic Perspective', in Frederic Grare and Amitabh Mattoo (eds), *Beyond the Rhetoric: The Economics of India's Look East Policy*, p. 25. New Delhi: CSH-Manohar.

Sarma, Atul and Paadeep Kumar Mehta. 2003. 'Indo-ASEAN Trade Prospects: A Study of Trade Complementarity', in Frederic Grare and Amitabh Mattoo (eds), *Beyond the Rhetoric: The Economics of India's Look East Policy*, p. 81. New Delhi: CSH-Manohar.

Samanta, R.K. (ed.). 1994. *India's North-East: The Process of Change and Development.* Delhi: B.R. Publication.

Sangma, Milton. (ed.). 1994. *Essays in North-East India*. New Delhi: Indus Publishing Company.

Sarkar, Sumit. 1983. *Modern India 1885–1947*. New Delhi: Macmillan.

Sharma, B.K. and S.N. Goswami. 2000. 'Border trade in Northeast India: An Overview', in Gurudas Das and R.K. Purkayastha (eds), *Border trade: North-East India and Neighbouring Countries*, p. 96. New Delhi: Akansha.

Sharma, S.K. and Usha Sharma (eds). 2005. *Discovery of North-East India* (Vol. 1). New Delhi: Mittal.

Sharma, Manorama. 2004. 'Socio-Economic History in Pre-colonial North-East India: Trends, Problems and Possibilities', in Cecile A Mawlong and Fozail Ahmad Qadri (eds), *Society and Economy in North-East India,*Mignonette Momin (Vol. 1), p. 1. New Delhi: Regency Publications.

Singh, B.P. 1987. *The Problem of Change: A Study of North-East India*. New Delhi: Oxford University Press.

Singh, A.K. Ranjit. 1990. 'Emergent Ethnic Processes in Manipur: A Reappraisal', in B. Pakem (ed.), *Ethnicity and Cultural Identity in North-East India*, p. 234. New Delhi: Omsons.

Singh, Jasjit (ed.). 1998. *Light Weapons and International Security*. New Delhi: Pugwash, IDSA & BASIC.

Singh, K.S. (ed.). 1986. *The Tribal Situation in India*. Shimla: Indian Institute of Advanced Studies.

Stubbs, Richard and Geoffrey R.D. Underhill (eds). 2000. *Political Economy and the Changing Global Order* (2nd edition). Canada: Oxford University Press.

Syiemlieh, D.R. 1985. 'The Political Integration of the Khasi States', in B. Pakem (ed.), *Regionalism in India: With Special Reference to North-East India*, p. 149. New Delhi: Har-Anand Publications.

Srinivas, M.N. and R.D. Sanwal. 1986. 'Some Aspects of Political Development in North-Eastern Hill Areas of India', in K.S. Singh (ed.), *The Tribal Situation in India*, p. 120. Shimla: Indian Institute of Advanced Studies.

Tarapot, Panthoujam. 1993. *Insurgency Movement in North Eastern India*. New Delhi: Vikas Publishing House.

Taylor, Charles. 1997. 'The Politics of Recognition', in Ajay Heble, Dona Palmatur and J.R. Struthers, *New Contexts of Canadian Criticism*, p. 105. Peterborough: Broadview Press.

Thakur, P. (ed). 1982. *India's North East*. Ludhiania: Gyan Publishers.

Thayer, Philip W. (ed.). 1956. *Nationalism and Progress in Free Asia*. Baltimore: John Hopkins Press.

Thet, Kyaw. 1956. 'Burma: The Political Integration of Linguistic and Religious Minority Groups', in Philip W. Thayer (ed.), *Nationalism and Progress in Free Asia*, pp. 161–62. Baltimore: John Hopkins Press.

Thomas, C. Joshua (ed.). 2005. *Polity and Economy: Agenda for Comtemporary North East India*. New Delhi: Regency.

———. 2006. *Engagement and Development: India's Northeast and Neighbouring Countries*. New Delhi: Akansha.

Umar, Ghulam. 1988. *SAARC: Analytical Survey*. Delhi: Renaissance Publishing House.

Upadhya, Shashi. 1995. 'Challenges before SAARC', in Ramakant and P.L. Bhola (eds), *Post Cold War Developments in South Asia*, p. 47. Jaipur: RBSA Publishers.

Upreti, B.C. 2000. *SAARC: Dynamics of Regional Cooperation in South Asia* (Vol. 1). New Delhi: Kalinga Publications.

van Ginkel, Hans and Luk Van Langenhove. 2003. 'Introduction and Context', in Hans Van Ginkel, Julius Court and Luk Van Langenhove, *Integrating Africa: Perspectives on Regional Integration and Development*, pp. 1–9. Tokyo: UNU press.

Verba, Sidney. 1965. 'Comparative Political Culture', in Lucian Pye and Sydney Verba (eds), *Political Culture and Political Development*, p. 513. Princeton, Princeton University Press.

Vanlawma, 1972. *Kan Ram le Kei*, p. 217. Aizawl: Self-published.

Verghese, B.G. 1996/2004. *India's Northeast Resurgent: Ethnicity, Insurgency, Governance, Development*. New Delhi: Konark Publishers.

———. 2006. 'Unfinished Business in Northeast', in Joshua Thomas (ed.), *Engagement and Development: India's Northeast and Neighbouring Countries*, p. 30. New Delhi: Akansha.

Weiner, Myron. 1978. *Sons of the Soil: Migration and Ethnic Conflict in India*. Princeton: Princeton University Press.

Wood, Francis. 2002. *The Silk Road: Two Thousand Years in the Heart of Asia*. Berkeley, CA: University of California Press.

Xaxa, V. 1990. 'Tribal Development in the North-East: Trends and Perspectives', in Ashish Bose, *Tribal Demography and Development in North-East India*, p. 25. Delhi: B.R. Publishing.

Yogi, Anand Kumar. 1991. *Development of the North East Region: Problems and Prospects*. Guwahati: Spectrums Publications.

Yonua, Asoso. 1974. *The Rising Nagas: A Historical and Political Study*. New Delhi: Vivek Publishing House.

Articles

Ahmad, Zarin. 8 March 2000. 'India: Package for the North East', *Institute of Peace and Conflict Studies*, 338. Available online at http://www.ipcs.org/article/india/india-package-for-the-north-east-338.html (downloaded on 07. 12. 2014).

Ake, Claude. April 1967. 'Political Integration and Political Stability: A Hypothesis', *World Politics*, 19 (3).

Bajpai, K. Shankar. February 1992. 'India in 1991: New Beginnings', *Asian Survey*, 32 (2). A Survey of Asia in 1991: Part II.

Banerjee, Paula, Sanjoy Hazarika, Monirul Hussain and Ranabir Samaddar. 4–10 September 1999. 'Indo-Bangladesh Cross-Border Migration and Trade', *Economic and Political Weekly*, 34 (36).

Baral, J.K. and J.N. Mahanty. Autumn 1992. 'India and the Gulf Crisis: The Response of a Minority Government', *Pacific Affairs*, 65 (3).

Baruah, Sanjib. June 2001. 'Generals as Governors: The Parallel Political Systems of Northeast India', *Himal South Asian*, 14 (6).

Batra, Amita. June 2009. 'India's Northeast and Southeast Asia: Strengthening and Integrated Space', *IPCS Issue Brief*, no. 107.

Bhagwati, Jagdish. September 1992. 'Regionalism versus Multilateralism', *The World Economy*, 15 (5).

Bhaumik, Subir. October 1998. 'Insurgency in North East', *Aakrosh*, 1 (1).

Bora, Jnananath. 1936. 'Kamrup Aru Bharat Varsha', *Awahan* (Assamese), 8 (3).

———. 1938. 'Asom Desh Bharatvarsha Bhitarat Jhakiba Kia?' *Awahan* (Assamese), 10 (3).

Chatterjee, Shibashis. 2007. 'Conceptions of Space in India's Look East Policy: Order, Cooperation or Community?' *South Asian Survey*, 14 (65).

Cocks, Peter. Winter 1980. 'Towards a Marxist Theory of European Integration', *International Organization*, 34 (1).

Coleman, James S. March 1955. 'The Problem of Integration in Emergent Africa', *The Western Political Quarterly*, 8 (1).

Connon, Walker. April 1972. 'Nation-Building or Nation-destroying'. *World Politics*, 24 (3).

Das, Gurudas. 1994. 'Understanding the Underdevelopment of North-Eastern region of India', *Journal of Indian Anthropological Society*, 29 (1 and 2).

———. 2002. 'Probable Options: Commenting the Faultlines in Assam'. *Faultines*, 11.

Das, Samir Kumar. Spring 2008. 'State against Minorities: State-Building Challenges in Contemporary North Eastern India', *Man and Society*, V.

Dasgupta, Jyotirindra. May 1997. 'Community, Authenticity, and Autonomy: Insurgence and Institutional Development in India's Northeast', *The Journal of Asian Studies*, 56 (2).

Datta, Sreeradha. 2000, 'Northeast Turmoil: Vital Determinants', *Strategic Analysis*, 23 (12): 2123–33.

Deutsch, Karl W. September 1961. 'Social Mobilization and Political Development', *American Political Science Review*, 55 (3).

Dutta, Binayak. 1998. 'Constructing India's North Eastern Tribal Policy and Verrier Elwin—A Review', Proceedings of the North East India History Association, 19th Session, Nagaland University, Kohima.

Edward D. Mansfield and Helen V. Milner. Summer 1999. 'The New Wave of Regionalism', *International Organization*, 53 (3).

Emerson, Rupert. February 1960. 'Nationalism and Political Development'. *The Journal of Politics*, 22 (1).

Ghosal, Baladas. January 1996. 'East Asian Miracle and India', *World Focus*, 17 (1).

Godbole, Madhav. January–March 2006. 'Illegal Migration from Bangladesh', *Dialogue*, 7 (3).

Goldman, Ralph M. Winter 1964. 'The Politics of Political Integration', *The Journal of Negro Education*, 33 (1).

Gonzales-Casanova, P. 1965. 'Internal Colonialism and National Development', *Studies in Comparative International Development*, 1 (4).

Gordon, Sandy. October 1995. 'South Asia after the Cold War: Winners and Losers', *Asian Survey*, 35 (10).

Haas, Ernst B. Spring 1976. 'Turbulent Fields and the Theory of Regional Integration', *International Organization*, 30 (2).

Harshe, Rajen. 8–14 May 1999. 'South Asian Regional Co-operation: Problems and Prospects', *Economic and Political Weekly*, 34 (19).

Henderson, William. November 1955. 'The Development of Regionalism in Southeast Asia', *International Organization*, 9 (4).

Hussain, Wassabir. 18 November 2004. 'Interaction on the North East', *Observer Research Foundation*. New Delhi.

Jafa, Vijendra Singh. July 1999. 'Administrative Policies and Ethnic Disintegration: Engineering Conflicts in India's North East', *Faultlines*, 2.

Jaffrelot, Christophe. April 2003. 'India's Look East Policy: An Asianist Strategy in Perspective', *India Review*, 2 (2).

Kurlander, Stetson Eric. March 2002. 'Multicultural and Assimilationist Models of Ethnopolitical Integration in the Context of the German *Nordmark*, 1890–1933', *The Global Review of Ethnopolitics*, 1 (3).

Lama, Mahendra P. July 2001. 'India's North-East States: Narcotics, Small Arms and Misgovernance', *Ethnic Studies Report*, 19 (2).

Lijphart, Arend. March 1971. 'Cultural Diversity and theories of Political Integration', *Canadian Journal of Political Science*, 4 (1).

Lindberg, Lenon N. Autumn 1970. 'Political Integration as a Multidimensional Phenomenon Requiring Multivariate Measurement', *International Organization*, 24 (4).

Litfin, Karen T. November 1997. 'Sovereignty in World Ecopolitics', *Mershon International Studies Review*, 41 (2).

Macdonald, Hamish and Jaya Sarkar. 11 March 1993. 'India: The Money Jagggernaut', *Far Eastern Economic Review*: 16–18.

Malik, J. Mohan. September 1991. 'India's Response to the Gulf Crisis: Implications for Indian Foreign Policy', *Asian Survey*, 31 (9).

Mattli, Walter. 2000. 'Sovereignty Bargains in Regional Integration', *International Studies Review*, 2 (2).

McDuie-Ra, Duncan. June 2013. 'Beyond the "Exclusionary City": North-east Migrants in Neo-liberal Delhi', *Urban Studies*, 50 (8): 1625.

Miri, Mrinal. October–December 2001. 'North-East: A Point of View', *Dialogue*, 3 (2).

Misra, Tilottoma. 9–15 August 1980. 'Assam: A Colonial Hinterland', *Economic and Political Weekly*, 15 (23).

Misra, Udayon. 22–28 May 1999. 'Immigration and Identity Transformation in Assam', *Economic and Political Weekly*, 34 (21).

Moses, Gopen. July–Spetember 2007. 'Drug Use, HIV/AIDS and Human Trafficking in the North-East', *Dialogue*, 9 (1).

Munro, Ross H. Summer 1993. 'The Loser: India in the Nineties', *National Interest*, 33.

Murayama, Mayumi. 8–14 April 2006. 'Borders, Migration and Sub-Regional Cooperation in Eastern South Asia', *Economic and Political Weekly*, 41 (14).

Mye, Joseph S., Jr. Autumn 1968. 'Comparative Regional Integration: Concepts and Measurement', *International Organization*, 22 (4).

Naidu, G.V.C. October–December 1996. 'India and Southeast Asia', *World Focus*, 17 (10, 11, 12).

Nayak, Nihar Ranjan. 8 July 2003. 'Narco-trafficking: Non-military threat in India's Eastern Border', *IPCS*, 1079. Available online at http://www.ipcs.org/article/india/narco-trafficking-non-military-threat-in-indias-eastern-border-1079.html (downloaded on 07. 12. 2014).

Nayar, Baldev Raj. Autumn 1998. 'Political Structure and India's Economic Reforms of the 1990s', *Pacific Affairs*, 71 (3).

Ohmae, Kenichi. 1993. 'The Rise of the Region State', *Foreign Affairs*, 172 (2).

Owen, N.H. 1975. 'Land, Politics and Ethnicity in a Carib Indian Community', *Ethnology*, 14 (5).

Padelford, Norman J. May 1954. 'Regional Organisation and the United Nations', *International Organisation*, 8 (2): 203–16.

Pal, Nabendu. September–October 2000. 'India's North-Eastern Region: Towards a more humane approach', *Bharat Rakshak Monitor*, 3 (2): 1–38.

Pommaret, Francoise. 'Ancient Trade Partners: Bhutan, Cooch Bihar and Assam (17th–19th Centuries)'. *Journal Asiatique*, 287: 285–303. English translation available online at http://www.bhutanstudies.org.bt/journal/vol2no1/v2n/ancienttrade.pdf (downloaded on 07.12. 2014).

Prabhakar, M.S. 6 October 1973. 'The North Eastern Council: Some Political Perspectives', *Economic and Political Weekly*, 8 (40).

Rao, Sangeeta. 2 October 1996. 'Otherwise? The Selling of Global Cultural Difference', *Sanskriti*, 7 (1).

Routray, Bibhu Prasad. September–October 2001. 'Analyzing an Insurgency: On the Trail of Nagalim', *Bharat Rakshak Monitor*, 4 (2).

Routray, Bihu Prasad. 25 June 2002. 'Is Development a Riposte to Insurgency?' *Institute of Peace and Conflict Studies*, 770. Available online at http://www.ipcs.org/article/terrorism/is-development-a-riposte-to-insurgency-770.html (downloaded on 07. 12. 2014).

Roy, J.N. January–March, 2007. 'The North-East needs New Approach', *Dialogue* 8, no. 3.

Sachdeva, Gulshan. April–June 2004. 'Fiscal Governance in the Northeast', *Dialogue*, 5 (4): 54.

———. January–March 2006. 'Demystifying Northeast', *Dialogue*, 7 (3): 77.

Sachdeva, Gulshan. 2000. 'India's Northeast: Rejuvenating a Conflict-riven Economy'. *Faultlines*, 6: 79–104.

Sahni, Ajay. 2001. 'Survey of Conflicts and Resolution in India's Northeast'. *Faultlines*, 12.

Sen, Rahul, Mukul G. Asher, and Ramkishen S. Rajan. 17–23 July 2004. 'ASEAN-India Economic Relations: Current Status and Future Prospects', *Economic and Political Weekly*, 39 (29).

Shen, Yi. 1999. 'The Miracle and Crisis of East Asia: Relation-Based Governance vs. Rule-Based Governance'. *Perspectives*, 1 (2).

Singh, B.P. 1987. 'North-East India: Demography, Culture and Identity Crisis', *Modern Asian Studies*, 21 (2).

Singh, Prakash. October–December 2006. 'India's Border Management Challenges', *Dialogue*, 8 (2).

Sinha, S.K. 2002. 'Violence and Hope in India's Northeast', *Faultlines*, 10.

Sreedhar. February 1994. 'Security Situation in Southern Asia', *Strategic Analysis*, 16 (11).

Tajena, Nisha. 17 March 2001. 'Informal Trade in SAARC Region', *Economic and Political Weekly*, 36 (11).

Upadhyay, Archana. 9 July 2005. 'Assam: The Infiltrators Issue', *Economic and Political Weekly*, 40 (28).

Weiner, Myron. March 1965. 'Political Integration and Political Development, *Annals of the American Academy of Political and Social Science*, 358 (1).

Wood, John R. November 1984. 'British versus Princely Legacies and the Political Integration of Gujarat', *The Journal of Asian Studies*, 44 (1).

World Bank. August–October 1993. 'The Making of the East Asian Miracle'. *World Policy Research Bulletin*, 4 (4).

Yahya, Faizal. September 2005. 'BIMSTEC and Emerging Patterns of Asian Regional and Inter Regional Cooperation', *Australian Journal of Political Science*, 40 (3).

Policy Briefs and Monographs

Bay of Bengal Initiative for Multi-Sectoral Technical and Economic Cooperation, et al. 2004. 'Future Directions of BIMSTEC: Towards a Bay of Bengal Economic Community.' Research and Information System for Developing Countries.

Das, Samir Kumar. 2007. 'Conflict and Peace in India's Northeast: The Role of Civil Society', *Policy Studies 42*, East West Centre.

'ECOSOC Promotes Regional Integration as a Prerequisite for Globalization'. *Regional Commissions Development Update*, Eleventh Issue, November 2001. Available online at http://www.un.org/Depts/rcnyo/newsletter/nl11/globalization.htm (downloaded on 07. 12. 2014).

Langenhove, L. Van. August 2003. 'Regional Integration and Global Governance', *UNUnexions*, 1(5), United Nations University, Tokyo.

Meek, Sarah (ed.). September 1998. 'Controlling Small Arms Proliferation and Reversing Cultures of Violence in Africa and the Indian Ocean', ISS monograph series no. 30, Pretoria: South Africa, Institute for Security Studies.

Rajagopalan, Swarna. 2008. 'Peace Accords in Northeast India: Journey over Milestones', *Policy Studies 46*, East-West Centre.

Research and Information System. March 2007. 'India's Engagement in ASEAN: Focus CLMV', *Mekong Ganga Policy Brief No. 1*, Research and Information System for Developing Countries publication on India-Mekong Economic Cooperation, New Delhi: 4.

Working, Occasional, Discussion and Theme Papers

Baru, Sanjay. February 2001. 'India and ASEAN: The Emerging Economic Relationship. Towards a Bay of Bengal Community', working paper no. 61, *Indian Council for Research on International Economic Relations (ICRIER)*.

Baruah, Sanjib. 2004. 'Between South and Southeast Asia: Northeast India and the Look East Policy', CENISEAS paper 4, Omeo Kumar Das Institute of Social Change and Development, Guwahati.

Biswas, Aparajita. 2008. 'Small Arms and Drug Trafficking in the Indian Ocean Region', working paper no. 4, Centre for African Studies.

Egreteau, Renaud. 2006. 'Instability at the Gate: India's Troubled Northeast and its External Connections', CSH occasional papers no. 16, Centre de humane Sciences, New Delhi.

Lombaerde, Philippe De and Luk Van Langenhove. 28 October 2004. 'Indicators of Regional Integration: Conceptual and Methodological Issues', UNU-CRIS occasional papers, 0-2004/15, United Nations University, Japan.

Ludden, David. 2003. *Where is Assam? Using Geographical History to Locate Current Social Realities*, CENISEAS Papers 1, Centre for Northeast India, South and Southeast Asia Studies, Guwahati, p. 12.

Mehta, Rajesh. January 2002. 'Establishment of Free Trade Arrangement among BIMST-EC Countries: Some Issues', RIS-Discussion Papers no. 23, New Delhi.

Morales, Isidro. September 2009. 'Post-NAFTA North America: Three Scenarios for the Near Future', UNU-CRIS Working Papers W-2009/19, Tokyo.

Nepram, Binalakshmi. December 2007. 'Armed Conflict, Small Arms Proliferation and Women's Responses to Armed Violence in India's Northeast', working paper no. 33, Heidelberg Papers in South Asian and Comparative Politics, Heidelberg.

Rahman, Mustafizur, Habibur Rahman and Wasel Bin Shadat. September 2007. 'BCIM Economic Cooperation: Prospects and Challenges', paper 64, Centre for Policy Dialogue, Dhaka, Dhaka.

Singh, Swaran. August 2007. 'Mekong-Ganga Cooperation Initiative: Analysis and Assessment of India's Engagement with Greater Mekong Sub-region', IRASEC occasional paper no. 3, Research Institute on Contemporary Southeast Asia, Bangkok.

Syiemlieh, David R. 1990. 'The Crown Colony Protectorate for North East India: The Tribal Response', Paper presented at the proceedings of the North East India History Association, Imphal.

Tschang, T. 2001. 'The Basic Characteristics of Skills and Organisational Capabilities in the Indian Software Industry', working paper no. 13, Asian Development Institute, Tokyo.

Verghese, B.G., B. Ahmed, G. Deshpande, N. Desai and R. Upadhyaya. 1980. 'Situation in Assam' (mimeo), Gandhi Peace Foundation, New Delhi.

Yong, Ong Keng. May 2005. 'Advancing the ASEAN-India Partnership in the New Millennium', RIS-Discussion Paper no. 96, New Delhi.

Zang, Dhong. 2006. 'India Looks East: Strategies and Impact', AUSAID working paper, September, Canberra, pp. 1–36.

Lectures, Seminars and Paper Presentations

Baruah, Sanjib. June 2005. 'The Problem', *Gateway to the East: A Symposium on Northeast India and the Look East Policy*, Seminar no. 550.

Bhaumik, Subir. February 2002. 'Disaster in Tripura', *Porous Border, Divided Selves*, Seminar no. 510.

———. June 2005. 'Guns, Drugs and Rebels', Seminar no. 550.

Datta, P.S. February 1990. 'Roots of Insurgency', *Northeast Special*, Seminar no. 366.

Ganguly, J.B. 1985. 'Economics of Development of the Tribal Villages of North East India', unpublished paper presented at the NEICSSR Seminar and Sequences in Development in the North-Eastern Region, Shillong, December.

Ginkel, Hans van. 2004. 'Regionalism and the United Nations', paper presented at UNU Global Seminar fourth Kanazawa Session on Globalization and Regionalism, 20–23 November.

Hettne, Bjorn. 1996. 'Globalization, the New Regionalism and East Asia', paper presented at the United Nations University Global Seminar '96 Shonan Session, on *Globalism and Regionalism,* Shonan International Village, Hayama, Kanagawa, Japan, 2–6 September.

Hussain, Wasbir. 2004. 'India's North-East: The Problem', paper presented as part of the Interaction on the North East, Observer Research Foundation, New Delhi, 18 November.

Kumar, Nagesh. 2005. 'Regional Economic Cooperation in Asia: Relevance and a Possible Roadmap for a Broader Asian Economic Community', paper presented at the 4th High-Level Conference on Asian Economic Integration: Towards an Asian Economic Community, RIS and ISEAS, New Delhi, 18–19 December.

Mohan, C. Raja. 2006. 'India's New Foreign Policy Strategy', draft paper presented at a Seminar in Beijing by China Reform Forum and the Carnegie Endowment for International Peace, Beijing, 26 May.

Ramesh, Jairam. 2004. 'Northeast India in a New Asia', inaugural lecture in CENISEAS Forum, *Towards a New Asia: Transnationalism and Northeast India*, Guwahati, 10–11 September.

Suryanarayan, V. March 2000. 'Prospects for a Bay of Bengal community'. Seminar no. 487.

Syiemlieh, David R. 2003. 'Response of the North East Hill Tribes of India Towards Partition, Independence and Integration: 1946–1950', *Pratibha Devi Memorial Lectures 2003*.

Verghese, B.G. 2001. 'Unfinished Business in the Northeast: Pointers towards Restructuring, Reform, Reconciliation and Resurgence', *Seventh Kamal Kumari Lecture*.

Newspaper Reports and Archives

Baruah, Sanjib. 2005. 'The Shadow of the Foreigner', *Indian Express*, New Delhi, 16 June.

———. 2005. 'Unfriendly Neighbourhood', *The Telegraph*, Kolkata, 8 June.

Bhagwati, Jagdish. 1993. 'Negotiating Trade Blocs', *India Today*, Mumbai, 15 July.

Deccan Herald, 2008. 24 June.

Jha, Prem Shankar. 1992. 'Stagnation and Sovereignty', *The Hindu*, New Delhi, 15 July.

Kaji, G.S. 1995. 'What East Asia has Achieved, India too can Emulate', *The Times of India*, New Delhi, 13 April.

Keesing's Contemporary Archives. 1947. North-Eastern Hill University, Shillong.

Malcolm, Subham. 1993. 'Sengupta returns with task half-fulfilled', *The Economic Times*, Mumbai, 10 August.

Parthasarathy, G. 2000. 'Look beyond "look east"', *The Pioneer*, New Delhi, 21 December.

People's Daily (English). 2001. 'China Opens 'Southern Silk Road' Tourism Route', *People's Daily*, Pingshan, 15 February.

Prabir De. 2008. 'Connecting Mekong Region with India through Infrastructure linkages', *Financial Express*, New Delhi, 5 February.

Ramchandran, S. 2006. 'India should aim at becoming part of Asian economic community', *The Hindu*, New Delhi, 9 April.

Ray, Sunanda K. Datta. 1980. 'Challenge of Diversity: Fringe peoples out in cold', *The Statesman*, Calcutta, 16 July.

Subham, Malcolm. 1993. 'Sengupta returns with task half-fulfilled', *The Economic Times*, Mumbai, 10 August.

The Indian Express. 1990. 'Fallout of Gulf Crisis: Indian Exports Suffer', *The Indian Express*, New Delhi, 27 September.

Thornhill, J. 2001. 'Enter the Dragon', *The Financial Times*, London, 20 February.

Internet Sources

Ahmed, E. 2006. 'Reinforcing "Look East" Policy.' Available online at http://www.meaindia.nic.in/interview/2006/01/17in01.htm (downloaded on 05.07.2007).

Association of Southeast Asian Nation (ASEAN) Official Website. Available online at http://www.aseansec.org/64.htm (downloaded on 22.08.2007).

For areas of SAARC cooperation, SAARC website, available online at http://www. saarc-sec.org/?t=2 (downloaded on 15.09. 2007).

Khanna, Sushil. 2008. 'Look East, Look South: Backward Border Regions in India and China.' Available online at www.burmalibrary.org/docs4/LookEast-LookSouth-08REVISED.pdf (downloaded on 18.07.2007).

MEA, 'Ganga–Mekong Swarnabhoomi Project.' Available online at http://meaindia. nic.in/onmouse/ganga1.htm (downloaded on 07.08.2007).

Menon, Sudha. 2007. 'Northeast India and Globalization: The Way Ahead'. *Digital Library of the Commons.* Available online at http://dlc.dlib.indiana. edu/archive/00002194/01/Northeast_the_way_ahead.pdf (downloaded on 29.01.2009).

'Overview of Association of Southeast Asian Nations.' Available online at http:// www.aseansec.org/64.htm (downloaded on 07.04.2007).

Shimray, U.A. 'Naga Issue and Nehru: A Brief Note.' Available online at http://ifp. co.in/ArticleFull.asp?ArticleID=486 (downloaded on 21.09.2008).

United Nations official website. Available online at http://www.un.org/aboutun/ charter (downloaded on 25.07.2006).

Index

About the Author

Thongkholal Haokip is an Assistant Professor of Political Science at Presidency University, Kolkata. He is the Editor of *Journal of North East India Studies*, and specialises in and writes extensively on India's policy towards its Northeastern region, the Look East policy, ethnicity and ethnic relations in Northeast India. He has recently edited *The Kukis of Northeast India: Politics and Culture* (2013).